PRENTICE HALL

SCIENCE EXPLORER

Earth's Waters

PRENTICE HALL
Needham, Massachusetts
Upper Saddle River, New Jersey

Earth's Waters

Program Resources

Student Edition
Annotated Teacher's Edition
Teaching Resources Book with Color Transparencies
Earth's Waters Materials Kits

Program Components

Integrated Science Laboratory Manual
Integrated Science Laboratory Manual, Teacher's Edition
Inquiry Skills Activity Book
Student-Centered Science Activity Books
Program Planning Guide
Guided Reading English Audiotapes
Guided Reading Spanish Audiotapes and Summaries
Product Testing Activities by Consumer Reports™
Event-Based Science Series (NSF funded)
Prentice Hall Interdisciplinary Explorations
Cobblestone, Odyssey, Calliope, and *Faces* Magazines

Media/Technology

Science Explorer Interactive Student Tutorial CD-ROMs
Odyssey of Discovery CD-ROMs
Resource Pro® (Teaching Resources on CD-ROM)
Assessment Resources CD-ROM with Dial-A-Test®
Internet site at www.science-explorer.phschool.com
Life, Earth, and Physical Science Videodiscs
Life, Earth, and Physical Science Videotapes

Science Explorer Student Editions

- *From Bacteria to Plants*
- *Animals*
- *Cells and Heredity*
- *Human Biology and Health*
- *Environmental Science*
- *Inside Earth*
- *Earth's Changing Surface*
- *Earth's Waters*
- *Weather and Climate*
- *Astronomy*
- *Chemical Building Blocks*
- *Chemical Interactions*
- *Motion, Forces, and Energy*
- *Electricity and Magnetism*
- *Sound and Light*

Staff Credits

The people who made up the *Science Explorer* team—representing editorial, editorial services, design services, field marketing, market research, marketing services, on-line services/multimedia development, product marketing, production services, and publishing processes—are listed below. Bold type denotes core team members.

Kristen E. Ball, **Barbara A. Bertell,** Peter W. Brooks, **Christopher R. Brown, Greg Cantone,** Jonathan Cheney, **Patrick Finbarr Connolly,** Loree Franz, Donald P. Gagnon, Jr., **Paul J. Gagnon, Joel Gendler,** Elizabeth Good, Kerri Hoar, **Linda D. Johnson,** Katherine M. Kotik, Russ Lappa, Marilyn Leitao, David Lippman, **Eve Melnechuk, Natania Mlawer,** Paul W. Murphy, **Cindy A. Noftle,** Julia F. Osborne, Caroline M. Power, Suzanne J. Schineller, **Susan W. Tafler,** Kira Thaler-Marbit, Robin L. Santel, Ronald Schachter, **Mark Tricca,** Diane Walsh, Pearl B. Weinstein, Beth Norman Winickoff

ISBN 0-13-434484-7
8 9 10   05 04 03 02 01

Cover: This waterfall in North Yorkshire, England, illustrates the force and beauty of water in motion.

Program Authors

Michael J. Padilla, Ph.D.
Professor
Department of Science Education
University of Georgia
Athens, Georgia

Michael Padilla is a leader in middle school science education. He has served as an editor and elected officer for the National Science Teachers Association. He has been principal investigator of several National Science Foundation and Eisenhower grants and served as a writer of the National Science Education Standards.

As lead author of *Science Explorer,* Mike has inspired the team in developing a program that meets the needs of middle grades students, promotes science inquiry, and is aligned with the National Science Education Standards.

Ioannis Miaoulis, Ph.D.
Dean of Engineering
College of Engineering
Tufts University
Medford, Massachusetts

Martha Cyr, Ph.D.
Director, Engineering
     Educational Outreach
College of Engineering
Tufts University
Medford, Massachusetts

Science Explorer was created in collaboration with the College of Engineering at Tufts University. Tufts has an extensive engineering outreach program that uses engineering design and construction to excite and motivate students and teachers in science and technology education.

Faculty from Tufts University participated in the development of *Science Explorer* chapter projects, reviewed the student books for content accuracy, and helped coordinate field testing.

Book Authors

Barbara Brooks Simons
Science Writer
Boston, Massachusetts

Thomas R. Wellnitz
Science Instructor
The Paideia School
Atlanta, Georgia

Contributing Writers

Greg Hutton
Science and Health Curriculum
     Coordinator
School Board of Sarasota County
Sarasota, Florida

Jeffrey C. Callister
Science Instructor
Newburgh Free Academy
Newburgh, New York

Jan Jenner, Ph.D.
Science Writer
Talladega, Alabama

Reading Consultant

Bonnie B. Armbruster, Ph.D.
Department of Curriculum
     and Instruction
University of Illinois
Champaign, Illinois

Interdisciplinary Consultant

Heidi Hayes Jacobs, Ed.D.
Teacher's College
Columbia University
New York, New York

Safety Consultants

W. H. Breazeale, Ph.D.
Department of Chemistry
College of Charleston
Charleston, South Carolina

Ruth Hathaway, Ph.D.
Hathaway Consulting
Cape Girardeau, Missouri

Teacher Reviewers

Stephanie Anderson
Sierra Vista Junior
    High School
Canyon Country, California

John W. Anson
Mesa Intermediate School
Palmdale, California

Pamela Arline
Lake Taylor Middle School
Norfolk, Virginia

Lynn Beason
College Station Jr. High School
College Station, Texas

Richard Bothmer
Hollis School District
Hollis, New Hampshire

Jeffrey C. Callister
Newburgh Free Academy
Newburgh, New York

Judy D'Albert
Harvard Day School
Corona Del Mar, California

Betty Scott Dean
Guilford County Schools
McLeansville, North Carolina

Sarah C. Duff
Baltimore City Public Schools
Baltimore, Maryland

Melody Law Ewey
Holmes Junior High School
Davis, California

Sherry L. Fisher
Lake Zurich Middle
    School North
Lake Zurich, Illinois

Melissa Gibbons
Fort Worth ISD
Fort Worth, Texas

Debra J. Goodding
Kraemer Middle School
Placentia, California

Jack Grande
Weber Middle School
Port Washington, New York

Steve Hills
Riverside Middle School
Grand Rapids, Michigan

Carol Ann Lionello
Kraemer Middle School
Placentia, California

Jaime A. Morales
Henry T. Gage Middle School
Huntington Park, California

Patsy Partin
Cameron Middle School
Nashville, Tennessee

Deedra H. Robinson
Newport News Public Schools
Newport News, Virginia

Bonnie Scott
Clack Middle School
Abilene, Texas

Charles M. Sears
Belzer Middle School
Indianapolis, Indiana

Barbara M. Strange
Ferndale Middle School
High Point, North Carolina

Jackie Louise Ulfig
Ford Middle School
Allen, Texas

Kathy Usina
Belzer Middle School
Indianapolis, Indiana

Heidi M. von Oetinger
L'Anse Creuse Public School
Harrison Township, Michigan

Pam Watson
Hill Country Middle School
Austin, Texas

Activity Field Testers

Nicki Bibbo
Russell Street School
Littleton, Massachusetts

Connie Boone
Fletcher Middle School
Jacksonville Beach, Florida

Rose-Marie Botting
Broward County
    School District
Fort Lauderdale, Florida

Colleen Campos
Laredo Middle School
Aurora, Colorado

Elizabeth Chait
W. L. Chenery Middle School
Belmont, Massachusetts

Holly Estes
Hale Middle School
Stow, Massachusetts

Laura Hapgood
Plymouth Community
    Intermediate School
Plymouth, Massachusetts

Sandra M. Harris
Winman Junior High School
Warwick, Rhode Island

Jason Ho
Walter Reed Middle School
Los Angeles, California

Joanne Jackson
Winman Junior High School
Warwick, Rhode Island

Mary F. Lavin
Plymouth Community
    Intermediate School
Plymouth, Massachusetts

James MacNeil, Ph.D.
Concord Public Schools
Concord, Massachusetts

Lauren Magruder
St. Michael's Country
    Day School
Newport, Rhode Island

Jeanne Maurand
Glen Urquhart School
Beverly Farms, Massachusetts

Warren Phillips
Plymouth Community
    Intermediate School
Plymouth, Massachusetts

Carol Pirtle
Hale Middle School
Stow, Massachusetts

Kathleen M. Poe
Kirby-Smith Middle School
Jacksonville, Florida

Cynthia B. Pope
Ruffner Middle School
Norfolk, Virginia

Anne Scammell
Geneva Middle School
Geneva, New York

Karen Riley Sievers
Callanan Middle School
Des Moines, Iowa

David M. Smith
Howard A. Eyer Middle School
Macungie, Pennsylvania

Derek Strohschneider
Plymouth Community
    Intermediate School
Plymouth, Massachusetts

Sallie Teames
Rosemont Middle School
Fort Worth, Texas

Gene Vitale
Parkland Middle School
McHenry, Illinois

Zenovia Young
Meyer Levin Junior
    High School (IS 285)
Brooklyn, New York

Contents

Earth's Waters

Activities

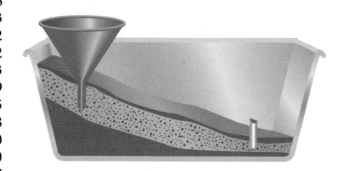

Interdisciplinary Activities

Life in a Sunless World

Dr. Cindy Lee Van Dover was born and raised in Eatontown, New Jersey. She is now Science Director of the West Coast National Undersea Laboratory at the University of Alaska, Fairbanks. She first studied ocean-floor shrimp as a graduate student at the Massachusetts Institute of Technology and as a researcher at the Woods Hole Oceanographic Institution in Massachusetts.

Oceanographer Cindy Lee Van Dover never thought that her childhood curiosity would lead her to this moment. But there she was, heading toward the cold, dark depths of the ocean floor. She was piloting the famous *Alvin*, a tiny research submarine known as a submersible. The *Alvin* would collect data and gather samples of rocks and delicate animals living deep in the ocean. Scientists usually leave the driving to trained submersible pilots. But because Dr. Van Dover wanted the full experience of exploring the ocean, she became the first scientist ever to qualify as a submersible pilot.

Light from the *Alvin* illuminates the dark sea floor where crabs and huge masses of shrimp feed around black smoker vents. ▶

Life on the Ocean Floor

Slowly, the *Alvin* entered the sunless world far beneath the surface of the Atlantic Ocean — one of the strangest and most remote places on Earth. As the *Alvin* approached an underwater mountain range, Dr. Van Dover could see colonies of animals swarming around undersea hot springs called "black smokers."

The black clouds that give these areas their name are not smoke at all. Rather they are streams of very hot water packed with minerals flowing from openings in the sea floor. Some microorganisms are able to use the minerals as their food source. Dr. Van Dover's special interest was in some very unusual shrimp that feed on these microorganisms.

▲ Black smoker vents are hot enough to glow. Water as hot as 350°C pours up from these hot springs. When the hot water mixes with the cold sea water, it quickly cools.

Endless Questions

How did Dr. Van Dover reach this moment in her life? As a child she was full of questions about everything in nature. "I had my bug period; I had my frog-and-tadpole period; I had my flower period and tree period and bird period. But I settled pretty firmly and quickly on marine invertebrates, sea animals without backbones," she explains. "That's because they were so unusual. I just loved all the odd structures they had, each with a function. Why does a crustacean have ten legs — or whatever number it might have? What does it use them all for?"

Could These Shrimp Have Eyes?

As she steered the *Alvin,* Dr. Van Dover thought about the shrimp she planned to observe. She knew that these shrimp live in the dark depths of the ocean. They lack eyestalks and the black, beady eyes of their better known relatives. She also knew that eyeless animals are common at depths too far beneath the surface for sunlight to reach.

Dr. Van Dover had made an interesting discovery about the shrimp in the lab. Her discovery

> **Other people told me I was crazy. There's no light on the sea floor. Why do they need eyes?**

came after she noticed odd, shiny patches on their backs. She asked herself what the function of the patches might be. "I dissected a shrimp in the laboratory," she recounts. "I found this pair of organs and pulled it out. It was very recognizable, and to my surprise, it was attached to what I took to be the brain of the shrimp.

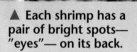

▲ **Each shrimp has a pair of bright spots— "eyes"— on its back.**

Light-sensitive shrimp swarm around "smoker" vents deep in the Atlantic Ocean. ▶

I looked at it and said, 'Looks like an eye!' Other people told me I was crazy. There's no light on the sea floor. Why do they need eyes?"

Dr. Van Dover kept an open mind and showed the structure to crustacean eye experts. They confirmed that it was not only an eye, but a very unusual one. It was able to detect very dim light. Immediately that raised another question: What could the shrimp be looking at?

"We thought about alternatives," Dr. Van Dover says. "The obvious thing is that these shrimp are only found around high-temperature black smokers. We all know that hot things glow. Did these vents glow?" The answer turned out to be yes. Those unusual eyes were just right for spotting undersea hot spots. Scientists hypothesize that the shrimp use these eyes to guide them toward the dim light in order to feed on the microorganisms. As the shrimp approach the vent, the light gets brighter. That signals the shrimp to keep a distance from the hottest water just emerging from the vent.

Looking Ahead

From time to time now, Dr. Van Dover thinks about the submersible that scientists plan to send to watery Europa, a moon of Jupiter. Scientists in a control room will pilot a robot version of *Alvin* under the oceans of Europa. "I'm delighted that I'm young enough that I'm going to see that," she says. When asked if she would like to be one of those scientists, she doesn't hesitate.

"Wouldn't that be sweet!" she says — and smiles.

▲ A surface ship lifts the *Alvin* from the ocean after a deep-sea expedition.

In Your Journal

Cindy Lee Van Dover's discoveries usually begin with her paying attention to details and then asking questions about what she finds. Think of a familiar place outdoors that you like to visit. Describe the place from memory. Jot down details. Then visit the place again to observe and record questions.

WHAT'S AHEAD

Every Drop Counts

With an almost deafening roar, water rushes over this waterfall and plunges into the rocky pool below. Every day, hundreds of thousands of liters of water flow over the falls. How do you think this amount compares with the amount of water that flows out of your faucets at home each day?

In this chapter, you will explore the many ways that living things depend on Earth's water. To learn how water is used in your own home and community, you will design a method for tracking water use over a one-week period.

Your Goal To monitor water use in your home and in another building in your community for one week.

To complete the project you will
◆ track your personal water use at home
◆ determine the total amount of water used in your home
◆ find out how much water is used by a business, school, hospital, or other building in your community

Get Started Begin now by brainstorming the ways you use water at home. Use this list to create a data table in which you will record each time you perform these activities during the week.

Check Your Progress You'll be working on this project as you study this chapter. To keep your project on track, look for Check Your Progress boxes at the following points.

Section 1 Review, page 22: Calculate your total water use.
Section 3 Review, page 35: Investigate water use at another building in your community.

Wrap Up At the end of the chapter (page 39), you will graph your household water-use data and share the information with your classmates.

Hikers in California's Yosemite National Park are awed by its thundering waterfalls.

DISCOVER •••ACTIVITY••••

Water, Water Everywhere?

1. Blow up a large, round balloon. Tie a knot at the end.

2. Pretend that your balloon is a globe. Using a permanent marker, draw the basic shapes of the continents at the size they would be if Earth were the size of your balloon. Shade the continents with the marker.

3. Now compare your balloon to an actual globe. Look at the amount of land compared to the amount of ocean on each.

North America
Eurasia
Africa
South America
Australia
Antarctica

Think It Over

Observing Does your balloon show more land area or ocean area? How do the areas of land and ocean actually compare on Earth?

GUIDE FOR READING

◆ How do people and other living things use water?

◆ How is Earth's water distributed among saltwater and freshwater sources?

Reading Tip As you read, use the headings to make an outline showing how water is important and where it is found.

Imagine a world without water. The planet is a barren desert. There are no cool green forests or deep oceans. The world is silent — no rain falls on rooftops; no birds or other animals stir. No clouds shield the planet from the hot sun. Even the shape of the land is different. Without water to wear them down, the mountains are jagged and rough. There are no Great Lakes, no Niagara Falls, and no Grand Canyon.

Can you imagine living in such a world? In fact, you could not survive there. The presence of water is essential for life to exist on the planet Earth. In this section, you will explore the ways that all living things depend on water.

How Do People Use Water?

Take a minute to list all of the ways you used water this morning. You probably washed your face, brushed your teeth, and flushed the toilet. Perhaps you drank a glass of water or used water to make oatmeal. These are some common uses of water in the home. But the water people use at home is just a small percentage of all the water used in the United States. **In addition to household purposes, people use water for agriculture, industry, transportation, and recreation.**

Agriculture Has your family ever had a garden? If so, you know that growing fruits and vegetables requires water. On a large farm, a constant supply of fresh water is essential.

Figure 1 The food processing industry requires large amounts of water. Before these juicy red tomatoes can be made into ketchup or spaghetti sauce, they must be washed.

Growing the wheat to make a single loaf of bread takes 435 liters of water, enough to fill 1,200 soft drink cans!

However, some parts of the United States don't receive enough regular rainfall for agriculture. For example, parts of California's Central Valley receive less than 26 centimeters of rain a year. Yet this area is one of the most productive farming regions in the country. How is it possible to farm in this dry place? The solution is irrigation. **Irrigation** is the process of supplying water to areas of land to make them suitable for growing crops. In the United States, more water is used for irrigating farmland than for any other single purpose.

Industry Think about the objects in a typical school locker. There's a jacket, some textbooks, a few pens without caps, and maybe a basketball or a flute for band practice. Did you know that water is needed to produce all these objects? Even though water is not part of the final products, it plays a role in the industrial processes that created them. For example, water is needed to make the paper in the textbooks. Wood chips are washed and then soaked in vats of water and chemicals to form pulp. The pulp is rinsed again, squeezed dry, and pressed into paper.

Industries use water in many other ways. For example, power plants and steel mills both need huge volumes of water to cool down hot machinery. Water that is used for cooling can often be recycled, or used again for another purpose.

Transportation If you live near a large waterway, you have probably seen barges carrying heavy loads of coal or iron. Oceans and rivers have been used for transporting people and goods since ancient times. If you look at a map of the United States, you will notice that many large cities are located on the coasts.

Water Used in the Home	
Task	**Water Used (liters)**
Showering for 5 minutes	95
Brushing teeth	10
Washing hands	7.5
Flushing standard toilet	23
Flushing "low-flow" toilet	6
Washing one load of laundry	151
Running dishwasher	19
Washing dishes by hand	114

Figure 2 Many common household activities involve water. *Interpreting Data How much water would a person save per flush by replacing a standard toilet with a "low-flow" toilet?*

Ocean travel led to the growth of port cities such as Boston, New York, and San Francisco. In early America, rivers also served as natural highways. St. Louis, Memphis, and Baton Rouge are some cities that began as trading posts along the Mississippi River.

Recreation   Do you like to swim in a neighborhood pool? Catch fish from a rowboat in the middle of a lake? Walk along a beach collecting seashells? Or maybe just sit on the edge of a dock and dangle your feet in the water? Then you know some ways water is used for recreation. And if you brave the winter cold to ski or skate, you are enjoying water in its frozen form.

☑ *Checkpoint* *List an agricultural use, an industrial use, and a household use of water that you relied on today.*

Water and Agriculture

Plants require a steady supply of water to grow. How have farmers throughout history provided their crops with water? This time line shows some methods developed in different parts of the world.

2000 B.C. Egypt

Egyptian farmers invented a way to raise water from the Nile River. The device, called a *shaduf,* acted as a lever to make lifting a bucket of water easier. The farmers then emptied the water into a network of canals to irrigate their fields. The *shaduf* is still in use in Egypt, India, and other countries.

3000 B.C.	2000 B.C.	1000 B.C.

3000 B.C. China

One of the oldest known methods of irrigation was developed for growing rice. Farmers built paddies, or artificial ponds with raised edges. The farmers flooded the paddies with water from a nearby stream. This ancient technique is still widely used throughout Southeast Asia.

700 B.C. Assyria

Sennacherib, king of the ancient nation Assyria, surrounded the capital city of Nineveh with fruit trees, cotton, and exotic plants. To help irrigate the plantations, he built a 10-kilometer canal and a stone aqueduct to transport water from the nearby hills.

Water and Living Things

INTEGRATING LIFE SCIENCE Here's a riddle for you: What do you and an apple have in common? You both consist mostly of water! In fact, water is a large part of every living thing. Water makes up nearly two thirds of your body. That water is necessary to keep your body functioning.

Water is essential for living things to grow, reproduce, and carry out other important processes. For example, plants use water, plus carbon dioxide and energy from the sun, to make food in a process called **photosynthesis** (foh toh SIN thuh sis). Animals and many other living things depend on the food made by plants. They may eat the plants directly or eat other organisms that eat plants.

In Your Journal

Find out more about one of these agricultural techniques. Imagine that you are a farmer seeing the method in action for the first time. Write a letter to a friend describing the new technique. What problem will it solve? How will it improve your farming?

A.D. 1870 United States

When homesteaders arrived on the dry Great Plains of the central United States, they had to rely on water stored underground. Windmills provided the energy to pump the groundwater to the surface. The farmers dug ditches to carry the water to irrigate their fields.

A.D. 1	A.D. 1000	A.D. 2000

A.D. 500 Mexico

To grow crops in areas covered by swampy lakes, the Aztecs built raised plots of farmland called *chinampas*. They grew maize on fertile soil scooped from the lake bottom. A grid of canals kept the crops wet and allowed the farmers to navigate boats between the *chinampas*.

Present Israel

Irrigation is the key to survival in desert regions. Today, methods such as drip irrigation ensure that very little water is wasted when crops are watered. Holes in the pipe allow water to drip directly onto the soil around the roots of each plant.

Sharpen your Skills

Calculating

ACTIVITY

This activity shows how Earth's water is distributed.

1. Fill a one-liter plastic bottle with water. This represents the total water on Earth.

2. First, measure 97 percent, or 970 milliliters (mL), of the water and pour it into a large bowl. This represents the salt water in Earth's oceans and salt lakes.

3. Next, you will demonstrate how the remaining fresh water is divided. Label five cups to match the fresh-water sources in Figure 3. Calculate how much of the remaining 30 mL of water you should pour into each cup to represent the percentage of Earth's fresh water found there.

4. Use a plastic graduated cylinder to measure out the amount of water for each cup. Use a plastic dropper to approximate amounts that are too small to measure accurately.

Which cups contain water that is available for humans to use? How does the amount of water in these cups compare to the original one liter?

Another way that living things use water is as a home. An organism's **habitat** is the place where it lives and that provides the things it needs to survive. Both fresh water and salt water provide habitats for many living things.

Water on Earth

Why do you think Earth is often called the "water planet"? Perhaps an astronaut suggested this name. From space, an astronaut can see that there is much more water than land on planet Earth. Oceans cover nearly 71 percent of Earth's surface.

Figure 3 shows how Earth's water is distributed. **Most of Earth's water — more than 97 percent — is salt water that is found in the oceans. Only 3 percent is fresh water.** Of that 3 percent, about three quarters is found in the huge masses of ice near the North and South Poles. A fraction more is found in the atmosphere. Most water in the atmosphere is invisible **water vapor,** the gaseous form of water. Less than 1 percent of the water on Earth is fresh water that is available for humans to use.

To explore where Earth's water is found, you can take an imaginary boat trip around the world. As you read, follow your route on the map in Figure 4.

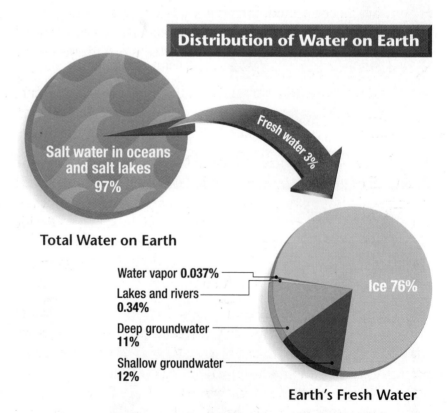

Distribution of Water on Earth

Salt water in oceans and salt lakes 97%

Fresh water 3%

Total Water on Earth

Water vapor 0.037%

Lakes and rivers 0.34%

Deep groundwater 11%

Shallow groundwater 12%

Ice 76%

Earth's Fresh Water

Figure 3 Most of Earth's water is salt water. Of the freshwater sources shown in the bottom circle graph, only the water in lakes, rivers, and shallow groundwater is available for human use.

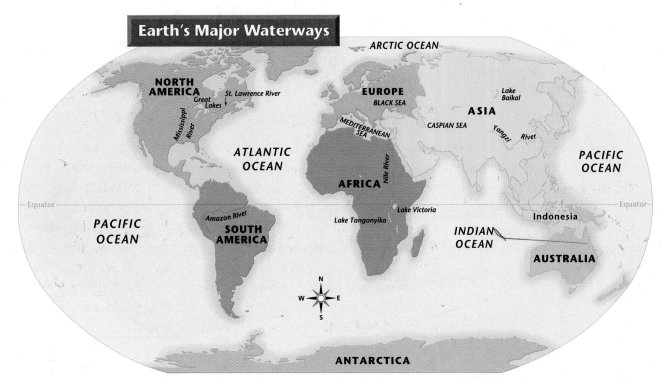

Earth's Major Waterways

ARCTIC OCEAN

NORTH AMERICA — Great Lakes — St. Lawrence River — Mississippi River

EUROPE — BLACK SEA — MEDITERRANEAN SEA

ASIA — Lake Baikal — CASPIAN SEA — Yangzi River

ATLANTIC OCEAN

AFRICA — Nile River

PACIFIC OCEAN

Equator

PACIFIC OCEAN

Amazon River — SOUTH AMERICA

Lake Tanganyika — Lake Victoria

Indonesia

INDIAN OCEAN

AUSTRALIA

Equator

N W E S

ANTARCTICA

Figure 4 Earth's oceans are all connected, enabling a ship to sail all the way around the world. This map also shows some of the world's major rivers and lakes. *Interpreting Maps* Which continents touch the Pacific Ocean? The Atlantic Ocean?

Oceans Your journey starts in Miami, Florida. From here, you can sail completely around the world without ever going ashore. Although people have given names to regions of the ocean, these regions are all connected, forming a single world ocean.

First you sail southeast across the Atlantic Ocean toward Africa. Swinging around the continent's southern tip, you enter the smaller but deeper Indian Ocean. After zigzagging among the islands of Indonesia, you head east across the Pacific Ocean, the longest part of your trip. This vast ocean, dotted with islands, covers an area greater than all the land on Earth put together.

Ice How can you get back to Miami? If you're not in a hurry, you could sail all the way around South America. But watch out for icebergs! These floating chunks of ice are your first encounter with fresh water on your journey. Icebergs in the southern Pacific and Atlantic oceans have broken off the massive sheets of ice that cover most of Antarctica. You would also find icebergs in the Arctic Ocean around the North Pole.

Rivers and Lakes To see examples of fresh water in rivers and lakes, you'll have to make a side trip inland. Sail north past Nova Scotia, Canada, to the beginning of the St. Lawrence Seaway. Navigate through the series of locks along the St. Lawrence River. Suddenly the river widens and you enter Lake Ontario, one of North America's five Great Lakes. Together, the Great Lakes cover an area nearly twice the size of New York state. They contain nearly 20 percent of all the water in the world's freshwater lakes.

Figure 5 This diagram shows an earthworm's view of the formation of groundwater. *Interpreting Diagrams* Why does the groundwater collect where you see it in this diagram?

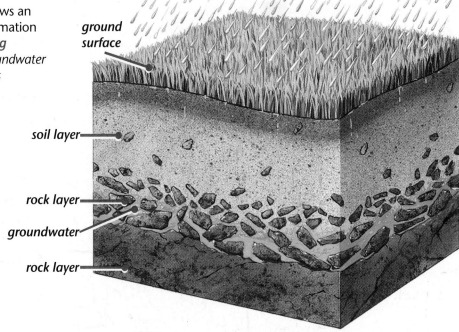

ground surface

soil layer

rock layer

groundwater

rock layer

Below Earth's Surface On your journey around the world, you would not see most of Earth's liquid fresh water. Far more fresh water is located underground than in all Earth's rivers and lakes. How did this water get underground?

As Figure 5 shows, when rain or snow falls some of the water soaks into the ground. The water trickles downward through spaces between the particles of soil and rock. Eventually the water reaches a layer that it cannot move through. Then the water begins to fill up the spaces above that layer. Water that fills the cracks and spaces in underground soil and rock layers is called **groundwater.** Chapter 2 explains more about groundwater, the source of much of the water used by humans.

Section 1 Review

1. What are five major ways that people in the United States use water?
2. Describe two ways that plants and other living things depend on water.
3. What percent of Earth's water is salt water? What percent is fresh water?
4. Where is most of the fresh water on Earth found?
5. **Thinking Critically Classifying** Classify the following as fresh water or salt water: groundwater, iceberg, ocean, and river.

Check Your Progress CHAPTER PROJECT 1
Complete your water-use data table by calculating the total amount of water you used during the week. Use Figure 2 to estimate the water used for some common activities. Then determine how much water your family used during the week. You can do this by reading your water meter, estimating based on your personal water use, or having your family members record their usage. (*Hint:* Convert all amounts to liters.)

SECTION 2 The Properties of Water

DISCOVER ········· ACTIVITY

What Are Some Properties of Water?

1. Pour a small amount of water into a plastic cup. Pour an equal amount of vegetable oil into a second cup.

2. Cut two strips of paper towel. Hold the strips so that the bottom of one strip is in the water and the other is in the oil.

3. After one minute, measure how high each substance climbed up the paper towel.

4. Using a plastic dropper, place a big drop of water onto a piece of wax paper.

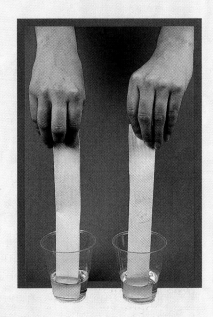

5. Using another dropper, place a drop of oil the same size as the water drop beside it on the wax paper.

6. Observe the shape of the two drops from the side.

7. Follow your teacher's instructions for disposing of the oil when you clean up after this activity.

Think It Over

Observing What differences do you notice between the water and the oil in each experiment?

How would you describe water to someone who had never seen it before? You might say that pure water has no color, no taste, and no odor. You might even say that water is a rather plain, ordinary substance. But if you asked a chemist to describe water, the response would be different. The chemist would say that water is very unusual. Its properties differ from those of most other familiar substances.

Are you and the chemist talking about the same substance? To understand the chemist's description of water, you need to know something about the chemical structure of water.

Water's Unique Structure

Like all matter, water is made up of atoms. Just as the 26 letters of the alphabet combine in different ways to form all the words in the English language, about 100 types of atoms combine in different ways to form all types of matter. Atoms attach together, or bond, to form molecules. Two hydrogen atoms bonded to an oxygen atom form a water molecule. A short way of writing this is to use the chemical formula for water, H_2O.

GUIDE FOR READING

◆ How does the chemical structure of water molecules cause them to stick together?

◆ How does water dissolve other polar substances?

◆ What are the three states in which water exists on Earth?

Reading Tip As you read, make a list of water's properties. Write a sentence describing each property.

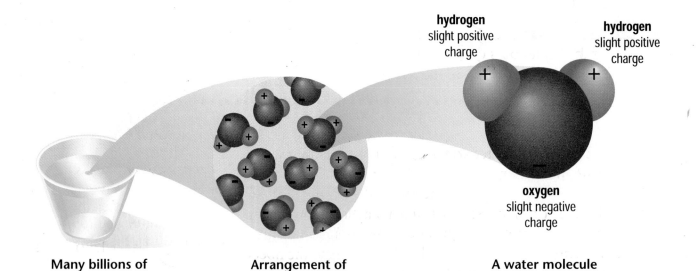

hydrogen
slight positive
charge

hydrogen
slight positive
charge

oxygen
slight negative
charge

**Many billions of
water molecules**

**Arrangement of
water molecules**

A water molecule

Figure 6 A glass of water contains many billions of water molecules. Notice how the water molecules are arranged in the center image. The positive ends of one molecule are attracted to the negative end of another molecule.

Figure 6 shows how the hydrogen and oxygen atoms are arranged in a water molecule. Each end of the molecule has a slight electric charge. The oxygen end has a slight negative charge. The hydrogen ends have a slight positive charge. A molecule that has electrically charged areas is called a **polar molecule**. Because water consists of polar molecules, it is called a polar substance.

Have you ever played with bar magnets? If so, you know that the opposite poles of two magnets attract each other. The same is true with polar molecules, except that an electric force rather than a magnetic force causes the attraction. **The positive hydrogen ends of one water molecule attract the negative oxygen ends of nearby water molecules. As a result, the water molecules tend to stick together.** Many of water's unusual properties occur because of this attraction among the polar water molecules.

☑ *Checkpoint* *Describe the arrangement of the atoms in a water molecule. What makes it a polar molecule?*

Surface Tension

Have you ever watched a water strider like the one at the left? These insects can skate across the surface of a pond without sinking. They are supported by the surface tension of the water. **Surface tension** is the tightness across the surface of water that is caused by the polar molecules pulling on each other. The molecules at the surface are being pulled by the molecules next to them and below them. The pulling forces the surface of the water into a curved shape. Surface tension also causes raindrops to form round beads when they fall onto a car windshield.

Figure 7 A water strider skips lightly across the surface of a pond. *Applying Concepts How do water's polar molecules keep the insect from falling into the water?*

Capillary Action

The next time you have a drink with a straw in it, look closely at the level of the liquid outside and inside the straw. You will see that the liquid rises higher inside the straw. Similarly, water will climb up into the pores of a brick or piece of wood. How does water move up against the force of gravity? Just as water molecules stick to each other, they also stick to the sides of a tube. As water molecules are attracted to the tube, they pull other water molecules up with them. The combined force of attraction among water molecules and with the molecules of surrounding materials is called **capillary action.** Capillary action allows water to move through materials with pores or narrow spaces inside.

Capillary action causes water molecules to cling to the fibers of materials like paper and cloth. You may have seen outdoor or athletic clothing that claims to "wick moisture away from the skin." The capillary action that occurs along the cloth's fibers pulls water away from your skin. By pulling the water away from your skin, the fibers keep you dry.

Water, the Universal Solvent

What happens when you make lemonade from a powdered mix? As you stir the powder into a pitcher of water, the powder seems to disappear. When you make lemonade, you are making a solution. A **solution** is a mixture that forms when one substance dissolves another. The substance that does the dissolving is called the **solvent.** In this example, the water is the solvent.

One reason that water is able to dissolve many substances is that it is polar. The charged ends of the water molecule attract the molecules of other polar substances. Sugar is a familiar polar substance. When you add a sugar cube to a cup of hot tea, the polar water molecules in the tea pull on the polar sugar molecules on the surfaces of the cube. As those sugar molecules

Follow That String

You can use a string to pour water sideways! Try this activity over a sink or outdoors.

ACTIVITY

1. Cut a piece of string as long as your arm. Wet the string.
2. Fill a pitcher with water. Tie the string to the handle.
3. Drape the string across the spout and let the other end dangle into a plastic cup. Tape the end of the string to the inside of the cup.

4. Hold the cup below the pitcher so that the string is pulled tight. As your partner gently pours the water into the cup, slowly move the cup to the right of the spout, keeping the string tight.

Inferring How do water's polar molecules cause it to follow the string?

Figure 8 Water's ability to dissolve limestone created the spiky stalactites and stalagmites in this cave in Arkansas' Ozark Mountains. As the water evaporated, the rock formations were left behind.

In this activity you will compare how well water and oil dissolve several substances.

1. Label six small plastic cups A, B, C, D, E, and F.

2. Add water to cups A, B, and C until they are half full. Add the same amount of vegetable oil to cups D, E, and F.

3. Make a table like the one shown below to help organize your observations.

Cup	Contents	Result
A	Water	
	Salt	

4. Now stir a spoonful of salt into cups A and D. Record your observations.

5. Stir a spoonful of baking soda into cups B and E. Record your observations.

6. Add two drops of food coloring to cups C and F. Do not stir. Record your observations.

Drawing Conclusions In which solvent did each substance dissolve better? Propose an explanation for your results. (*Hint:* Think about the difference between polar and nonpolar molecules.)

dissolve, other sugar molecules are exposed to the water. Eventually the sugar cube dissolves into many individual molecules too small to see. The result is a solution of sweetened tea.

Water dissolves so many substances that it is often called the "universal solvent." It can dissolve solids, such as salt and soap, and liquids, such as bleach and rubbing alcohol. Water also dissolves many gases, including oxygen and carbon dioxide. These dissolved gases are important for organisms that live in the water.

However, some substances, such as oils and wax, do not dissolve in water. You have observed this if you have ever seen the oil separate from the vinegar and water in salad dressing. The molecules of oil are nonpolar molecules — they have no charged regions. Nonpolar molecules do not dissolve well in water.

☑ *Checkpoint* List a solid, a liquid, and a gas that dissolve in water.

Changing State

It's a hot, humid summer day. To cool down, you put some ice cubes in a glass and add cold water. Is there anything unusual about this scene? Surprisingly, yes! You are interacting with water in three different **states,** or forms: solid, liquid, and gas. **The ice is a solid, the water is a liquid, and the water vapor in the air is a gas.** In terms of chemistry, this is a remarkable situation. Water is the only substance on Earth that commonly exists in all of its different states.

As you know if you have ever boiled water or made ice cubes, water can change from one state to another. Most other substances require extremes of hot or cold to change state. A steel car door doesn't melt in a July heat wave. In fact, steel would remain a solid even inside your kitchen oven. The air you breathe remains a gas whether the weather is hot or cold. Water, however, can change states within the range of Earth's normal temperatures.

Melting To understand how temperature is related to change of state, start by thinking about an ice cube. The ice is a solid. It has a regular shape because its molecules are arranged in a rigid structure. Suppose that the temperature of the ice is −10°C. What does the temperature tell you? Temperature is a measurement of the average speed of the molecules. Although you can't see them, all the molecules in a substance are constantly moving. At −10°C, the molecules in the ice cube are vibrating back and forth, but they are not moving fast enough to break free of their structure.

Now suppose that you put the ice cube in a pan on the stove. As heat energy is added, the molecules in the ice start moving faster. The temperature rises. When the temperature reaches 0°C, the solid ice melts and becomes liquid water.

Boiling and Evaporation As you know, liquid water looks very different from solid ice. The liquid flows and takes the shape of the pan. This is true because the molecules in liquid water have more energy than the molecules in ice. The molecules move more freely, bouncing off each other.

What happens if you continue to heat the water on the stove? As more energy is added to the liquid water, the speed of the molecules increases and the temperature rises. At 100°C, the water boils and another change of state occurs. The molecules have enough energy to escape the liquid and become invisible water vapor. The molecules in a gas move even more freely than those in a liquid. They spread out to fill their container — in this example, your whole kitchen!

Another way that liquid water can become a gas is through evaporation. **Evaporation** is the process by which molecules at the surface of a liquid absorb enough energy to change to the gaseous state. If you let your hair air-dry after going swimming, you are taking advantage of evaporation.

Condensation As water vapor cools down, it releases some of its energy to its surroundings. The molecules slow down and the temperature decreases. As the temperature of the gas reaches the boiling point, the water vapor begins to change back to the liquid state. The process by which a gas changes to a liquid is called **condensation.** When you fog up a window by breathing on it, you are seeing the effects of condensation. The invisible water vapor in your breath is cooled by the window and forms visible drops of liquid water.

Figure 9 Water exists on Earth in all three states: solid, liquid, and gas. **A.** The molecules in solid ice are close together and form a rigid structure. **B.** In liquid water, the molecules move more freely and the water takes the shape of its container. **C.** The molecules in gaseous water vapor move very freely and spread out to fill a space. *Comparing and Contrasting In which state do the molecules move the slowest? The fastest?*

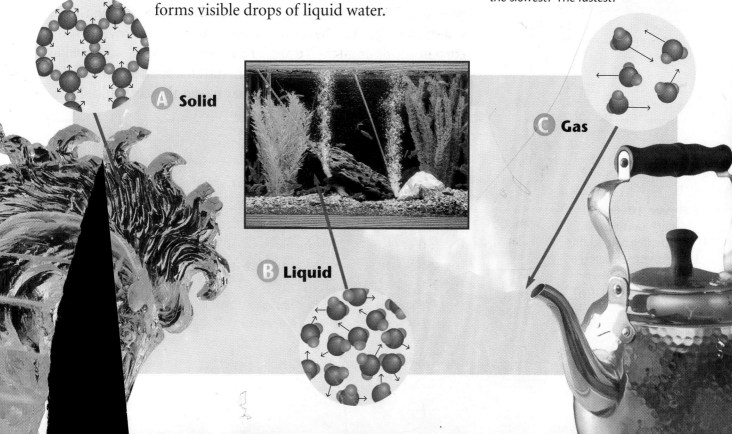

Ⓐ **Solid**

Ⓑ **Liquid**

Ⓒ **Gas**

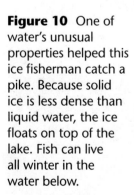

Language Arts
CONNECTION

Imagine that you work at an advertising agency. Your agency has just been hired to design an advertising campaign for water. You know that water has many properties that make it unique. Your plan is to highlight one or more of these properties in an ad to show people what an unusual substance water is.

In Your Journal

Before you begin to write, decide which properties you will highlight in your ad. Write down some facts about each property that you think will interest people. Now you are ready to create the ad. Use humor, pictures, and everyday examples to make your point in an appealing way. Will your ad convince people that water is a unique substance?

Freezing If the liquid water continues to be cooled, the molecules continue to lose energy. They move more and more slowly. At 0°C, the liquid water freezes, changing back into solid ice. If you have ever observed an icicle forming from water dripping off a roof, you have seen this change of state in progress.

☑ *Checkpoint* **In which state do water molecules have the most energy?**

Why Ice Floats

You know from experience that ice cubes in a glass float at the top of the water. If you combine the solid and liquid forms of most other substances, the solid sinks to the bottom. You have observed this if you have ever melted wax to make candles. The solid wax pieces sink to the bottom of the hot liquid wax.

As most liquids cool, their molecules slow down and move closer together until they reach their compact solid form. But surprisingly, something different happens to water. When water cools below about 4°C, the molecules begin to line up in a gridlike crystal structure. The molecules take up more space in this crystal structure than as a liquid. Frozen water in an ice cube tray contains the same amount of matter as when it was a liquid. However, the water takes up more space as ice than it did as a liquid. This means that ice is less dense than liquid water. Less dense substances, like the ice, float on more dense substances, like the liquid water.

 INTEGRATING LIFE SCIENCE The fact that ice floats has important consequences for fish and other organisms that live in water. When lakes and ponds freeze in the winter, the ice stays at the top. The ice layer shelters the water below from the coldest winds and air. The fish are able to live in the water below the ice and find food on the bottom of the lake. If water acted as most substances do when they freeze, the ice would sink to the bottom of the lake as it formed.

Figure 10 One of water's unusual properties helped this ice fisherman catch a pike. Because solid ice is less dense than liquid water, the ice floats on top of the lake. Fish can live all winter in the water below.

Specific Heat

Imagine a steamy July day. The air is hot, the sidewalk is hot, and the sandy beach is hot. You jump into a pool or the ocean, and the water is surprisingly cool! But if you go for an evening swim, the water is warm compared to the cool air.

You feel this difference in temperature because of water's unusually high specific heat. **Specific heat** is the amount of heat needed to increase the temperature of a certain mass of a substance by 1°C. Compared to other substances, water requires a lot of heat to increase its temperature.

Water's high specific heat is due to the many attractions among water molecules. Other substances, such as air and rocks, have fewer attractions between their molecules. Their temperature increases more quickly as they are heated than water that is heated the same amount.

One effect of water's high specific heat is that land areas located near large bodies of water experience less dramatic temperature changes than areas far inland. In the summer, the sun's heat warms the land more quickly than the water. The warm land heats the air above it to a higher temperature than the air over the ocean. As a result, the air is warmer inland than on the coast. Just the opposite effect occurs in the winter. The land loses heat to the air more quickly than the water. The water remains warm and keeps the air above it warmer than the air over the cold land.

Figure 11 What could be more refreshing than a swim on a hot summer day? This swimmer is taking advantage of water's high specific heat. *Applying Concepts How does this property of water help the swimmer cool off?*

Section 2 Review

1. What causes water molecules to be attracted to each other?
2. Why does sugar dissolve well in water?
3. Describe what is happening to the water molecules as ice melts.
4. What unusual fact about ice causes it to float in liquid water?
5. **Thinking Critically Predicting** If you place a cup of sand and a cup of water in the sun, which one will heat up faster? Explain your prediction in terms of a property of water.

Science at Home

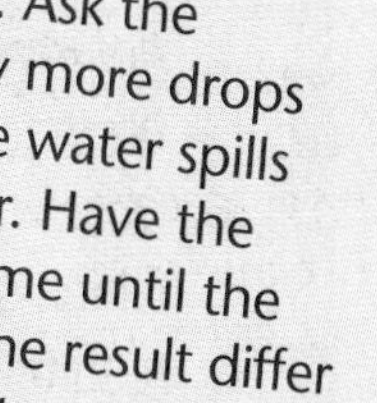

Put a penny on a piece of paper. With a plastic dropper or a toothpick, have a family member place a single drop of water on the penny. Ask the person to predict how many more drops he or she can add before the water spills off the penny onto the paper. Have the person add drops one at a time until the water overflows. How does the result differ from the prediction? Explain to your family member which property of water might account for this result.

Speeding Up Evaporation

You have just learned that water changes from a liquid to a gas through evaporation. In this lab, you will develop hypotheses as you investigate this process.

Problem

What factors increase the rate at which water evaporates?

Materials

water   3 index cards
plastic dropper   paper towels
2 plastic petri dishes   stopwatch
1 petri dish cover   lamp

Procedure

Part 1 Effect of Heat

1. Copy the data table into your notebook.
2. How do you think heating a water sample will affect how fast it evaporates? Record your hypothesis in the data table.
3. Place each petri dish on an index card.
4. Add a single drop of water to each of the petri dishes. Try to make the two drops the same size.
5. Position the lamp over one of the dishes as a heat source. Turn on the light. Make sure the light does not shine on the other dish. **CAUTION:** *The light bulb will become very hot. Avoid touching the bulb or getting water on it.*
6. Observe the dishes every 3 minutes to see which sample evaporates faster. Record your result in the data table.

DATA TABLE	
Part 1 Effect of Heat	
Hypothesis	
Result	
Part 2 Effect of a Cover	
Hypothesis	
Result	
Part 3 Effect of Wind	
Hypothesis	
Result	

Part 2 Effect of a Cover

7. How do you think placing a cover over the water sample will affect how fast it evaporates? Record your hypothesis in the data table.
8. Dry both petri dishes and place them side by side over the index cards. Add a drop of water to each dish as you did in Step 4.
9. Place a cover over one dish. Leave the other dish uncovered.
10. Observe the dishes after 10 minutes to see which sample evaporates faster. Record your result in the data table.

Part 3 Effect of Wind

11. How do you think fanning the water sample will affect how fast it evaporates? Record your hypothesis in the data table.
12. Dry both petri dishes and place them over the index cards. Add a drop of water to each dish as you did in Step 4.

13. Use an index card to fan one of the dishes for 5 minutes. Be careful not to fan the other dish as well.

14. Observe the dishes to see which sample evaporates faster. Record your result in the data table.

Analyze and Conclude

1. In which cases were your hypotheses correct? In which cases were they incorrect?

2. For each part of the experiment, explain why the water evaporated faster in one dish than the other. (*Hint:* Think about what happened to the water molecules in each dish.)

3. Make a general statement about factors that increase the rate at which water evaporates.

4. Based on this experiment, predict what would happen in each of the following situations.

   a. Would a wet swimsuit dry faster in a plastic bag or out in the open? Explain.

   b. Would wet clothes on a clothesline dry faster on a windy day or on a calm day? Explain.

   c. Would wet clothes dry faster if they were hung on a clothesline located on the sunny side of a house or on the shady side? Explain.

5. **Think About It** What knowledge or everyday experiences helped you make your hypotheses at the beginning of the experiment? Explain how hypotheses differ from guesses.

More to Explore

How do you think increasing the surface area of a water sample will affect how fast it evaporates? Write your hypothesis and then design an experiment to test it. Be sure to check your plan with your teacher before carrying out your experiment.

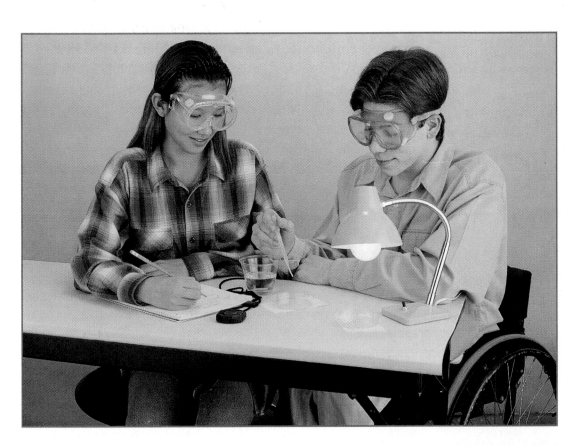

Where Does the Water Come From?

1. Fill a glass with ice cubes and water, being careful not to spill any water. Set the glass aside for 5 minutes.

2. Observe the outside of the glass and the surface it was sitting on.

Think It Over

Inferring Where did the water on the outside of the glass come from? How do you think it got there?

◆ How does Earth's water move through the water cycle?

◆ In what ways do living things depend on the water cycle?

Reading Tip Before you read, preview *Exploring the Water Cycle* on the facing page. Make a list of any unfamiliar words in the diagram.

The next time it rains, cup your hand and catch some raindrops. Think about where a single water molecule in one of those raindrops may have traveled. Most recently, it was part of the gray cloud overhead. Last year, it may have tumbled over a waterfall or floated down the Nile River. Perhaps it spent years as part of the Pacific Ocean. The same water molecule may even have fallen as rain on a dinosaur millions of years ago.

How could one water molecule reappear in so many different places and forms? In fact, all the water on Earth has been through similar changes. Water is naturally recycled through the water cycle. The **water cycle** is the continuous process by which water moves through the living and nonliving parts of the environment. **In the water cycle, water moves from bodies of water, land, and living things on Earth's surface to the atmosphere and back to Earth's surface.** The sun is the source of energy that drives the water cycle.

Water Evaporates

Water moves continuously through the water cycle. The cycle has no real beginning or end. You can follow a water molecule through one complete cycle in *Exploring the Water Cycle* on the facing page.

Think about a molecule of water floating near the surface of an ocean. The sun is shining and the air is warm. Soon, the molecule has absorbed enough heat energy to change state. It evaporates and becomes water vapor. Although the water comes from the salty ocean, it becomes fresh through the process of evaporation. The salt remains in the ocean.

Large amounts of water evaporate constantly from the surfaces of oceans and large lakes. In addition, small amounts evaporate from the soil, puddles, and even from your skin.

A significant amount of water is given off by plants. Plants draw in water from the soil through their roots. Eventually the water is given off through the leaves as water vapor in a process called **transpiration.** You may be surprised to learn how much water plants release to the atmosphere through transpiration.

EXPLORING *the Water Cycle*

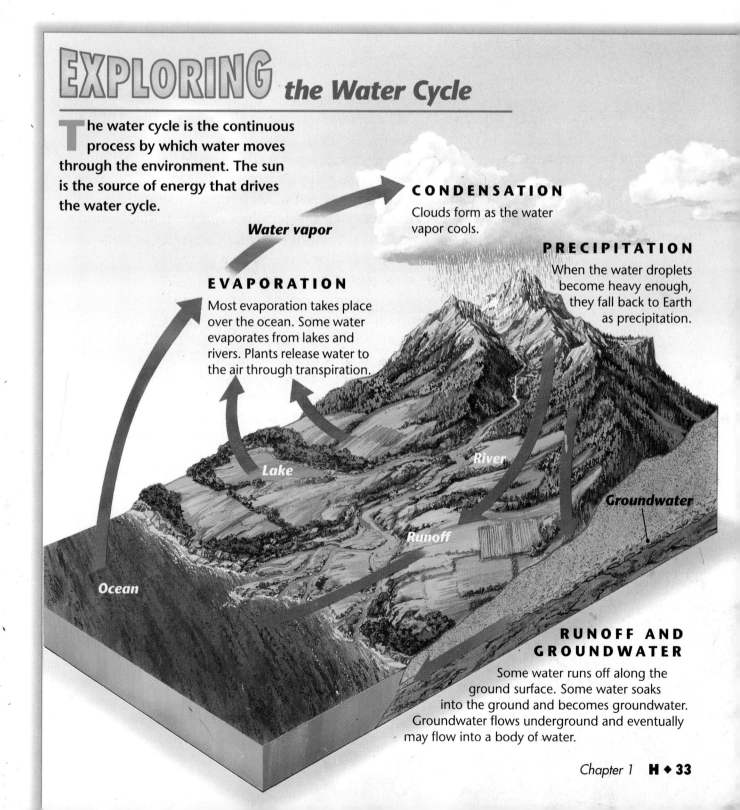

The water cycle is the continuous process by which water moves through the environment. The sun is the source of energy that drives the water cycle.

Water vapor

CONDENSATION
Clouds form as the water vapor cools.

PRECIPITATION
When the water droplets become heavy enough, they fall back to Earth as precipitation.

EVAPORATION
Most evaporation takes place over the ocean. Some water evaporates from lakes and rivers. Plants release water to the air through transpiration.

Lake

River

Groundwater

Runoff

Ocean

RUNOFF AND GROUNDWATER
Some water runs off along the ground surface. Some water soaks into the ground and becomes groundwater. Groundwater flows underground and eventually may flow into a body of water.

Figure 12 Clouds and mist blanket this lush rain forest in Costa Rica. *Relating Cause and Effect Describe how the processes of evaporation and condensation can cause clouds to form.*

Tabletop Water Cycle

In this activity  you will build a model of the water cycle.

1. Put on your goggles. Pour enough water into a flat-bottomed bowl to cover the bottom. Fill a small jar with sand and place it in the bowl.

2. Loosely cover the top of the bowl with plastic wrap. Secure with a rubber band.

3. Place a rock on top of the plastic, directly over the jar.

4. Place the bowl in direct sunlight or under a lamp. After one hour, observe the bowl and plastic wrap.

Making a Model What features of the water cycle are represented in your model?

The thousands of leaves on a single birch tree, for example, may give off 260 liters of water in one day — enough to fill nine kitchen sinks!

Have you ever seen your breath on a cold day? If so, you have observed another way that water vapor enters the atmosphere. Small amounts of water vapor are released by animals when they exhale. Tiny amounts of water vapor also enter the air from ice, when water passes directly from the solid state to the gaseous state.

☑ *Checkpoint* **List three places from which water evaporates.**

Clouds Form

Once a water molecule has found its way into the atmosphere, what happens next? Warm air carries the water molecule higher into the atmosphere. Higher up, the air tends to become much colder. Cold air holds less water vapor than warm air. Some of the water vapor cools and condenses into liquid water. Condensed droplets of water clump together around tiny dust particles in the air, forming clouds. In even colder parts of the upper atmosphere, the water vapor sometimes forms ice crystals rather than water droplets.

Water Falls As Precipitation

As more water vapor condenses, the water droplets in a cloud grow larger and larger. Eventually, the drops become so heavy that they fall back to Earth. Water that falls to Earth as rain, snow, hail, or sleet is called **precipitation.** Most water molecules probably spend only about 10 days in the atmosphere before falling back to Earth. Most precipitation falls directly into the oceans. Water in the ocean may stay there for many years before evaporating, thus continuing the cycle.

When precipitation falls on land, some of the water evaporates again immediately. Some runs off the surface of the land into rivers and lakes. From there, it may eventually evaporate or flow back into the ocean. Some water trickles down into the ground and forms groundwater. Groundwater may move underground until it reaches a river, lake, or ocean. Once groundwater reaches the surface, it can continue through the cycle by evaporating again.

Before returning to the atmosphere, some water passes through living things. Animals drink the water and eventually release it back to the environment as a waste product. Plants use the water to grow and to produce food. When these living things die, their bodies are broken down slowly, and the water returns to the environment.

A Global Process

Precipitation is the source of all fresh water on and below Earth's surface. The water cycle renews the usable supply of fresh water on Earth. For millions of years, the total amount of water on Earth has remained fairly constant. The worldwide amounts of evaporation and precipitation balance each other. This may not seem believable if you live in an area where there is either a lot of precipitation or very little. It is possible for parts of India to receive as much as 1,000 centimeters of precipitation in a year, while the Sahara, a desert in Africa, may get only 5 centimeters. But in the world as a whole, the rates of evaporation and precipitation are balanced.

Figure 13 These thirsty zebras are a part of the water cycle. The water they drink passes through their bodies and is released in their wastes.

Section 3 Review

1. Describe the general path of water as it moves through the water cycle.
2. How does the water cycle renew Earth's supply of fresh water?
3. What is the source of the energy that drives the water cycle?
4. **Thinking Critically Relating Cause and Effect** How might cutting down trees affect the amount of evaporation in an area?

Check Your Progress
CHAPTER PROJECT 1

By now you should have chosen a building in your community to monitor. How will you determine the amount and type of water usage there? Be sure to check with your teacher before contacting anyone at the site. (*Hint:* A building manager or facilities manager often has information about water use. You may find it helpful to write down your questions before you interview the person.)

Water From Trees

Trees play many important roles in the environment—they keep the soil from washing away, remove carbon dioxide from the air, and produce oxygen. Trees are also a vital part of the water cycle. In this lab you will discover how trees help to keep water moving through the cycle.

DATA TABLE

Starting mass of bags, ties, and pebbles	
Mass of bags, ties, and pebbles after 24 hours	
Difference in mass	

Problem

How much water do the leaves on a tree give off in a 24-hour period?

Skills Focus

observing, calculating, inferring

Materials

3 plastic sandwich bags   balance
3 small pebbles   3 twist ties

Procedure

1. Copy the data table into your notebook.
2. Place the sandwich bags, twist ties, and pebbles on a balance. Determine their total mass to the nearest tenth of a gram.
3. Select an outdoor tree or shrub with leaves that are within your reach.
4. Put one pebble into a sandwich bag and place the bag over one of the tree's leaves as shown. Fasten the twist tie around the bag, forming a tight seal around the stem of the leaf.
5. Repeat Step 4 with the other plastic bags on two more leaves. Leave the bags in place on the leaves for 24 hours.
6. The following day, examine the bags and record your observations in your notebook.

7. Carefully remove the bags from the leaves and refasten each twist tie around its bag so that the bag is closed tightly.
8. Place the three bags, including pebbles and twist ties, on the balance. Determine their total mass to the nearest tenth of a gram.
9. Subtract the original mass of the bags, ties, and pebbles that you found in Step 2 from the mass you found in Step 8.

Analyze and Conclude

1. Based on your observations, how can you account for the difference in mass?
2. What is the name of the process that caused the results you observed? Explain the role of that process in the water cycle.
3. A single birch tree may transpire as much as 260 liters of water in a day. How much water would a grove of 1,000 birch trees return to the atmosphere in a year?
4. **Apply** Based on what you learned from this investigation, what is one reason that people may be concerned about the destruction of forests around the world?

More to Explore

Find another type of tree and repeat this experiment. What might account for any differences in the amount of water the two trees transpire?

SECTION 1 — How Is Water Important?

Key Ideas

◆ People use water for many purposes, including household use, industry, agriculture, transportation, and recreation.

◆ All living things need water to carry out their life processes.

◆ About 97 percent of Earth's water is salt water stored in the oceans. Less than 1 percent is usable fresh water.

Key Terms

irrigation   photosynthesis   habitat
water vapor   groundwater

SECTION 2 — The Properties of Water

INTEGRATING CHEMISTRY

Key Ideas

◆ A water molecule consists of two hydrogen atoms bonded to an oxygen atom. The hydrogen ends of the molecule have a slight positive charge. The oxygen end of the molecule has a slight negative charge.

◆ The charged ends of water's polar molecules attract the charged ends of other water molecules. Water molecules are also attracted to other charged particles.

◆ Some properties caused by the attractions among water molecules are surface tension, capillary action, and high specific heat.

◆ Water dissolves so many substances that it is sometimes called the "universal solvent."

◆ Water on Earth exists in three states: liquid water; ice, a solid; and water vapor, a gas.

◆ Energy must be added or released for water molecules to change state.

◆ Unlike most other substances, the solid form of water is less dense than the liquid form.

Key Terms

polar molecule   surface tension   capillary action
solution   solvent   state
evaporation   condensation   specific heat

SECTION 3 — The Water Cycle

Key Ideas

◆ In the water cycle, water evaporates from Earth's surface into the atmosphere. The water forms clouds, then falls back to Earth as precipitation. The sun's energy drives the water cycle.

◆ The water cycle renews Earth's supply of fresh water. In the world as a whole, the rates of evaporation and precipitation balance each other.

Key Terms

water cycle   transpiration   precipitation

USING THE INTERNET

ACTIVITY

www.science-explorer.phschool.com

Reviewing Content

For more review of key concepts, see the Interactive Student Tutorial CD-ROM.

Multiple Choice

Choose the letter of the best answer.

1. The process of supplying land areas with water to make them suitable for farming is
   a. transpiration.   b. irrigation.
   c. condensation.   d. capillary action.

2. More than 97 percent of Earth's total water supply is found in
   a. ice sheets.
   b. the atmosphere.
   c. the oceans.
   d. groundwater.

3. A molecule with electrically charged parts is a
   a. nonpolar molecule.
   b. solution.
   c. polar molecule.
   d. gas.

4. When you stir salt into water, you are making a
   a. solution.   b. solvent.
   c. solid.   d. molecule.

5. The energy that drives the water cycle comes from the
   a. Earth.   b. sun.
   c. rain.   d. ocean.

True or False

If the statement is true, write true. If it is false, change the underlined word or words to make the statement true.

6. The process in which plants use water, light, and carbon dioxide to make food is called <u>photosynthesis</u>.

7. Most of Earth's liquid fresh water is found in the form of <u>lakes</u>.

8. The property of <u>surface tension</u> allows insects to walk on water.

9. In the water cycle, precipitation returns <u>salt</u> water to Earth.

10. The process by which the leaves of plants give off water into the atmosphere is <u>condensation</u>.

Checking Concepts

11. How is the water supplied to plants important for many other living things on Earth?

12. Explain why Earth is called the "water planet."

13. Explain why so little of Earth's water is available for human use.

14. Draw a diagram of a water molecule that shows how it is polar. Be sure to include labels in your diagram.

15. Give examples of two properties of water that are caused by the attractions between water molecules.

16. Describe two changes of state that occur during the water cycle.

17. **Writing to Learn** As the information officer aboard a starship, you are assigned to write a handbook describing Earth's waters to visitors from other galaxies. Write a description in which you explain how water is important to living things on Earth.

Thinking Visually

18. **Cycle Diagram** Copy the cycle diagram onto a sheet of paper and complete it to show one possible path for a water molecule. Add a title. (For more on cycle diagrams, see the Skills Handbook.)

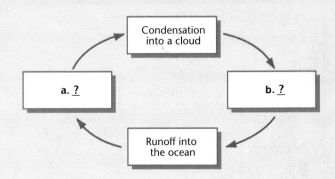

Applying Skills

Use this circle graph to answer questions 19–21.

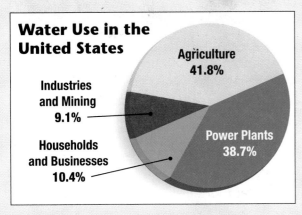

Water Use in the United States

- Agriculture 41.8%
- Industries and Mining 9.1%
- Households and Businesses 10.4%
- Power Plants 38.7%

19. Interpreting Data Which category represents the largest use of water in the United States? Which is the smallest?

20. Calculating If the total daily usage of water in the United States is 1,280 billion liters, how many liters are used each day by power plants?

21. Predicting How would an increase in the amount of irrigation affect this graph?

Thinking Critically

22. Making Generalizations Explain why towns and cities are often located along bodies of water.

23. Comparing and Contrasting Compare the three states of water in terms of the speed and arrangement of their molecules.

24. Applying Concepts You may have heard the saying, "Oil and water don't mix." Explain this statement in terms of the chemistry of water.

25. Predicting The city of Charleston, South Carolina, is located on the Atlantic coast. The city of Macon, Georgia, is located about 340 kilometers inland to the west. Predict which city is likely to be cooler in the summer. Explain your answer.

26. Relating Cause and Effect A molecule of water is likely to evaporate more quickly from the Caribbean Sea near the equator than from the Arctic Ocean. Explain why this statement is true.

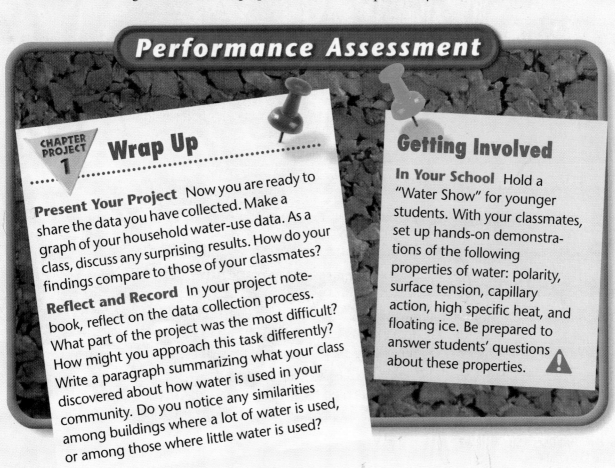

Performance Assessment

CHAPTER PROJECT 1 — Wrap Up

Present Your Project Now you are ready to share the data you have collected. Make a graph of your household water-use data. As a class, discuss any surprising results. How do your findings compare to those of your classmates?

Reflect and Record In your project notebook, reflect on the data collection process. What part of the project was the most difficult? How might you approach this task differently? Write a paragraph summarizing what your class discovered about how water is used in your community. Do you notice any similarities among buildings where a lot of water is used, or among those where little water is used?

Getting Involved

In Your School Hold a "Water Show" for younger students. With your classmates, set up hands-on demonstrations of the following properties of water: polarity, surface tension, capillary action, high specific heat, and floating ice. Be prepared to answer students' questions about these properties.

WHAT'S AHEAD

PROJECT 2

Build a Watershed

The bull moose plunges into the stream, sending shimmering drops of water flying in all directions. In addition to a refreshing dip, the stream provides the moose with drinking water and a place to find food. A stream is one place you can find fresh water on Earth. In this chapter you will explore fresh water as it moves and changes the land, as it collects in lakes and ponds and provides a home for living things, and as it flows underground. Throughout the chapter, you will be making a model showing how water moves over the land.

Your Goal To design and build a three-dimensional model of a watershed and river system.

Your model should
◆ include a main river and at least two tributaries
◆ show at least one example of a body of standing water
◆ be constructed of materials that allow water to run over it
◆ be built following the safety guidelines in Appendix A

Get Started Begin by previewing Section 1 to see some parts of a river system. Look at the shape of the land surrounding different parts of rivers. Start thinking about materials you could use to make your landscape.

Check Your Progress You'll be working on this project as you study this chapter. To keep your project on track, look for Check Your Progress boxes at the following points.
Section 1 Review, page 52: Sketch a design for your watershed.
Section 3 Review, page 64: Revise your design to include all features.
Section 5 Review, page 74: Build your model watershed.

Wrap Up At the end of the chapter (page 77), you will use a spray bottle to demonstrate your watershed in action!

A bull moose shakes himself off following a dip in an Alaskan stream.

 SECTION 4 Glaciers and Icebergs

Discover How Can Ice Change the Land?

 SECTION 5 Water Underground

Discover Where Does the Water Go?
Sharpen Your Skills Drawing Conclusions
Real-World Lab Soil Testing
Try This An Artesian Well

① Streams and Rivers

DISCOVER · ACTIVITY · · · ·

What Affects How Water Moves?

1. Cover the bottom of a pan with a mixture of sand and pebbles.
2. Press a small piece of porcelain tile onto the sand mixture to represent pavement. In another area of the pan, press a clump of soil and grass into the sand.
3. Prop up one end of the pan so it slopes gently.
4. Using a watering can, sprinkle "rain" onto the pan's contents.
5. Observe how the water moves when it falls on the sand mixture, on the tile, and on the grass.
6. Wash your hands when you are finished with this activity.

Think It Over

Predicting How would the movement of the water change if you poured the water all at once? If you tilted the pan more steeply?

GUIDE FOR READING

◆ What is a river system?

◆ How does a river change the land around it?

◆ What conditions can cause a flood?

Reading Tip Before you read, use the section headings to make an outline. Leave space to take notes as you read.

Standing on a bridge in Albuquerque, New Mexico, you look through your binoculars at the waters of the Rio Grande—the "Big River." The name fits this broad, deep stretch of water. But 700 kilometers upstream, the Rio Grande looks very different. The river begins as trickles of melting snow high in the San Juan Mountains in Colorado. As more water joins the river, it carves deep, narrow canyons out of the rock.

By the time it reaches Albuquerque the river has grown wider. It continues into Texas, winding back and forth across the dusty desert valley. In places, the river is so shallow that it may even dry up during the summer. When the Rio Grande finally empties its water into the Gulf of Mexico, it is sluggish and heavy with mud.

Spanish explorers once gave different names to three parts of the Rio Grande. They thought they had seen three different rivers! In this section, you will discover how rivers change, and how they change the land around them.

How Do Rivers Begin?

Have you ever helped out at a car wash for your school or youth group? Think about what happened to the water that sloshed onto the pavement. First the water ran in little trickles, which then joined together into a larger stream. The water followed the slope of the pavement down to the street or into a storm drain. A river begins in much the same way—trickles of water run over the ground and join together in larger streams.

When rain falls, some of the water evaporates immediately. Some soaks into the soil. The remaining water that flows over the ground surface is called **runoff.** Runoff also comes from melting ice and snow, like the runoff that forms the beginnings of the Rio Grande.

Figure 1 In addition to washing a car, these teens are demonstrating how ground surface affects the formation of runoff. *Applying Concepts What happens to the water that lands on the pavement? The grass?*

Factors That Affect Runoff

What determines whether water soaks into the ground or flows over it as runoff? One factor is the nature of the ground surface. Water soaks into some types of ground covering more easily than others. How much water soaks in depends on the amount of space between the particles that make up the ground cover. For example, there is more space between the particles of soil than between the particles of pavement. As a result, water soaks into soil more easily than into pavement. Since plant roots also absorb water, ground that is covered with grass or trees absorbs water more easily than bare soil.

The rate of rainfall is a second factor that affects the amount of runoff. During a heavy downpour, so much rain falls in a short time that it can't all soak into the ground. Instead some becomes runoff.

A third factor is whether the land is flat or hilly. The force of gravity pulls water downhill, just as it pulls you downhill on a sled or skateboard. Water flows faster down a steep slope than over flat ground. Because the water is moving so quickly, it runs off instead of soaking in. As runoff flows along a trench, or channel, it forms a stream. This is the beginning of the process that forms a river.

☑ *Checkpoint* List three factors that affect the amount of runoff.

River Systems

If you were hiking in the San Juan Mountains, you could observe the path of the runoff from melting snow. As you followed one small stream downhill, you would notice that the stream reached a larger stream and joined it. You could then continue along this stream until it flowed into a small river. Eventually this path would lead you to the Rio Grande itself.

Tributaries are the smaller streams and rivers that feed into a main river. **A river and all its tributaries together make up a river system.** The tributaries flow toward the main river following a downhill path due to the pull of gravity. Even a land area that appears flat can have small differences in height that affect how water flows.

Watersheds Just as all the water in a bathtub flows toward the drain, all the water in a river system drains into the main river. The land area that supplies water to a river system is called a **watershed.** Watersheds are also called drainage basins.

A river can flow into another, larger river. When rivers join another river system, the areas they drain become part of the largest river's watershed. You can identify a river's watershed on a map by drawing an imaginary line around the region drained by all its tributaries. Some watersheds are very small. The watershed of a stream that flows down a hill into a river is just that hillside—maybe a square kilometer or two. By contrast, the watershed of the Mississippi River covers more than 3 million

Figure 2 This map shows the watersheds of several large rivers in the United States. Each river's watershed consists of the region drained by the river and all its tributaries. *Interpreting Maps Name five tributaries of the Mississippi River. Which tributary has the largest watershed?*

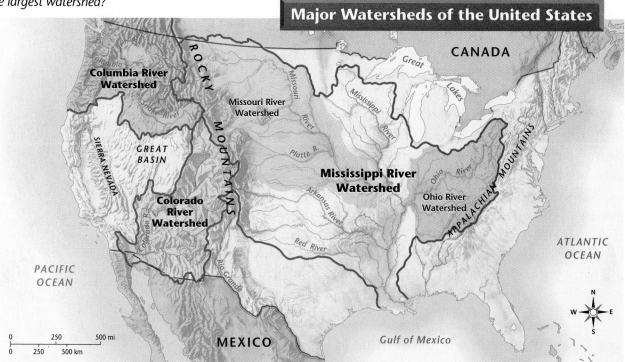

Major Watersheds of the United States

square kilometers! With your finger, trace the boundary of the Mississippi's watershed on Figure 2. Notice that it includes the watersheds of the Ohio River and the Missouri River, its two largest tributaries.

Divides One watershed is separated from another by a ridge of land called a **divide.** Streams on each side of the divide flow in different directions. The Continental Divide, the longest divide in North America, follows the line of the Rocky Mountains. Locate the Rocky Mountains on Figure 2. West of the Continental Divide, water either flows toward the Pacific Ocean or into the dry Great Basin, where the water usually evaporates. Between the Rocky Mountains and the Appalachian Mountains, water flows toward the Mississippi River or directly into the Gulf of Mexico.

☑ *Checkpoint* *Into what ocean do rivers east of the Appalachian Mountains flow?*

Rivers Shape the Land

The next time it rains, watch the rainwater flow along the side of a road. Notice how the water picks up leaves and twigs and carries them away. Bits of paper and small pebbles bounce and swirl along in the flow. Even a tiny stream has the power to move objects.

Picture a stream ten times larger, and you will start to get an idea of how running water can cause erosion. **Erosion** is the process by which fragments of soil and rock are broken off from the ground surface and carried away. These fragments are carried along by the moving water until they are eventually dropped, or deposited, in a new location. **Deposition** is the process by which soil and rock are left behind. **Rivers wear away landforms through erosion and build new landforms through deposition.** The particles of rock and soil that are picked up and moved by erosion and deposition are called **sediments.**

A river's speed affects its ability to wear away, or erode, the land. The faster the water flows, the more energy it has. A river traveling at a speed of 1 kilometer an hour

The Knuckle Divide

Make your hand into a **ACTIVITY** fist and put it on a paper towel, knuckles facing up. With your other hand, dribble water from a spoon so that it falls onto your knuckles. Observe how the water flows over your hand.

Making a Model How are your knuckles similar to a mountain range on land? What parts of your hand represent a watershed?

Figure 3 A hiker carefully avoids the collapsed edge of this dirt road, evidence of moving water's power to erode soil.

has enough energy to move pebbles along. At 18 kilometers an hour it can move a boulder the size of an armchair! When a river slows down, its energy decreases. It can no longer move heavy objects. The river deposits heavier sediment particles first, then lighter ones.

One factor that affects how fast a river flows is the steepness of its slope. Water flows faster down a mountainside than over a flat plain. A second factor that affects a river's speed is the volume of water in the river. An increase in the amount of water in a river

Interpreting Data

How Fast Does a Stream Flow?

In this lab, you will interpret data to see how different factors affect stream flow. First, you will build a model called a stream trough.

Problem

How do the slope of a stream and the volume of water it contains affect its speed?

Materials

meterstick	water
pencil with eraser	stopwatch
several wooden blocks	plastic tub

2 100-mL beakers with pour spouts
rain gutter section, 120 cm or longer
food coloring in squeeze-top bottle

Procedure

1. Copy the data table into your notebook. Label it "Experiment number 1."
2. Use the pencil to mark an "S" at one end of the gutter. This represents the stream's source. Mark an "M" at the other end of the gutter. This represents the stream's mouth.
3. About 10 cm from the source end, draw a dark line across the inside of the gutter.

DATA TABLE

Experiment number: _____

Number of blocks: _____

Number of beakers: _____

Trial Number	Time (seconds)
Trial 1	
Trial 2	
Trial 3	

Average time: _____

Average stream speed: _____

4. Measure 100 cm toward the mouth end from the first line. Draw a second line across the gutter.
5. Place the plastic tub under the mouth end of the gutter to collect the water.
6. Place enough blocks under the source end to raise it 5 cm above the tub. Record the number of blocks in the data table.
7. Write "1" after "Number of beakers" in the data table.

causes the river to flow faster. A third factor is the shape of the channel through which the river flows. As the water in the river rubs against the sides and bottom of its channel, it creates friction. This friction slows the water's movement. In a shallow, narrow channel, almost all the water is in contact with the sides or bottom, and it moves slowly. In a broad, deep channel, however, most of the water can flow without any friction, so the river flows faster.

8. One person should slowly pour water from one beaker into the source end of the gutter, trying not to spill any water out the back end. A second person should add one drop of food coloring at the source end, above the "S" line. A third person should begin timing when the food coloring first reaches the "S" line. Stop timing when the food coloring reaches the "M" line. Record the time on your data table. Be sure the water is collecting in the tub at the mouth end.

9. Repeat Step 8 twice, pouring the water at the same rate each time. Record your results.

10. Copy the data table again, labeling it "Experiment number 2." Repeat Steps 8 and 9 with an increased water volume in the stream. Increase the water volume by pouring water into the stream from two beakers at the same time. Try to pour both at the same rate.

11. Now increase the slope of the stream, adding blocks to raise the source end 5 cm higher.

12. Copy the data table two more times for Experiment numbers 3 and 4. For Experiment 3, repeat Steps 8 and 9 at this steeper slope. For Experiment 4, repeat Step 10.

Analyze and Conclude

1. Average the three trials for each experiment. Record the average times on your data table.

2. Calculate the average stream speed for each experiment using the following formula:

$$\text{Speed of stream (cm/s)} = \frac{\text{distance (100 cm)}}{\text{average time (s)}}$$

3. How did the speed of the stream change when you increased the volume of water?

4. How did the speed of the stream change when you increased the slope?

5. **Think About It** What errors might have affected your data? How could they be reduced?

More to Explore

The volume of sediments picked up and carried by a stream indicates how much erosion is occurring. How could you modify this experiment to test how the amount of erosion is affected by a stream's speed? Obtain your teacher's permission to try the experiment.

Profile of a River

Imagine taking a rafting trip along the entire length of a river to observe how it changes firsthand. You can follow the journey in *Exploring a River.*

The Headwaters Your trip starts near the river's beginning, or source, in the mountains. The many small streams that come together at the source of the river are called the **headwaters.** Your ride through the headwaters is quite bumpy as your raft bounces through rapids, dropping suddenly over a small waterfall. You notice how the fast-flowing water breaks off clumps of soil from

EXPLORING *a River*

As you follow this river from its headwaters to its mouth, notice how its speed, volume, and shape change. Each part of the river forms a different habitat for living things.

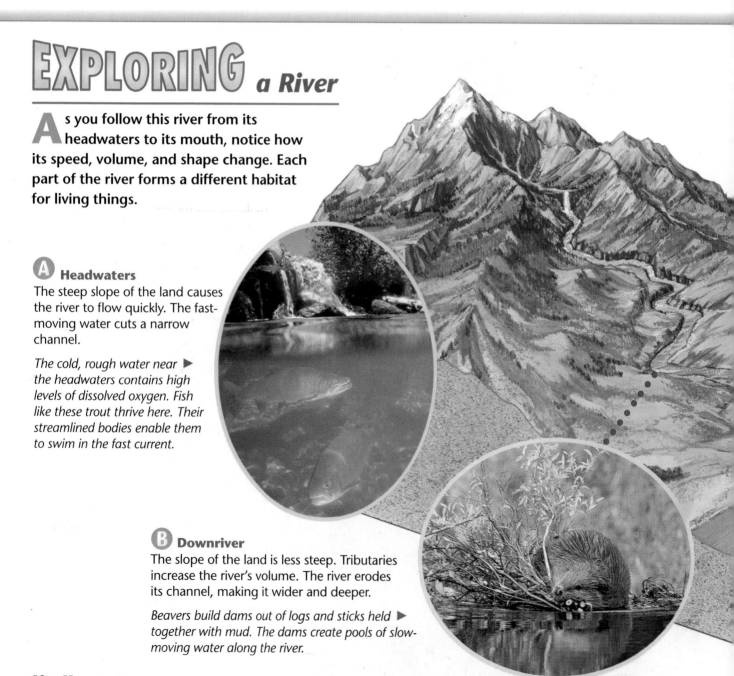

A Headwaters
The steep slope of the land causes the river to flow quickly. The fast-moving water cuts a narrow channel.

The cold, rough water near ▶ the headwaters contains high levels of dissolved oxygen. Fish like these trout thrive here. Their streamlined bodies enable them to swim in the fast current.

B Downriver
The slope of the land is less steep. Tributaries increase the river's volume. The river erodes its channel, making it wider and deeper.

Beavers build dams out of logs and sticks held ▶ together with mud. The dams create pools of slow-moving water along the river.

the riverbanks and carries them along. As the river continues this erosion, it wears away the sides and cuts into the bottom of its channel. The channel gradually becomes wider and deeper.

Downriver As you continue downriver, your ride becomes smoother. The land around the river is less steep than it was near the headwaters. Some smaller streams have joined the river, increasing the volume of water. Since less of the water is in contact with the channel, there is less friction slowing it down. As a result, although the slope is less steep, the river continues to flow fairly swiftly.

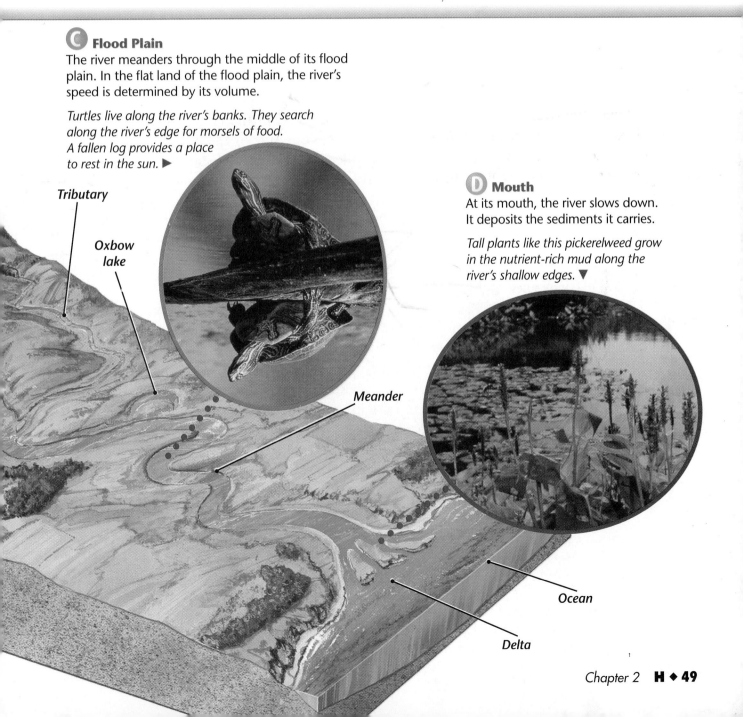

C Flood Plain

The river meanders through the middle of its flood plain. In the flat land of the flood plain, the river's speed is determined by its volume.

Turtles live along the river's banks. They search along the river's edge for morsels of food. A fallen log provides a place to rest in the sun. ▶

Tributary

Oxbow lake

Meander

D Mouth

At its mouth, the river slows down. It deposits the sediments it carries.

Tall plants like this pickerelweed grow in the nutrient-rich mud along the river's shallow edges. ▼

Ocean

Delta

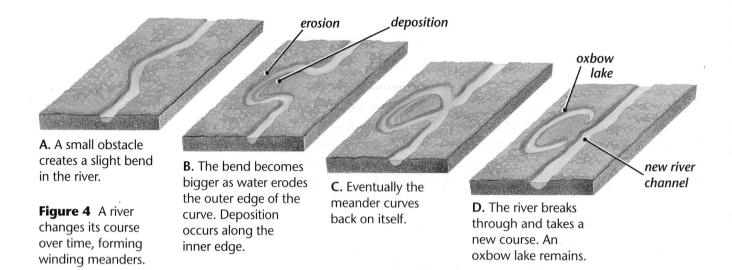

erosion   deposition

oxbow
lake

new river
channel

A. A small obstacle creates a slight bend in the river.

B. The bend becomes bigger as water erodes the outer edge of the curve. Deposition occurs along the inner edge.

C. Eventually the meander curves back on itself.

D. The river breaks through and takes a new course. An oxbow lake remains.

Figure 4 A river changes its course over time, forming winding meanders.

The Flood Plain Next your raft travels through the middle of a wide valley. The river created this valley over time by eroding the land along its banks. The broad, flat valley through which the river flows is called the **flood plain.**

In places, small obstacles in the river's channel cause the water to flow slightly to one side or the other. This movement creates a bend in the river. As Figure 4 shows, the water erodes the outer edge of the curve, where it flows faster. The river deposits sediments along the inner edge, where it flows slower. This process gradually forms looping curves in the river called **meanders.** Eventually the river may break through the ends of the meander, carving a new channel. The crescent-shaped, cutoff body of water that remains is called an **oxbow lake.**

The Mouth Your raft trip is nearly over as you approach the river's mouth. The **mouth** is the point where a river flows into another body of water—a larger river, a lake, or an ocean. When the fast-moving waters of a river hit the slower waters of a lake or ocean, the river suddenly slows down. As it slows, the river deposits most of its sediment. These deposits at the river's mouth build up, forming an area called a **delta.** The sediment deposits are rich in nutrients and minerals. As a result, the soil in delta areas is very fertile for farming.

Habitats Along a River Recall that an organism's habitat

INTEGRATING
LIFE SCIENCE

provides the things that the organism needs to live. As you saw in *Exploring a River,* a river provides habitats for many living things. Some organisms live in the river and obtain nutrients and dissolved gases from the water. Others find shelter and food along its banks.

☑ *Checkpoint* *How does a river's volume change between its headwaters and mouth?*

Sharpen your Skills

Inferring

ACTIVITY

Many of the world's rivers flow from north to south. However, the Nile River in Egypt flows from south to north. What can you infer about the slope of the land through which the Nile flows? (*Hint:* Think about the factors that determine how a river system forms.)

Rivers and Floods

Spring floods occur frequently on rivers in the Midwest, but the floods of 1997 were far worse than usual. The residents of Fargo, North Dakota, had already used a million sandbags, and the Red River of the North was still rising! As the flood waters rose, people piled the sandbags higher around their houses, hoping no water would break through. People moved their belongings to their attics, then watched as water flowed through their homes.

The Red River floods went on for weeks, fed by rain and melting snow. A spring blizzard added more snow. Other nearby rivers also flooded. Parts of North Dakota, South Dakota, and Minnesota were declared a disaster area. Weary residents just waited for the waters to recede so they could start to repair the damage.

What caused the Red River to flood so badly? **A flood occurs when the volume of water in a river increases so much that the river overflows its channel.** As rain and melting snow added more and more water, the river gained in speed and strength. Recall that as the speed of a river increases, so does the amount of energy it has. A flooding river can uproot trees and pluck boulders from the ground. As it overflows onto its floodplain, the powerful water can even wash away bridges and houses.

Throughout history, people have both feared and welcomed floods. Ancient Egyptians, for instance, called their fertile cropland "the gift of the Nile." Deposition from regular floods left a layer of rich soil on each side of the river, creating a green strip of good land in the middle of the desert. But floods can also destroy farms, towns, and crops. In the United States, 20 million people live in places where flooding is likely. Even in the last century, floods have killed millions of people around the world, many of them in the heavily populated flood plains of China, Bangladesh, and India.

Figure 5 A flood can be disastrous for nearby residents, such as the owners of this house. *Making Generalizations Explain how floods can be both harmful and helpful to people.*

Can Floods Be Controlled?

INTEGRATING TECHNOLOGY As long as people have lived on flood plains, they have tried to control floods. Building dams is one method of flood control. A dam is a barrier across a river that may redirect the flow of a river to other channels or store the water in an artificial lake. Engineers can open the dam's floodgates to release water in dry seasons. Dams work fairly well to control small floods. During severe floods, however, powerful flood waters can wash over the top of a dam or break through it.

Sediment deposits actually build a natural defense against floods. As a river overflows onto its flood plain, it slows down, depositing the heavier sediments alongside the channel. Over time, these deposits build up into long ridges called **levees.** These natural levees help keep the river inside its banks. People sometimes build up the natural levees with sandbags or stone and concrete to provide further protection against floods.

But building up levees can sometimes backfire. These walls prevent the natural channel-widening process that rivers normally undergo as their volume increases. As a result, during a flood, the water has nowhere to go except downstream. Although built-up levees can work well to prevent small floods, they often make heavy flooding worse for areas farther downstream. The full power of the surge of flood water is passed on to flood the downstream areas.

Figure 6 These people are working together to protect their community during a flood. *Applying Concepts How do sandbags help control flooding?*

Section 1 Review

1. What bodies of water make up a river system?
2. Name and describe the two major processes by which a river changes the land.
3. How might a period of very heavy rain cause a flood to occur?
4. Describe one method of controlling floods.
5. **Thinking Critically Applying Concepts** Is a river more likely to erode the land around its headwaters or at its mouth? Why?

Check Your Progress **CHAPTER PROJECT 2**
Begin sketching your model watershed. How will you shape the land to form the main river and tributary? What materials would be easy to shape and allow runoff to occur? Use the sketch to help estimate amounts of materials you will need. *(Hint:* Decide what to use as a base for your model. Draw your sketch on a piece of paper the same size as the base.)

DISCOVER

What's in Pond Water?

1. Using a hand lens, observe a sample of pond water.

2. Make a list of everything you see in the water. If you don't know the name of something, write a short description or draw a picture.

3. Your teacher has set up a microscope with a slide of pond water. Observe the slide and add any new items to your list. Wash your hands with soap when you are done.

Think It Over

Classifying Use one of these systems to divide the items on your list into two groups: moving/still, living/nonliving, or microscopic/visible without a microscope. What does your classification system tell you about pond water?

What do a glass of water, a canoe, and a snowstorm have in common? They're three things that could connect you to a nearby lake. Lake Michigan, for example, is a source of drinking water; a place to go boating and swimming; and the source of winter snowstorms on its shores.

While water in streams and rivers is always on the move, the water in lakes and ponds is still, or standing, water. Although there is no definite rule to determine whether a body of water is called a pond or a lake, ponds are generally smaller and shallower than lakes. Sunlight usually reaches to the bottom of all parts of a pond. Most lakes have parts where the water is too deep for sunlight to reach all the way to the bottom.

Ponds and lakes form when water collects in hollows and low-lying areas of land. Rainfall, melting snow and ice, and runoff supply water to ponds and lakes. Others are fed by rivers or groundwater. Eventually, water may flow out of a pond or lake into a river, or evaporate from its surface.

GUIDE FOR READING

◆ How do ponds and lakes form?

◆ What is the result of lake turnover?

Reading Tip Before you read, predict one way in which ponds and lakes are similar and one way in which they are different. As you read, add to your explanation.

EXPLORING *a Pond*

Many organisms live in the different habitats within a pond. From the shallow edges to the muddy bottom, conditions in each habitat vary in important ways.

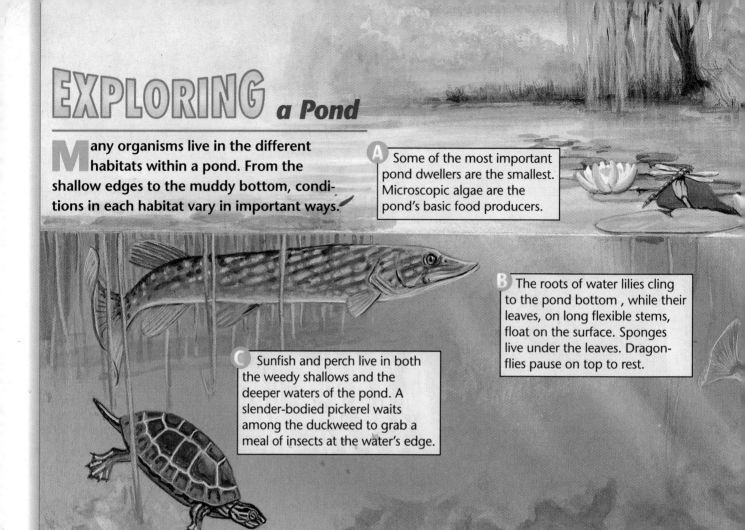

A Some of the most important pond dwellers are the smallest. Microscopic algae are the pond's basic food producers.

B The roots of water lilies cling to the pond bottom , while their leaves, on long flexible stems, float on the surface. Sponges live under the leaves. Dragonflies pause on top to rest.

C Sunfish and perch live in both the weedy shallows and the deeper waters of the pond. A slender-bodied pickerel waits among the duckweed to grab a meal of insects at the water's edge.

Ponds

INTEGRATING LIFE SCIENCE Compared to a tumbling mountain stream, a pond seems still and peaceful at first glance. Silvery minnows glide smoothly below the surface. A dragonfly touches the water, then whirs away. Lily pads with broad, green leaves and waxy, white blossoms float on the surface. This quiet pond is actually a thriving habitat, supporting a wide diversity of living things.

If you have ever waded in a pond, you know that the muddy bottom is often covered with weeds. Because the water is shallow enough for sunlight to reach the bottom, plants grow throughout a pond. Plantlike organisms called algae also live in the pond. As the plants and algae use sunlight to make food through photosynthesis, they also produce oxygen. Animals in the pond use the oxygen and food provided by plants and algae. You can see some common pond organisms in *Exploring a Pond*.

D. The shore is edged with grasses and trees that require a lot of water, such as willows and maples. These plants provide shelter and nesting places for redwing blackbirds and other birds.

E. Frogs lay eggs in the shallow water near shore. They hatch in the water as tadpoles and move to the land as adults.

F. Snails find food on the soft bottom of the pond. Crayfish lie buried in the mud, waiting for bits of food to drift down.

Not all ponds exist year-round. For example, some ponds in the northern and western United States appear only in the spring, when runoff from spring rains and melting snow collects in low areas. The ponds dry up by midsummer as the shallow water quickly evaporates in the heat.

Ponds in colder climates often freeze over during the winter. As you learned in Chapter 1, ice floats because it is less dense than liquid water. As a result, ice forms on the surface of the pond, while the living things survive in the liquid water below.

☑ *Checkpoint* *Why can plants grow throughout a pond?*

Lakes

Suppose you suddenly found yourself on a sandy beach. Waves break on the shore. The water stretches as far as your eye can see. Gulls screech overhead. Where are you? Although you might think you're at the ocean, this immense body of water could

Figure 7 Standing water is found in lakes and ponds. **A.** The cold waters of Crater Lake in Oregon fill the hollow of an ancient volcano. **B.** Water lilies float in a Colorado pond. *Interpreting Photographs In which of these bodies of water does sunlight reach the bottom? Give evidence to support your answer.*

actually be a lake! You could be on a beach in Indiana, on the shore of Lake Michigan.

Although most lakes are not as large as Lake Michigan, they are generally bigger and deeper than ponds. Most lakes are deep enough that sunlight does not reach all the way to the bottom. A lake bottom may consist of sand, pebbles, or rock. The bottom of a pond is usually covered with mud and algae.

Lake Formation Lakes form in many ways. As you read in Section 1, a cut-off river meander may become an oxbow lake. Ice sheets that melted at the end of the Ice Age created depressions that became lakes. Some lakes were created by movements of Earth's crust. Such movements created the deep valleys in central Africa that lie below Lake Tanganyika and Lake Victoria. Other lakes are the result of volcanoes. An erupting volcano can cause a flow of lava or mud that blocks a river and forms a lake. Some lakes, like the one in Figure 7, form in the empty craters of volcanoes.

People can also create a lake by building a dam across a river. The lake may be used for supplying drinking water, for irrigating fields, and for boating and fishing. A lake that stores water for human use is called a **reservoir.** One of the largest reservoirs in the United States is Lake Mead in Nevada, behind Hoover Dam on the Colorado River.

Lake Habitats Like a pond, a lake provides habitats for many

INTEGRATING LIFE SCIENCE

organisms. In the shallow water near shore, the wildlife is similar to that in a pond. Water beetles scurry over the slippery, moss-covered rocks.

Loons and kingfishers pluck fish from the open water. But unlike a pond, sunlight does not reach the bottom at the center of a lake. Without sunlight, plants cannot live in the deep water. As a result, fewer other organisms live in the chilly, dark depths of the lake. A few worms and mollusks do live on the bottom. They feed on food particles that drift down from the surface. The deep waters of lakes are also the home of large, bony fish such as pike and sturgeon. These fish eat the tiny bottom dwellers. They also swim to the surface to feed on fish and even small birds.

☑ *Checkpoint* *List four possible ways a lake might form.*

Changes in a Lake

Particularly in cool, northern areas of North America, many lakes undergo changes with the seasons. In the summer, the sun warms the upper layer of water in the lake. The warm water floats on top of the cooler, denser lower layer. But in the fall, the top layer cools off, too. As the water cools, it becomes denser and sinks. This causes the lake waters to mix together. **As the water mixes, minerals, plant matter, and other nutrients rise from the lake bottom to the surface. Called lake turnover, this seasonal change refreshes the supply of nutrients throughout the lake.**

A second type of change that occurs in a lake happens over a long period of time. The organisms in a lake constantly release waste products into the water. The wastes and the remains of dead organisms contain nutrients such as nitrates and phosphates. Algae feed on these nutrients. Over many years, the nutrients build up in the lake in a process called **eutrophication** (you troh fih KAY shuhn). As eutrophication causes more algae to grow, a thick, green scum forms on the

Figure 8 This island floating on Lake Titicaca is woven from totora reeds.

Social Studies
CONNECTION

Imagine living on a floating island in the middle of a deep, cold lake. The island is a mat made of thick reeds you have woven tightly together. During a storm, you must anchor your island or it could be swept away. If you were a member of a group of Native Americans who live on Lake Titicaca in South America, such an island might be your home.

Lake Titicaca lies high in the Andes Mountains. Around the edges of the lake grows a hollow reed called totora. The people weave totora reeds together to form "islands" that are strong enough to hold homes and livestock. They also make ropes, boats, tea, and even medicine from the totora reeds.

In Your Journal

How would living on a totora reed island on Lake Titicaca affect your daily routine? Write a journal entry describing what a typical day might be like if you lived on a floating island.

A. The process begins as algae and other organisms add nutrients to the lake. These nutrients support more plant growth.

B. Soil, fallen leaves, and decaying matter pile up on the lake bottom. The lake becomes shallower and marshy.

C. Eventually, the plants completely fill the lake, creating a grassy meadow.

Figure 9 A lake environment gradually changes over time. *Predicting Would you expect the water temperature in the lake to be higher in A or B?*

surface of the water. Have you ever forgotten to clean a fish tank for a few weeks? You may have observed the process of eutrophication as algae began to grow on the sides of the tank.

When the algae layer becomes so thick that it begins to block out the sunlight, plants in the lake cannot carry out photosynthesis. They stop producing food and oxygen and die. As dead organisms in the lake decay, the amount of oxygen in the water decreases. The lake environment changes. Many of the fish and other animals no longer have enough oxygen to live. Material from decaying plants and animals piles up on the bottom, and the lake becomes more shallow. The sun warms the water to a higher temperature. Now many plants take root in the rich mud on the lake bottom. Eventually, the lake becomes completely filled with plants. The remaining water evaporates, and a grassy meadow takes the place of the former lake.

Section 2 Review

1. Explain how ponds and lakes form.
2. How does lake turnover renew the supply of nutrients in the water?
3. Give three examples of typical pond organisms. Describe where in a pond each is found.
4. What are two uses of reservoirs?
5. **Thinking Critically Relating Cause and Effect** How is the depth of the water in the middle of a lake related to the variety of living things there?

Science at Home

Ask a family member to crumple up a piece of waxed paper. Straighten out the paper to model a landscape with hills and valleys. Have the person use a permanent marker to draw lines along the highest divides of the landscape. Then have the person draw circles where lakes and ponds will form on the landscape. After placing the waxed paper in a sink to catch any overflow, tell the person to sprinkle water over the landscape to simulate rain. Point out where the water collects. Which would you classify as ponds and which as lakes?

SECTION 3 Wetland Environments

DISCOVER ··· ACTIVITY

Wet or Dry?

1. Hold a kitchen sponge under water until it is soaked. Then squeeze out the water until the sponge is just damp.

2. Place the damp sponge next to a dry sponge in a pan. The sponges represent areas of wet and dry land.

3. Pour water into two paper cups until each is half full.

4. Hold one cup in each hand so that the cups are about 10 centimeters above the pan. Pour the water onto both sponges at the same time.

Think It Over

Observing Which of the two sponges absorbs water faster? How would you relate your observations to what might happen in areas of wet and dry land?

Your canoe slips quietly through the brown-tinged waters of the marsh in South Dakota's Lacreek National Wildlife Refuge. Paddling among the thick clumps of velvety golden cattails, you scan for birds' nests. A spot of red catches your eye, and you realize you are only centimeters away from a black-and-white grebe sitting still atop a nest of dry rushes. Suddenly, a loud honking sound breaks the silence, as a huge flock of Canada geese flies by. You gasp as some of the black and brown birds land on a grassy mound nearby. Their outspread wings must be almost as long as your canoe!

The waters of this marsh serve as an important stopover for thousands of geese, swans, and other migrating birds. Birds stop to feed on grass and seeds as they fly south to their winter homes. Like other wetlands, the Lacreek marsh is a vital habitat for birds and many other living things.

What Is a Wetland?

What image does the word *wetland* bring to mind? As the photographs on the next page show, not all wetlands are dark, smelly swamps oozing with mud. A **wetland** is an area of land that is covered with a shallow layer of water during some or all of the year. Wetlands form in places where

GUIDE FOR READING

◆ What features of wetlands make them good habitats for living things?

◆ How do wetlands help control flooding?

Reading Tip Before you read, write a short description of what you think a wetland is. As you read, add details and examples to your description.

▼ *Western grebe*

water is trapped in low areas or where groundwater seeps onto the surface of the land. They can range in size from a water-filled roadside ditch to an area covering thousands of square kilometers. Some wetlands fill up during spring rains and dry up over the summer. Others, like the Lacreek marsh, are covered with water year-round.

Marshes, swamps, and bogs are three common types of freshwater wetlands. Marshes generally are grassy areas covered by a shallow layer or stream of water. They contain cattails, rushes, tule, and other tall grass-like plants. Swamps look more like flooded forests, with trees and shrubs growing in the water. In the United States, many swamps are located in the South, where trees grow quickly in the warm, humid climate. The cypress swamps of Mississippi and Louisiana are examples of wooded swamps. Bogs, which are more common in cooler northern states, often form in depressions left by melting ice sheets thousands of years ago. The water in bogs tends to be acidic. Many types of mosses thrive in the conditions found in bogs.

Wetlands along coasts usually contain both fresh and salt water. Coastal wetlands, which you will learn more about in Chapter 5, include salt marshes and mangrove forests. Salt marshes are found along both coasts of the United States. They often contain tall, strong grasses growing in a rich, muddy bottom. Mangrove forests, which are found along the central and southern coasts of Florida, consist of short trees with a thick tangle

Figure 10 Freshwater wetlands come in many forms. **A.** In Montana, colorful flowers dot a bed of velvety moss in an alpine bog. **B.** Water flows slowly through a marsh in Oregon's Willamette Valley. **C.** Curtains of Spanish moss hang from cypress trees in a Louisiana swamp. *Comparing and Contrasting How are these three environments similar? How are they different?*

of roots. The tough roots anchor the mangroves against tropical winds and storms.

☑ *Checkpoint* *Name three types of freshwater wetlands.*

Wetland Habitats

If you've ever enjoyed tart cranberry sauce or crunchy wild rice, you've eaten plants that grow in wetlands. The layer of water covering a wetland can range from several centimeters to a few meters deep. Dead leaves and other plant and animal material serve as natural fertilizer, adding nitrogen, phosphates, and other nutrients to the water and soil. **Because of their sheltered waters and rich supply of nutrients, wetlands provide habitats for many living things.**

Many year-round residents of wetlands are similar to those in other freshwater habitats. As in a pond, frogs, salamanders, turtles, raccoons, muskrats, and many types of insects find food and shelter among the wetland plants. Birds nest in and around the wetlands, feeding on the plants and insects there.

Wetlands also have many temporary residents. Many ducks, geese, and other waterfowl travel from Alaska and Canada to their winter homes in the South along a "flyway." For example, birds traveling along the Central Flyway through Montana, Minnesota, the Dakotas, Nebraska, and Iowa depend on the millions of small, shallow marshes called prairie potholes along their route. Like the geese at Lacreek Refuge, birds stop there to rest, feed, and mate. In the spring, thousands of birds build their nests in the prairie pothole region.

A Natural Filter

This activity demonstrates one important role wetlands play in the environment.

1. Cover your work surface with newspaper. In one end of a loaf pan, build a sloping hill of damp soil.
2. Add water to the other end of the pan to form a lake.
3. Use a watering can to sprinkle rain onto the hill. Observe what happens to the hill and the lake.
4. Empty the water out of the pan and rebuild the hill.
5. Now push a sponge into the soil across the bottom of the hill to model a wetland.

6. Repeat Steps 2 through 4. Follow your teacher's instructions for cleaning up.

Observing What happened to the soil with and without the wetland? How did the lake look in each case?

The Importance of Wetlands

Imagine coming home from a long trip, only to find that your house is gone and in its place is a parking lot! That happened to thousands of migrating birds before people began to understand the importance of wetlands. Farmers and builders once considered the soggy soil of wetlands to be "wasteland." This land could not be used unless it was drained and filled in. Thousands of square kilometers of wetlands were developed for farmland or for building homes and businesses. Beginning in the 1970s, however, the government enacted laws to protect wetland habitats.

Wetlands serve important functions for people as well as for wildlife. For example, wetlands provide natural water filtration. As water moves slowly through a wetland, waste materials settle out. The thick network of plant roots traps silt and mud. **Wetlands also help control floods by absorbing extra runoff from heavy rains.** They act like giant sponges, storing water and gradually releasing it as it drains or evaporates. When wetlands are drained or paved over, the water cannot be absorbed. Instead, it runs off the land quickly and can cause floods.

Figure 11 Many unusual species live in the freshwater wetland habitats of the Everglades.

Roseate spoonbills

Great egret

Snowy egret

Little blue heron

Sawgrass

Anhinga

Florida panther

The Everglades: A Unique Environment

Walking down a path in Florida's Everglades National Park, you would feel the ground squish under your feet. Water is the key to the Everglades, a unique region of wetlands. A shallow layer of water moves slowly over the gently sloping land from Lake Okeechobee south to Florida Bay. Tall, sharp-edged blades of sawgrass grow in the water. The thick growth of sawgrass gave this region its Native American name, *Pa-hay-okee*, which means "river of grass." Low islands called hammocks are scattered throughout the sawgrass marsh. Trees like gumbo limbos and palms grow on the hammocks.

Everglades Wildlife As in other wetlands, water means life for many Everglades creatures. Fish and snakes gobble up tiny organisms in the warm, muddy water. Wading birds in a rainbow of colors—pink flamingoes, white egrets, and purple gallinules—stand on skinny legs in the water. A raccoon digs for alligator eggs, unaware of the alligator lying low in the sawgrass nearby.

The Everglades provide habitats for many rare or endangered species. The endangered Florida panther lives deep in the wilderness portions of the Everglades. Many species of birds, such as the wood

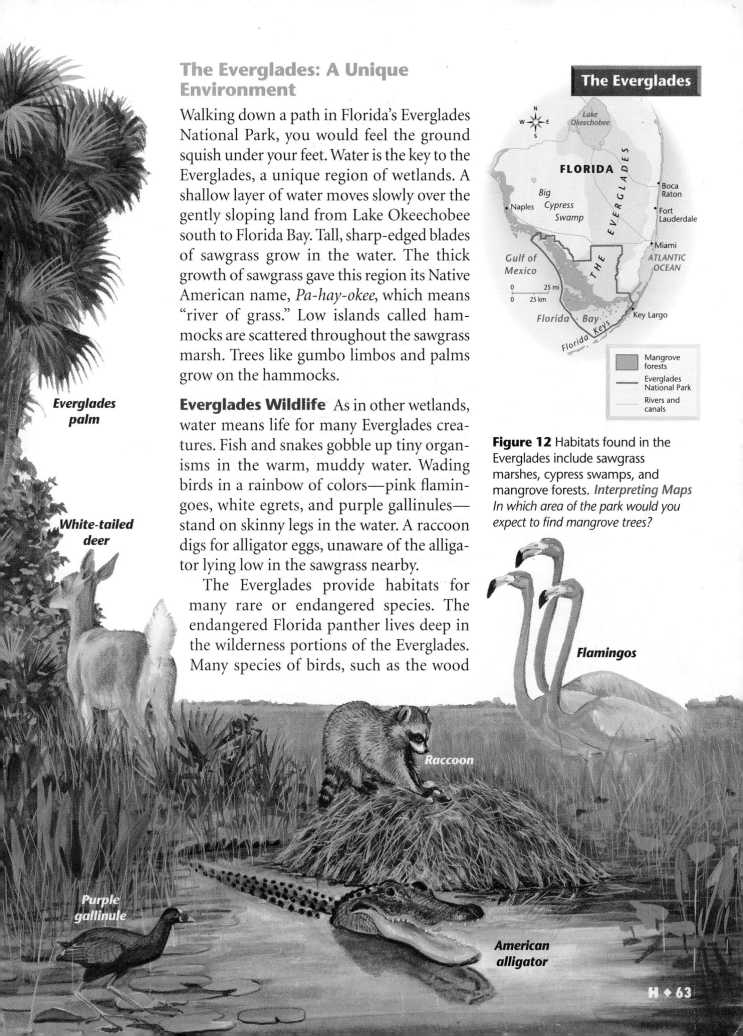

Everglades palm

White-tailed deer

The Everglades

Mangrove forests

Everglades National Park

Rivers and canals

Figure 12 Habitats found in the Everglades include sawgrass marshes, cypress swamps, and mangrove forests. *Interpreting Maps* In which area of the park would you expect to find mangrove trees?

Flamingos

Raccoon

Purple gallinule

American alligator

stork and the roseate spoonbill (named for the unusual shape of its beak), depend on the Everglades as a nesting area. The awkward-looking manatee, or sea cow, lives in the mangrove forests along the coast, grazing on water hyacinths. Because manatees swim so slowly, they are easily injured by the propellers of powerboats. They have become an endangered species as a result of increased boating in Florida Bay.

Threats to the Everglades The Everglades are a fragile environment. Nearby farming has introduced new chemicals into the slow-moving water of the marsh, upsetting the balance of nutrients. Outside the protected limits of the national park, developers have filled in areas of wetland to build new homes and roads. New organisms brought into the area accidentally or for pest control compete with other organisms for space and food.

Figure 13 A manatee floats in the warm waters of Florida Bay. This species is threatened by the increased use of coastal waters around the Everglades.

Water that once flowed into the Everglades from Lake Okeechobee has been diverted for farming. New canals and levees built to provide drinking water for nearby communities and to control flooding have changed the flow of water into and out of the Everglades. Some areas are drying up, while others are flooded.

Preserving the Everglades Scientists and government officials have been trying for many years to develop a plan to preserve the Everglades and save its endangered wildlife. One plan involves building an elaborate system of pipes and canals to refill some drained areas with fresh water. The National Park Service, the State of Florida, and the U.S. Army Corps of Engineers are working together to manage the supply of water to areas around and within the Everglades.

Section 3 Review

1. How are wetlands important to wildlife?
2. Explain how wetlands help control floods.
3. How are the Everglades unusual?
4. **Thinking Critically Making Judgments** Some of the plans to restore the Everglades will require millions of dollars and will negatively affect local farmers. What information would you want to have to help decide what plan of action to take to save the Everglades?

Check Your Progress

CHAPTER PROJECT 2

At this point, add the body of standing water to your watershed sketch. If your model will include any wetland areas, what materials will you use to model them? (*Hint:* Be sure to consider how water will enter and leave the body of water.)

4 Glaciers and Icebergs

DISCOVER • ACTIVITY

How Can Ice Change the Land?

1. Your teacher will give you two ice cubes, one of which has some sand and gravel frozen into its bottom side.

2. Rub each ice cube slowly along a piece of cardboard, pressing down slightly.

3. Observe the piece of cardboard. Wash your hands when you are finished with this activity.

Think It Over

Inferring How might a large, moving block of ice and rocks affect the surface of the land?

Standing on a mountaintop more than 4,800 meters above sea level, sparkling ice and snow surround you in every direction. The temperature is −29°C, and the wind whistles around your ears. Where is this chilly spot? It's Vinson Massif, the highest point on the continent of Antarctica.

Recall that more than two thirds of the fresh water on Earth exists in the form of ice. About 85 percent of that ice is part of the massive ice sheet that covers Antarctica. This ice sheet is larger than the United States and Europe put together! The rest of the ice on Earth is found in other ice sheets and in icebergs.

Glaciers

The ice sheet that covers Antarctica is one form of a glacier. A **glacier** (GLAY shur) is a huge mass of ice and snow that moves slowly over the land.

Glaciers form in cold places where more snow falls each year than melts. Layers of snow pile on top of more layers of snow. **Over time, the weight of the layers presses the particles of snow so tightly together that they form a solid block of ice.** If you have ever squeezed a handful of fluffy snow until it became an icy ball, you have modeled the way a glacier forms.

Ice sheets that spread over a large area of land are called continental glaciers. Today, continental glaciers are

GUIDE FOR READING

◆ How does a glacier form?

◆ Why are icebergs dangerous to ships?

Reading Tip As you read, make a list of main ideas and supporting details about glaciers and icebergs.

▲ *Gentoo penguins in Antarctica*

Figure 14 The massive Beloit Glacier towers above Prince William Sound in Alaska. *Classifying Which type of glacier is the Beloit Glacier? Explain your answer.*

found only in Antarctica and Greenland. The Antarctic glacier covers high mountain ranges and even active volcanoes. In some spots it is 3,000 meters thick. That's higher than six Empire State Buildings stacked on top of each other.

Most present-day glaciers are valley glaciers. These glaciers form in the mountains. They look like thick rivers of ice sliding down into the valley. As a valley glacier descends into warmer regions, it gradually melts. Valley glaciers are found mainly in high, cold mountain ranges such as the Alps in Europe, the Rockies in the United States, and the Himalayas in Asia.

Like moving water, moving ice can cause erosion. As a glacier forms, rocks, gravel, and other debris are frozen into the ice. Like a giant piece of sandpaper, the glacier scrapes against the ground as it moves. Over time, glaciers grind away rock and change the surface of the land.

☑ *Checkpoint* *How does a glacier change the shape of the land?*

Icebergs

It was a dark night in the spring of 1912. The gleaming new ocean liner *Titanic* sailed through the North Atlantic on its first voyage, from Southampton, England, to New York City. Suddenly a huge white wall loomed out of the darkness in front of the ship! It was an iceberg, the terror of ships at sea. Underwater, the jagged ice tore a series of cuts in the *Titanic's* side. As the ship sank to the bottom of the ocean, nearly 1,500 people died.

Icebergs like the one that sank the *Titanic* form when a glacier reaches the seacoast. With a loud roar, large chunks

Figure 15 The *Titanic* sank on its first voyage when it hit an iceberg in the North Atlantic Ocean.

TITANIC DISASTER GREAT LOSS OF LIFE
EVENING NEWS

break off, or calve, and float away. Although icebergs are found in the salty ocean, remember that they consist of fresh water.

In the North Atlantic and Arctic oceans, about 10,000 new icebergs form every year. Many of these icebergs calve from Greenland's continental glacier. As they drift south, the icebergs break into chunks as big as houses. They begin to melt in the warmer water.

The ocean around Antarctica is filled with even larger icebergs. Flat-topped pieces calve from the edges of the glaciers along the coast. In 1995, a giant iceberg broke off Antarctica's Larsen Ice Shelf. Scientists flying over the new iceberg reported that it was about 70 kilometers long and 25 kilometers wide — more than half the size of the state of Rhode Island!

The thought of a chunk of floating ice that big is scary enough, but it's more frightening to realize that only about 10 percent of an iceberg is visible above the water. **About 90 percent of an iceberg lies below the surface. The underwater part is a hazard to ships because it is often much wider than the visible part of the iceberg.** Icebergs are also a threat to floating platforms that support rigs for drilling oil from the ocean floor.

After the *Titanic* disaster, countries involved in Atlantic shipping set up the International Ice Patrol. The Patrol, which is managed by the United States Coast Guard, uses ships, planes, and satellites to track icebergs. The Patrol's warnings have saved many people aboard ships and floating oil rigs from disasters like the *Titanic*.

Figure 16 If you could see an entire iceberg at once, how would it look? An artist created this composite photograph to reveal the hidden part of the iceberg. *Applying Concepts What percentage of the ice is underwater?*

Section 4 Review

1. Describe the process by which a glacier forms.
2. Why is it hard to determine the size of an iceberg from the deck of a ship?
3. How do icebergs form?
4. Name the two types of glaciers. Where is each type of glacier found?
5. **Thinking Critically Making Judgments** How might the fact that glaciers and icebergs consist of fresh water make them useful to people?

Science at Home

With a family member, make a model iceberg. Fill the cut-off bottom of a milk or juice carton with water and freeze. When the water has frozen, peel the carton away from the iceberg. Add salt to a large bowl of water to create an "ocean." Float the iceberg in the bowl. Help your family member use a ruler to measure how much of the iceberg's thickness is above the surface of the water and how much is below. Use these measurements to explain why icebergs can be dangerous to ships.

SECTION 5 Water Underground

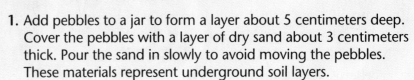

DISCOVER

Where Does the Water Go?

1. Add pebbles to a jar to form a layer about 5 centimeters deep. Cover the pebbles with a layer of dry sand about 3 centimeters thick. Pour the sand in slowly to avoid moving the pebbles. These materials represent underground soil layers.

2. Sprinkle water onto the sand to simulate rainfall.

3. Looking through the side of the jar, observe the path of the water as it soaks through the layers. Wash your hands when you are finished with this activity.

Think It Over

Observing Describe what happens when the water reaches the bottom of the jar.

GUIDE FOR READING

◆ How does water move through underground layers of soil and rock?

◆ How do people obtain water from an aquifer?

Reading Tip As you read, create a flowchart that shows one possible path of water from a rainstorm to a well.

When you were younger, did you ever dig a hole in the ground hoping to find a buried treasure? Though you probably never found a trunk full of gold, you could have found a different kind of treasure without even realizing it. If you continued to dig deeper, past tangled grass roots and small stones, you would have noticed the soil begin to feel heavier and wetter. If you dug deep enough, the bottom of your hole would have started to fill up with water. You would have "struck groundwater!" In the days before pipes and public water systems, such a discovery was like finding a treasure. A usable source of fresh water enabled people to build a house or farm and settle on that land. Today, many people still rely on the water underground to meet their water needs.

Underground Layers

Where does this underground water come from? Like the water in rivers, lakes, and glaciers, it comes from precipitation. Recall what can happen to precipitation when it falls. It can evaporate right away, run off the surface, or soak into the ground. The water that soaks in trickles downward, following the pull of gravity.

If you pour water into a glass full of pebbles, the water trickles down around the pebbles until it reaches the bottom of the glass. Then the water begins to fill up the spaces between the pebbles. **In the same way, water underground trickles down between particles of soil and through cracks and spaces in layers of rock.**

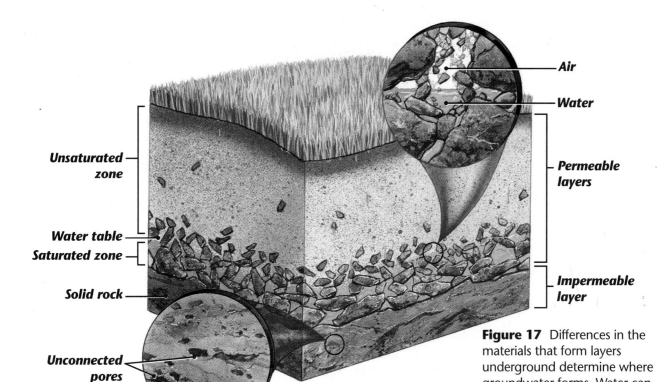

Unsaturated zone

Water table

Saturated zone

Solid rock

Unconnected pores

Air

Water

Permeable layers

Impermeable layer

Figure 17 Differences in the materials that form layers underground determine where groundwater forms. Water can move through the pores of permeable layers, but not through impermeable layers. *Interpreting Diagrams* What is the difference between the saturated and unsaturated zone?

Different types of rock and soil have different-sized spaces, or **pores,** between their particles. How easily water moves through the material depends not only on the size of the pores, but also on whether the pores are connected to each other. Materials that allow water to easily pass through, or permeate, are called **permeable.** Sand and gravel are permeable materials.

As water soaks down through permeable rock, it eventually reaches layers of material that it cannot pass through. These materials have few or no pores or cracks for the water to flow through. Materials that water cannot pass through easily are called **impermeable.** Clay and granite are impermeable materials.

Once water reaches an impermeable layer, it is trapped. It can't soak any deeper. Instead, the water begins to fill up the spaces above the impermeable rock. The area of permeable rock or soil that is totally filled, or saturated, with water is called the **saturated zone.** The top of the saturated zone is the **water table.** Knowing the depth of the water table in an area tells you how deep you must dig to reach groundwater.

Soil and rock layers above the water table contain some moisture, too. But here the pores contain air as well as water. They are not saturated with water. Therefore, the layer of rocks and soil above the water table is called the **unsaturated zone.**

☑ *Checkpoint* *Give an example of a permeable material other than sand or gravel.*

Drawing Conclusions

You have just bought some land and need to dig a well. By drilling a number of holes on your property, you learn that there is a layer of impermeable granite rock located approximately 12 meters underground. If the saturated zone is 3 meters thick, how deep should you dig your well? (*Hint:* Drawing a diagram may be helpful.)

SOIL TESTING

In what type of soil is it best to site a well? This is a question that hydrologists, scientists who study groundwater, need to answer before new houses or other buildings can be constructed. In this lab, you will compare different soil types to learn more about their water-holding properties.

Problem

How fast does water move through sand, clay, and pebbles?

Skills Focus

observing, measuring, drawing conclusions

Materials (per group)

hand lens	3 100-mL beakers
sand, 100 mL	water, 300 mL
stopwatch	pebbles, 100 mL
3 rubber bands	

powdered potter's clay, 100 mL
3 squares of cheesecloth
3 large funnels or cut-off plastic soda bottle tops

Procedure

1. Copy the data table into your notebook.

HELP WANTED

Hydrologists to conduct soil tests for new housing development. Homes will have private wells. Engineers must test soil permeability to select best locations. Please send resumé and references to

2. Use a hand lens to observe each of the three material samples closely. Record your observations in your data table.

3. Place a piece of cheesecloth over the bottom of each funnel or bottle top and secure it with a rubber band.

4. Place the sand in one funnel, the pebbles in another, and the clay in another. Be sure that there is at least 5 cm of space above the material in each funnel.

5. Place each funnel on top of a beaker.

6. Slowly pour 100 mL of water into the funnel containing the sand. Do not let the water overflow the funnel.

7. Start the stopwatch when the water begins to flow or drip out of the bottom of the funnel.

DATA TABLE

Material	Observations	Time for Water to Stop Dripping
Sand		
Clay		
Pebbles		

8. Stop the stopwatch when the water stops dripping out of the funnel or after 5 minutes. Record the time to the nearest second in your data table.

9. Repeat Steps 6 through 8 with the pebbles and then with the clay. When you are finished with this activity, dispose of your materials according to your teacher's instructions. Wash your hands thoroughly with soap.

Analyze and Conclude

1. Through which material did water move the fastest? The slowest?

2. What can you conclude about the permeability of the three materials?

3. Based on your observations of each sample, suggest an explanation for the differences in their permeability.

4. Based on the results of this lab, would you expect to get more water from a well dug in sand, pebbles, or clay? Explain.

5. **Apply** Why might gardeners and landscapers need to know about the permeability of different soil types?

More to Explore

Which of the soil samples that you tested do you think the soil of the grounds at your school most resembles? Design an experiment to test your hypothesis. With your teacher's permission, carry out your experiment.

An Artesian Well

In this activity you will build **ACTIVITY** a model of an artesian well. Before you start, cover your desk or table with newspaper.

1. Cover the bottom of a loaf pan with clay. Pile the clay higher at one end.

2. Cover the clay with about 4 cm of moist sand.

3. Cover the sand with a thin sheet of clay. Seal the edges of the clay tightly against the sides of the pan.

4. Push a funnel into the high end so that the bottom of the funnel is in the sand.

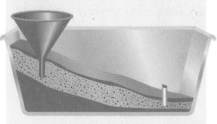

5. Insert a short piece of plastic straw through the clay and into the sand layer at the low end. Remove the straw, discard it, and then insert a new piece of straw in the same hole.

6. Slowly pour water into the funnel. Do not let the water overflow the funnel.

7. Observe the level of water in the straw. Wash your hands after this activity.

Making a Model What real-world feature does each part of your model represent? How is your model like a real artesian well? How is it different?

Aquifers

Any underground layer of rock or sediment that holds water is called an **aquifer.** Aquifers can range in size from a small underground patch of permeable material to an area the size of several states. The huge Ogallala aquifer lies beneath the plains of the midwest, stretching from South Dakota to Texas. Millions of people obtain their drinking water from this underground storehouse. The Ogallala aquifer also provides water for crops and livestock.

Maybe you picture groundwater as a large, still pool beneath Earth's surface. In fact, the water is actually in motion, seeping through the layers of rock. How fast it moves depends largely on how steeply the aquifer slopes and how permeable the rocks are. Groundwater in some aquifers moves only a few centimeters a day. At that rate, the water moves about 10 meters a year—less than the length of a typical classroom. Groundwater may travel hundreds of kilometers and stay in an aquifer for thousands of years before coming to the surface again.

☑ *Checkpoint* *What factors affect how fast water moves in an aquifer?*

Bringing Groundwater to the Surface

Look at Figure 18 and notice how the level of the water table generally follows the shape of the underground rock layers. The depth of the water table can vary greatly even over a small area of land. Heavy rain or lots of melting snow raise the level of the water table. The level falls in dry weather.

In places where the water table meets the ground surface, groundwater seeps onto the surface. The groundwater may feed a stream or pond, or form a wetland. People can also bring groundwater to the surface.

Wells Since ancient times, people have brought groundwater to the surface for drinking and other everyday uses. **People can obtain groundwater from an aquifer by drilling a well below the water table.** Locate the well near the center of Figure 18. Because the bottom of the well is in the saturated zone, the well contains water. Notice the level of the bottom of the dry well in the diagram. Because this well does not reach below the water table, water cannot be obtained from it.

Long ago, people dug wells by hand. They lined the sides of the well with brick or stone to keep the walls from collapsing. To bring up water, they lowered and raised a bucket. Today, most wells are dug with well-drilling equipment. Pumps bring up the groundwater.

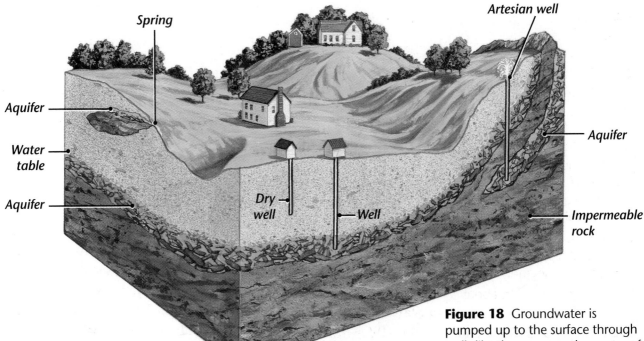

Spring

Aquifer

Water table

Aquifer

Dry well

Well

Artesian well

Aquifer

Impermeable rock

Figure 18 Groundwater is pumped up to the surface through wells like the one near the center of the diagram. At the right, pressure causes water to spurt from an artesian well. Where an aquifer meets the ground surface, at the left, a spring may form.
Interpreting Diagrams Why does the dry well not contain any water?

Pumping water out of an aquifer lowers the water level near the well. If too much water is pumped out too fast, the well may run dry. It will be necessary either to dig deeper to reach the lowered water table, or to wait for rainfall to refill the aquifer. New water that enters the aquifer from the surface is called **recharge**.

Artesian Wells In some aquifers, groundwater is trapped between two layers of impermeable rock or sediment. This water is under great pressure from the weight of the water above it. If the top layer of rock is punctured, the pressure sends water spurting up through the hole. Water flows without pumping from a well dug in such an aquifer. A well in which water rises because of pressure within the aquifer is called an **artesian well** (ahr TEEZH uhn well).

Springs and Geysers

Imagine that you are walking through a strange-looking land full of bubbling mud pools and mineral-filled ponds. With a loud roar, a column of boiling hot water and white steam suddenly erupts from the ground in front of you. The towering fountain soars high into the air as the hot steam blows around you. Although you might think you've landed on another planet, these are common sights in Wyoming's Yellowstone National Park.

Springs In Yellowstone, groundwater seeps, flows, and erupts onto the surface in very dramatic ways. But in most other places, groundwater comes to the surface more quietly. Places

Figure 19 A crowd of tourists is amazed by Yellowstone's most famous geyser, Old Faithful. The geyser's regular eruptions can reach as high as an eight-story building.

where groundwater bubbles or flows out of cracks in the rock are called **springs.** Most springs contain water at normal temperatures, but some springs, like those in Yellowstone, contain water that is warmed by the hot rocks deep below the surface. The heated water bubbles to the surface in hot springs. Not surprisingly, two places in the United States where such springs occur are Warm Springs, Georgia, and Hot Springs, Arkansas!

Geysers The fountain in Yellowstone that shot into the air is a geyser. A **geyser** (GY zur) is a type of hot spring from which the water bursts periodically into the air. The word *geyser* comes from an Icelandic word, *geysir,* which means "gusher."

A geyser forms when very hot water that has been circulating deep underground begins to rise through narrow passages in the rock. Heated gases and bubbles of steam are forced up these passages by the pressure of the hot water boiling below. Just as pressure builds up in a partly blocked water pipe, the pressure within these narrow openings in the rock increases. Finally the gases, steam, and hot water erupt high into the air. Outside the United States, many dramatic geysers are found in Iceland, New Zealand, Kenya, and Indonesia.

Section 5 Review

1. Describe what happens to water that soaks into the ground.
2. Why is it important to know the depth of an aquifer before drilling a well?
3. Draw a cross section of the ground that includes the following labeled features: permeable layer, saturated zone, unsaturated zone, impermeable layer, and water table.
4. What force causes a geyser to erupt?
5. **Thinking Critically Inferring** During the winter, a small spring flows on your property. Every summer, the spring dries up. What might be the reason for the change?

Check Your Progress

CHAPTER PROJECT 2

Now you are ready to build your model watershed. Be sure to follow the plan you have drawn. When your model is finished, do a practice run of your demonstration. (Hint: Some materials need to be worked with quickly before they harden. Others need time to dry before you can pour water over them. Be sure to leave yourself enough time to build your model and let it dry before your presentation.)

SECTION 1 — Streams and Rivers

Key Ideas

◆ Runoff from precipitation forms streams, which flow together to form rivers. The area drained by a river system is its watershed.

◆ Rivers wear away landforms through erosion and build new ones through deposition.

◆ As a river flows from its headwaters to its mouth, the slope, speed, and volume change.

◆ Floods occur when a river overflows its channel and spreads out over its floodplain.

Key Terms

runoff	tributary	watershed
divide	erosion	deposition
sediment	headwaters	flood plain
meander	oxbow lake	mouth
delta	levee	

SECTION 2 — Ponds and Lakes

Key Ideas

◆ Ponds and lakes are bodies of standing water that form when fresh water collects in depressions in the land.

◆ Because sunlight reaches the bottom of a pond, plants can grow throughout the pond.

◆ Lake turnover is a seasonal mixing that refreshes the nutrient supply in the lake.

Key Terms

reservoir   eutrophication

SECTION 3 — Wetland Environments

INTEGRATING LIFE SCIENCE

Key Ideas

◆ Wetlands are covered with a shallow layer of water for all or part of the year.

◆ Wetlands provide nesting and feeding areas for birds and other wildlife. Wetlands also filter water and help control floods.

Key Term

wetland

SECTION 4 — Glaciers and Icebergs

Key Ideas

◆ Glaciers form when layers of snow pile up. The pressure from the mass of the layers packs the snow into ice.

◆ Icebergs form when the edges of glaciers reach the ocean and break off. About 90 percent of an iceberg is located underwater.

Key Term

glacier

SECTION 5 — Water Underground

Key Ideas

◆ As water soaks into the ground, it moves through the pores between particles of soil and rock. Water moves easily through permeable materials, but does not move easily through impermeable materials.

◆ People dig wells to obtain groundwater from aquifers. To supply water, a well must reach below the level of the water table.

◆ Water pressure brings groundwater to the surface naturally in artesian wells, springs, and geysers.

Key Terms

pore	permeable	impermeable
saturated zone	unsaturated zone	
water table	aquifer	recharge
artesian well	spring	geyser

ACTIVITY

USING THE INTERNET

www.science-explorer.phschool.com

Reviewing Content

 For more review of key concepts, see the Interactive Student Tutorial CD-ROM.

Multiple Choice

Choose the letter of the best answer.

1. Rain that falls on a steep, paved street during a thunderstorm will most likely become
   a. groundwater.　　b. runoff.
   c. a spring.　　　　d. a reservoir.

2. Which of the following features is most typical of the headwaters of a river?
   a. broad flat valley
   b. waterfalls and rapids
   c. winding meanders
   d. muddy, slow-moving water

3. Lakes that store water for human use are called
   a. reservoirs.　　b. aquifers.
   c. oxbow lakes.　　d. wetlands.

4. More than two thirds of Earth's fresh water is found in
   a. rivers and streams.
   b. ponds and lakes.
   c. wetlands.
   d. glaciers and icebergs.

5. Groundwater is stored in
   a. wetlands.
   b. water tables.
   c. aquifers.
   d. impermeable layers.

True or False

If the statement is true, write true. If it is false, change the underlined word or words to make the statement true.

6. In the process of <u>erosion,</u> moving water breaks off rocks and soil and carries them downstream.

7. <u>Dams</u> are ridges that build up naturally alongside rivers that frequently flood.

8. <u>Continental</u> glaciers move like rivers of ice down mountain slopes.

9. Water moves easily through <u>permeable</u> rock layers.

10. To supply water, the bottom of a well must be located in the <u>saturated zone</u>.

Checking Concepts

11. What are two factors that affect amount of runoff?

12. Explain how a meander forms in a river.

13. Describe how temperature changes in the fall and spring can help distribute nutrients throughout a lake.

14. Explain how wetlands are important to migrating birds.

15. Describe one way that groundwater can come to the surface naturally.

16. **Writing to Learn** Imagine that you are on summer vacation in one of three different places: a river valley, a pond, or a lake. Write a letter to a friend describing the kinds of wildlife you see and the sports and other activities you are enjoying at the spot you chose.

Thinking Visually

17. **Concept Map** Copy the concept map about wetlands onto a sheet of paper. Complete it and add a title. (For more on concept maps, see the Skills Handbook).

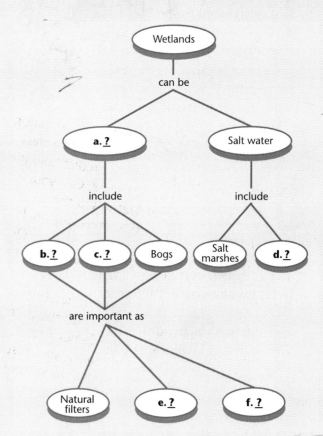

Applying Skills

Use the diagram of underground layers to answer Questions 18–20.

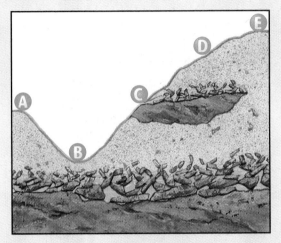

18. **Drawing Conclusions** Would point D or point E be a better location to dig a well? Explain your reasoning.
19. **Inferring** At which location could you obtain groundwater without having to pump it up? What is such a place called?

20. **Predicting** Draw a simple diagram showing how this area might look during a very rainy season.

Thinking Critically

21. **Comparing and Contrasting** How is the variety of organisms you would find in the center of a pond different from those you would find in deep water at the center of a lake?
22. **Classifying** Which of the following materials are permeable? Which of the materials are impermeable? Aluminum foil, cotton, plastic wrap, glass, paper towel, and bread.
23. **Problem Solving** Suppose that the water table in your area is located 8 meters below the ground surface in the spring. By the end of the summer, the level of groundwater drops 2 meters. How deep should you dig a well to be sure that it does not run dry?

Performance Assessment

CHAPTER PROJECT 2 Wrap Up

Present Your Project Before presentation day, show your watershed model to a classmate. Ask your classmate to predict how the water will flow over the model. Can your classmate identify the features of the watershed? If you need to make any final adjustments to your model, do so now. On presentation day, use a spray bottle to spray rain onto your model.

Reflect and Record In your notebook, explain what you would change about your model now that you have demonstrated it. What aspect of freshwater flow was most difficult to model? What other watershed features might you add?

Getting Involved

In Your Community Obtain permission from your teacher and family to conduct a survey of lakes, ponds, and wetlands in your community. Choose one location and, with an adult family member, take an inventory of the wildlife you find there. If possible, sketch or photograph plants, birds, small mammals, frogs, and other wildlife. Prepare an exhibit for your local library that highlights the natural features of this water environment.

PROJECT 3

A Precious Resource

If you lived in Rajasthan, India, you might walk two kilometers every morning to collect a heavy bucket of water from a spring-fed oasis. Your family would use this water for breakfast, washing dishes, and laundry. When you came home from school, you would fetch more water for the evening meal and bathing.

In this chapter, you will explore water as a resource. You will discover what happens when water is scarce, and how water can become polluted. You will also learn how people can use freshwater resources more wisely, and how water pollution can be prevented or cleaned up. Throughout the chapter, you will be building your own model water treatment system.

Your Goal To design and build a water treatment system to clean one liter of dirty water.

Your treatment system should
- consist of at least two treatment steps
- be made from materials that have been approved by your teacher
- recover as much of one liter of clean water as possible
- be built following the safety guidelines in Appendix A

Get Started Your teacher will give you a sample of dirty water. Begin now by using your senses to observe your sample. Make a list of all your observations. Think about what types of substances might be present in this water. **CAUTION:** *Never taste or drink the water samples before or after treatment.*

Check Your Progress You'll be working on this project as you study this chapter. To keep your project on track, look for Check Your Progress boxes at the following points.

Section 1 Review, page 89: Plan the steps of your system.
Section 3 Review, page 104: Assemble your treatment system.
Section 4 Review, page 108: Test and modify your system.

Wrap Up At the end of the chapter (page 111), you will demonstrate how well your system cleans up the dirty water sample.

SECTION 4
Integrating Physics
Water As an Energy Resource

Discover Can Water Do Work?
Try This Making a Water Wheel

These residents of Rajasthan, India, balance steel and brass containers of water on their heads for the walk home from the oasis.

How Hard Is It to Move Water?

1. Line two large trash barrels with heavy plastic bags. Fill one barrel with about 100 liters of water. This is about how much water a person uses during a five-minute shower.

2. Form a line of students between the barrels. Your goal is to transfer all the water from the first barrel to the second barrel. Avoid spilling the water. Be careful of slippery floors if you are doing this activity indoors.

3. The first person in line should fill a large plastic pitcher with water, put the cover on, and hand it to the next person.

4. Pass the pitcher to the end of the line, where the last person should empty it into the second barrel. Hand the empty pitcher back down the line to the first person.

5. Repeat Steps 3 and 4 until all the water has been transferred to the second barrel. How many times did you pass the pitcher down the line?

Think It Over

Calculating Suppose a person uses an average of 250 liters of water a day. How many times would you have to pass the pitcher to move the amount of water this person would use in a day? In a year?

GUIDE FOR READING

◆ What is the goal of drinking-water treatment?

◆ What happens to wastewater in most large communities?

Reading Tip Before you read, rewrite the section headings as how, why, or what questions. As you read, find answers to these questions.

At first, doctors in Milwaukee, Wisconsin, thought that 1993 was just a bad year for the flu. Patient after patient complained of nausea, fever, and other flulike symptoms. Within just a few weeks, about 400,000 people came down with symptoms of the disease. Public health officials began looking for another explanation for the epidemic.

The investigators discovered that all the victims had drunk water from the same water treatment plant. Tests revealed that the water contained a tiny parasite, a protist called *Cryptosporidium*. One sip of water could contain enough *Cryptosporidium* to make a person ill! This parasite had not been killed by the chemicals used to treat water at the plant. The scientists hypothesized that the *Cryptosporidium* might have come from runoff from fields where cows grazed. Although most of the victims recovered after a few weeks, about 100 deaths were blamed on the contamination.

Figure 1 An aqueduct carries water from one place to another. This aqueduct, the Pont du Gard in France, was built by the Romans more than 2,000 years ago. *Inferring Why do you think the Romans found it necessary to construct aqueducts?*

Milwaukee's experience was a reminder of the importance of a safe, clean water supply. In this section, you will follow drinking water on its journey to and from homes, schools, and businesses.

Sources of Drinking Water

Where does the water in your kitchen faucet come from? The first step in tracing the path of your water supply is to identify its source. Recall that Earth's liquid fresh water is found on the surface in rivers, lakes, and reservoirs, and underground in rock layers called aquifers. Most people in the United States get their drinking water from one of these sources.

If you live near a large lake or river, your water may come from that source. A distant lake or reservoir could also supply your drinking water. For instance, the city of Los Angeles draws much of its water from the Sierra Nevada Mountains, halfway across California. Or you may rely on groundwater as a source of drinking water. About half the people in the United States, including most people in rural areas, pump drinking water from aquifers.

Your drinking water comes from either a public or private water supply. Most large communities maintain public water supplies. These communities collect, treat, and distribute water to residents. In smaller communities and rural areas, people rely on private wells that supply water for individual families.

☑ *Checkpoint* *List three possible sources of drinking water.*

Treating Drinking Water

After you have identified the source of your drinking water, what is the next step in its journey to your faucet? **Water from both public and private supplies often needs some treatment to ensure that the water is safe and appealing to drink.** Treatment can range from a simple filter on a household well to complex processes at public treatment plants.

Appearance and Taste Picture a glass of water. What observations would affect whether or not you were willing to take a sip? What if the water were cloudy, or had a funny smell? What if the water were rust-colored? Cloudiness, odor, and color are three factors that affect water quality. **Water quality** is a measurement of the substances in water besides water molecules. Some substances, such as iron, can affect the taste or color of water but are harmless unless present at very high levels. Other

You, the Consumer

Testing the Waters

How does the bottled water sold in supermarkets differ from the water that comes out of your kitchen faucet? In this lab, you will discover some differences among various types of water.

Problem

How do distilled water, spring water, and mineral water differ from tap water?

Skills Focus

observing, inferring, drawing conclusions

Materials

hot plate
ruler
tap water, 200 mL
spring water, 200 mL
4 200-mL beakers
4 pieces of pH paper
25-mL graduated cylinder
4 paper cups per person

liquid soap
wax pencil
distilled water, 200 mL
mineral water, 200 mL
4 test tubes and stoppers
pH indicator chart

Procedure

1. Copy the data table into your notebook.

2. Label the beakers A, B, C, and D. Pour 100 mL of tap water into beaker A. Pour 100 mL of the other water samples into the correct beaker (refer to the data table).

3. Heat each water sample on a hot plate until about 20 mL remains. Do not allow the water to boil completely away. **CAUTION:** *Do not touch the hot plate or beakers.*

4. After the water samples have cooled, look for solids that make the water cloudy. Rank the samples from 1 to 4, where 1 has the fewest visible solids and 4 has the most visible solids. Record your rankings in the data table.

5. Label the test tubes A, B, C, and D. Pour 10 mL of each water sample from the source bottle into the correct test tube.

6. Dip a piece of pH paper into test tube A to measure its acidity. Match the color of the pH paper to a number on the pH indicator chart. Record the pH (0–14) in your data table.

substances, such as certain chemicals and microorganisms, can be harmful to your health.

Acidity The **pH** of water is a measurement of how acidic or basic it is, on a scale of 0 to 14. Pure water is neutral, meaning it is neither an acid or a base, and has a pH of 7. The lower the pH, the more acidic the water. Acidic water can cause problems by dissolving lead or other metals from the pipes it passes through. The higher the pH, the more basic the water.

DATA TABLE				
Water Sample	Visible Solids (1–4)	pH (0–14)	Soapsud Height (cm)	Taste
A - Tap water				
B - Distilled water				
C - Spring water				
D - Mineral water				

7. Repeat Step 6 for the other samples.
8. Add 0.5 mL of liquid soap to test tube A. Put a stopper in the test tube and shake it 30 times. With the ruler, measure the height of the soapsuds in the test tube. Record the measurement in your data table.
9. Repeat Step 8 for the other samples.
10. Label the four cups A, B, C, and D. Write your name on each cup.
11. Pour a little tap water into cup A directly from the original source bottle. Taste the tap water. In your data table, describe the taste using one or more of these words: salty, flat, bitter, metallic, refreshing, tasteless.
    CAUTION: *Do not conduct the taste test in a lab room. Use a clean cup for each sample and discard it after use.*
12. Repeat Step 11 with the other samples.

Analyze and Conclude

1. Review your data table. Compare each of the bottled water samples to the tap water sample. What similarities and differences did you detect?
2. Rank the samples from the one with the fewest soapsuds to the one with the most. Compare this ranking to the one for visible solids. What pattern do you see? What do both of these tests have to do with the hardness of water?
3. What other information about the water samples might you need before deciding which one to drink regularly? Explain.
4. **Apply** Based on your results, which sample would you most want to use for (a) drinking, (b) boiling in a kettle, and (c) washing laundry? Which sample would you least want to use for each purpose? Explain.

Getting Involved

Conduct a survey to find out what percentage of people buy bottled mineral water, distilled water, and spring water. Why do they buy each type of water and how do they use it in their homes?

Parts per . . .

Concentrations are often measured in parts per million (ppm) or parts per billion (ppb). What do these units mean? If you own one compact disc by your favorite band, and the disc sells one million copies, your disc is one of the one million sold, or one part per million. When you see a concentration written in this form, you can rewrite it as a fraction:

1. Suppose the concentration of iron in a water sample is 500 parts per million.

2. Write this concentration as a fraction by putting the number of parts on top, and the "whole" on the bottom:

$$500 \text{ parts per million} = \frac{500}{1,000,000}$$

Hardness The level of two minerals—calcium and magnesium—in water is referred to as **hardness.** Hard water contains high levels of these minerals. The minerals come from rocks such as limestone that water flows through. For most people, the main drawback of hard water is that it does not form suds well when mixed with soap. That means that it takes more soap or detergent to get laundry clean in hard water. The minerals in hard water also form deposits that can clog pipes and machinery. Soft water, on the other hand, contains lower levels of calcium and magnesium. Soft water leaves fewer deposits and forms better soapsuds than hard water.

Disease-Causing Organisms Another factor affecting water quality is the presence of disease-causing organisms. The coliform count measures the number of *Escherichia coli* bacteria. Since these bacteria are found in human and animal wastes, their presence in the water shows that it contains waste material. A high coliform count is an indicator, or sign, that the water may also contain other disease-causing organisms.

Standards of Quality The Environmental Protection Agency (EPA), which is responsible for protecting the quality of water and other natural resources in the United States, has developed water-quality standards for drinking water. These standards set concentration limits for certain chemicals, minerals, and bacteria in drinking water. A **concentration** is the amount of one substance in a certain volume of another substance. For example, the concentration of letters in alphabet soup might be written as the number of letters per liter of soup. Figure 2 shows the standards for some different substances.

☑ *Checkpoint* List five factors that affect water quality.

Figure 2 The EPA has set standards for the amounts of various substances in drinking water. *Interpreting Data Based on this table, is a concentration of 0.09 ppm of arsenic in drinking water acceptable? Is a concentration of 0.05 ppm of cyanide acceptable?*

Selected Water-Quality Standards	
Substance	**Limit**
Arsenic	0.05 parts per million (ppm)
Carbon tetrachloride	0.005 ppm
Copper	1.3 ppm
Cyanide	0.2 ppm
Lead	0.015 ppm
Coliform count	No more than 5% of samples taken in a month can be positive.
pH	6.5–8.5

Source: U.S. Environmental Protection Agency, National Primary and Secondary Drinking-Water Standards.

A Typical Treatment Plant

Follow the water from river to faucet in *Exploring Drinking-Water Treatment* to see what happens in a typical water treatment plant.

The first step in treating water from a lake or river is usually filtration. **Filtration** is the process of passing water through a series of screens that allows the water through, but not larger solid particles. During this first step, trash, leaves, branches, and other large objects are removed from the water.

In the second step, a chemical such as alum is added to cause sticky globs, called **flocs,** to form. Other particles in the water stick to the flocs, a process called **coagulation.** The heavy clumps sink to the bottom in the settling basins. The water is then filtered again.

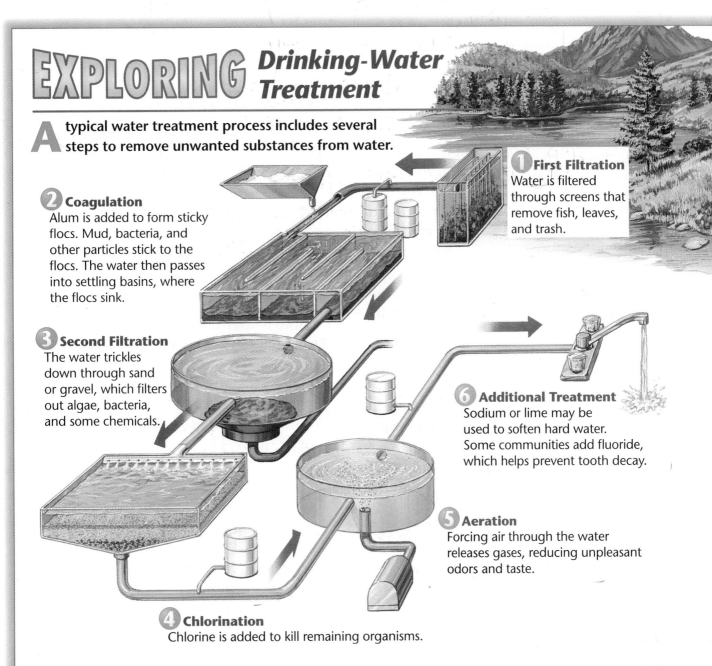

EXPLORING Drinking-Water Treatment

A typical water treatment process includes several steps to remove unwanted substances from water.

1 First Filtration
Water is filtered through screens that remove fish, leaves, and trash.

2 Coagulation
Alum is added to form sticky flocs. Mud, bacteria, and other particles stick to the flocs. The water then passes into settling basins, where the flocs sink.

3 Second Filtration
The water trickles down through sand or gravel, which filters out algae, bacteria, and some chemicals.

4 Chlorination
Chlorine is added to kill remaining organisms.

5 Aeration
Forcing air through the water releases gases, reducing unpleasant odors and taste.

6 Additional Treatment
Sodium or lime may be used to soften hard water. Some communities add fluoride, which helps prevent tooth decay.

Moving Water Uphill

In this activity you will see  how a device called a siphon can be used to move water.

1. Pile a stack of books on a table. Place one bowl on top of the books and another bowl on the table. Pour water into the higher bowl until it is about half full.

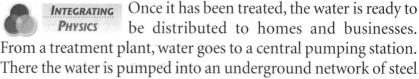

2. Submerge a piece of plastic tubing in the water in the upper bowl. When the tubing is full of water, put a finger over each end.

3. Keeping one end of the tubing underwater, place the other end in the lower, empty bowl. Release both fingers and watch what happens.

Observing In what direction does the water first have to travel to get out of the higher bowl? Can you explain this movement?

The next step is to chlorinate the water. If you have ever been to a public swimming pool, you are familiar with the smell of chlorine. Chlorine is added to drinking water for the same reason it is added to swimming pools—to kill disease-causing microorganisms. At this point, the water is usually ready to be distributed to homes. Sometimes other chemicals are added to kill specific organisms, such as the *Cryptosporidium* you read about earlier.

Water from an aquifer may require less treatment than water from a lake or river. Flowing through the rocks or sand naturally filters and purifies the water. However, most public water supplies that use a groundwater source still add chlorine to kill disease-causing organisms.

Public health officials regularly test samples from water treatment plants to assess water quality. They test for the substances covered by the drinking-water standards, including chemicals, dissolved solids, pH, hardness, and disease-causing organisms. Private well owners should also test their water regularly to make sure no treatment is needed.

☑ *Checkpoint* What is the goal of most drinking-water treatment systems?

Water Distribution

INTEGRATING PHYSICS Once it has been treated, the water is ready to be distributed to homes and businesses. From a treatment plant, water goes to a central pumping station. There the water is pumped into an underground network of steel or concrete pipes called water mains. The water mains branch off to smaller pipes. These feed into smaller copper or plastic pipes that carry water into houses and other buildings.

Water pressure causes the water to move through this system of pipes. Whenever water is in an enclosed space, it exerts pressure in all directions. For example, water pressure pushes water through a garden hose. If the hose springs a leak, a jet of water sprays out of the hole into the air. The pressure pushes the water out through the hole.

Pumping stations are designed to keep water pressure steady throughout the system. If there is a leak in one of the pipes, water escapes—just as it did from the garden hose—and the pressure drops. A typical distribution system can push water up against the downward force of gravity about five or six stories. High-rise buildings must use additional pumps to raise the water to higher floors.

Rather than use a central pumping station, some communities store their water high in the air! No, not as clouds or water vapor, but in a water tower or tank on top of a hill. Treated

Figure 3 These firefighters rely on water pressure to force streams of water through the air. *Predicting If the diameter of the firehose were larger, would the spray be more powerful or less powerful?*

water is pumped up into the water tower. When the water is released, the weight of the water supplies additional pressure that sends the water rushing downward, filling the town's water mains and pipes.

Treating Wastewater

Finally, after a long journey, the water reaches your house. You take a shower, flush the toilet, or wash a load of laundry. What happens now to the used water that goes down the drain? That wastewater and the different kinds of wastes in it are called **sewage.** You might be surprised to learn that this water could someday return as part of your drinking water! No need to worry, however. The wastewater goes through many changes to make this possible.

In many communities, a network of pipes called sanitary sewers carries sewage away from homes. Sanitary sewers are separated from storm sewers, which drain rainwater and runoff from sidewalks, lawns, and parking lots.

Cities and towns have had sanitary sewer systems for only about the last 200 years. Before then, wastewater was often dumped into open gutters and allowed to run directly back into rivers or oceans. Although people eventually realized that this practice helped spread disease, it still occurs in some places, both in the United States and the rest of the world. Coastal cities, in particular, sometimes still pump untreated sewage into the oceans.

Most communities treat their wastewater to make it safe to return to the environment. Different communities may use different treatment processes.

Figure 4 If your community has a sanitary sewer system, you may have seen a sewer cover like this one in the street. Sanitary sewers carry wastewater away from homes and businesses.

You can follow one typical wastewater treatment process, called a trickling filter system, in *Exploring Wastewater Treatment*.

During primary treatment, deposits of fine solids called **sludge** settle out from the wastewater. Despite its unappetizing name, sludge is a useful material. It can be treated with heat and chemicals and used as fertilizer. Sludge can also be reused in secondary treatment. In one method, bacteria are added to the sludge to create "activated sludge." The activated sludge is mixed into the wastewater. The bacteria then break down the remaining sewage in the water.

If necessary, additional treatment may remove other substances from the water, such as metals and industrial chemicals. Once wastewater has gone through an effective treatment process, it is safe to return to the environment. It may be released

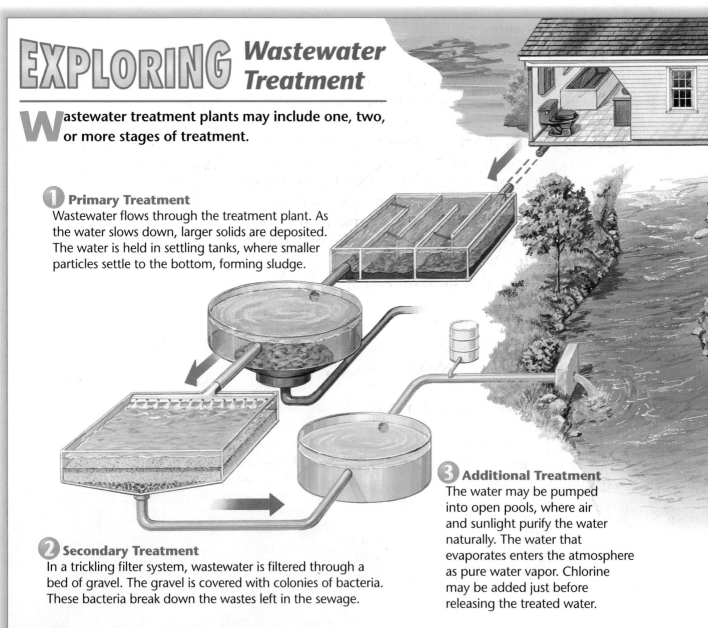

EXPLORING Wastewater Treatment

Wastewater treatment plants may include one, two, or more stages of treatment.

1 Primary Treatment
Wastewater flows through the treatment plant. As the water slows down, larger solids are deposited. The water is held in settling tanks, where smaller particles settle to the bottom, forming sludge.

2 Secondary Treatment
In a trickling filter system, wastewater is filtered through a bed of gravel. The gravel is covered with colonies of bacteria. These bacteria break down the wastes left in the sewage.

3 Additional Treatment
The water may be pumped into open pools, where air and sunlight purify the water naturally. The water that evaporates enters the atmosphere as pure water vapor. Chlorine may be added just before releasing the treated water.

back into lakes, rivers, and oceans or pumped back into the ground. The water rejoins the water cycle. Eventually, it could return to the same reservoir or aquifer that is the source of your water supply.

Treated wastewater that is not quite clean enough for drinking can still be used in other ways. For instance, some communities use this "gray water" to water the grass on golf courses or public parks. Gray water can also be used for irrigation or as cooling water in factories.

Septic Systems

Just as some people rely on private wells rather than public water supplies, many people are not connected to public sanitary sewer systems. They use other methods to dispose of sewage, such as a septic system. A septic system like the one in Figure 5 includes a **septic tank,** an underground tank containing bacteria that treat wastewater as it passes through. Sludge settles to the bottom of the tank and must be cleaned out regularly so it does not fill up the tank. The remaining water filters out through holes in the septic tank into the ground around it. The area around the septic tank that the water filters through is called a **leach field.** Over time, the remaining wastes break down naturally in the soil of the leach field.

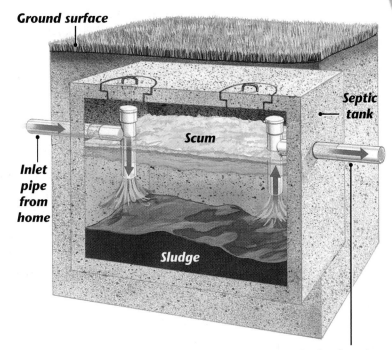

Figure 5 Sewage flows into a septic tank, where bacteria break down the waste material. Cleaner water leaves the tank and flows into a leach field. There, the water slowly releases the remaining dissolved minerals into the soil.

Section 1 Review

1. How does drinking-water treatment improve water quality?
2. What is the goal of wastewater treatment?
3. List the main sources of drinking water. Classify each source as surface water or groundwater.
4. Describe how drinking water is delivered to homes and businesses in a community.
5. **Thinking Critically Inferring** Explain why it is important to know the depth and location of drinking-water wells before deciding where to build a septic tank.

Check Your Progress

CHAPTER PROJECT 3

Now you are ready to plan the steps of your water treatment system. What will each step accomplish? What materials will you use to perform each step? Draw a diagram of your system and a flowchart showing how it will work. Check your plans with your teacher. (Hint: Be sure to consider how your treatment unit will be constructed. How will you hold the pieces in place?)

2 Balancing Water Needs

DISCOVER •• ACTIVITY••••

Can You Reach a Balance?

1. 🖐 Fill a large measuring cup with water to represent a reservoir. Record the level of the water. One partner, the water supplier, should have a plastic dropper and a small bowl of water. The other partner, the water user, should have a spoon and an empty bowl.

2. Start a stopwatch. For two minutes, the water supplier should add water to the measuring cup one dropperful at a time. Each time the water supplier adds a dropperful of water, the water user should remove one spoonful of water from the reservoir.

3. At the end of two minutes, record the level of water in the cup.

4. Now increase the rate of water use by removing two spoonfuls of water for every dropperful added.

5. After another two minutes, record the level of water in the cup again.

Think It Over

Predicting What changes will you need to make so that the water level in the reservoir stays constant?

GUIDE FOR READING

◆ What conditions can result in a water shortage?

◆ What are some ways industries can conserve water?

Reading Tip Before you read, write an explanation of what you think water conservation means. As you read, add to your explanation.

Has this ever happened to you? You're eating dinner with your family and you ask someone to pass the rolls. As the basket makes its way around the table, each person takes a roll. By the time it gets to you, there's nothing left in the basket but crumbs!

This scenario is an example of a limited resource, the rolls, being used by many people. The same thing can happen to a river! For example, the Colorado River holds a resource that is precious in the Southwest—water. In this desert region there is little precipitation to provide water for people's needs. As the river flows through five states and into Mexico, it is tapped again and again to provide water for drinking, irrigation, and other uses. The river's mouth at the Gulf of California is now often only a dry riverbed.

Figure 6 Cracks appear in the dry soil of an empty riverbed.

Water Supply and Demand

States along a river such as the Colorado have to decide how much water each one can take from the river. The deserts of Nevada and Arizona are home to some of the fastest-growing cities in the country. As more people move to Las Vegas, Phoenix, and Tucson, these cities need more water. They increase their demand on already scarce water supplies. Meanwhile, farmers claim a large share to irrigate their fields. Mining companies use water to cool down machinery and flush out the mines they dig. The cities, farms, and mines compete for water rights—the legal right to take water from a particular source.

The Southwest is just one of many places in the world where there doesn't seem to be enough water to go around. As you know, the water cycle ensures that water is a renewable resource. However, the water supply in a specific area is only renewed when there is enough time for rainfall to replace what has been used. **A water shortage occurs when there is too little water or too great a demand in an area—or both.**

Figure 7 Farmers require large amounts of water to irrigate crops in the dry desert. *Relating Cause and Effect What are two factors that might result in a shortage of water available for irrigation?*

Drought Places that normally get enough precipitation may experience a few years of scarce rainfall, a condition known as a **drought.** A drought affects the supply of groundwater as well as surface water. Without precipitation to recharge the aquifer, the amount of groundwater in the aquifer decreases. What happens to a well as the level of the water table falls? Imagine trying to drink from a tall glass of milk through a straw the length of a toothpick. When the level of the milk falls below the bottom of the straw, you can no longer reach it to drink. In the same way, when the water table falls below the bottom of a well, the well runs dry.

Aquifer Overuse Even without droughts, the demands of

INTEGRATING TECHNOLOGY growing populations can result in overuse of aquifers. When water is used up faster than the aquifer can be recharged, the aquifer is depleted, or emptied.

When too much water is pumped out of an aquifer, the ground above the aquifer can sink or collapse. The ground is no longer supported by the pressure of the water inside it. To

prevent collapse, engineers can artificially recharge an aquifer. One method is to pump water from wastewater treatment plants or industrial cooling water into shallow ponds that feed the aquifer. Another method is to inject water down wells directly into the saturated zone. However, because these techniques require expensive equipment and additional water, it is a better solution not to overuse the aquifer.

☑ *Checkpoint* *How can a drought cause a well to run dry?*

Conserving Water

During a water shortage, people often pay more attention to how they use water. They look for ways to avoid wasting water both at home and at work. Using a resource wisely so that it will not be used up is called **conservation.**

In the Home Most people in the United States have access to as much clean, safe water as they want. As a result, it is often easy to use more water than needed without thinking much about it. But as Figure 8 shows, there are some simple things you can do to help conserve water around your home.

Can these suggestions really make a difference? Figure it out. How long do you stand under the shower? For every minute, you use about 18 liters of water. If you stand under the shower for 10 minutes, that's about 180 liters. But if you showered for 5 minutes instead, you would use only 90 liters. And if each student in a class of 25 showered for 5 minutes instead of 10, they would save a total of 2,250 liters of water—enough to fill 22 trash barrels! As you can see, small efforts by many individuals can add up to a lot of water savings.

In Agriculture As you learned in Chapter 1, the biggest use of water in the United States is for agriculture. In the last few decades, farmers have found new ways to use less water. When water is carried into fields in open canals or ditches, much of it is lost through evaporation. Using pipes to carry water reduces the time that water is exposed to the air. Two such methods are sprinkler irrigation and drip irrigation. Sprinkler irrigation sprays water onto crops from overhead pipes. Drip irrigation distributes water through pipes with tiny holes. The water drips directly onto the soil near the plants' roots so that very little is wasted.

In Industry Paper mills, oil refineries, chemical factories, and other industries have made changes in manufacturing processes to use less water. For example, in the 1950s it took about 227,000 liters of water to make 1,000 kilograms of writing paper. By the 1980s, paper mills needed only half that much water to produce the same amount of paper.

New water-saving techniques help industries save money in water costs and meet the requirements of environmental laws. **Reducing water use, recycling water, and reusing water are three major forms of water conservation by industries.** These approaches conserve water while also reducing the amount of wastewater that plants release. For example, some factories that use water to cool machinery are building lagoons on their property. The heated water cools off in the lagoons and then can be used again. Other factories are replacing water-cooling systems with cooling systems that use air. Another change is to use high-pressure water sprays to clean products and equipment instead of dipping the objects in large tanks of water.

Fresh Water for the Future

As the number of people in the world increases, so does the need for water. Where can people find new sources of water for the future? One obvious place would seem to be the other 97 percent of water on Earth—the salt water in the oceans. For thousands

Sharpen your Skills

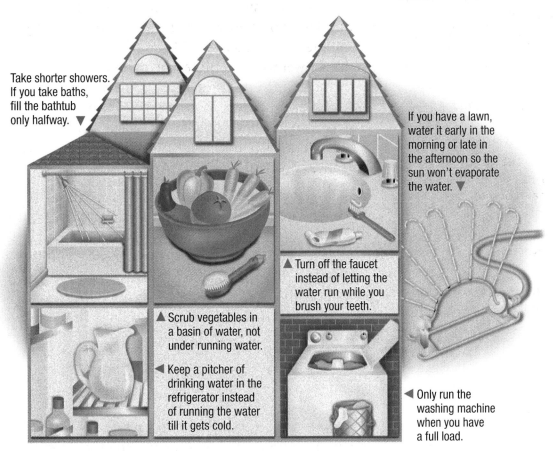

Take shorter showers. If you take baths, fill the bathtub only halfway. ▼

If you have a lawn, water it early in the morning or late in the afternoon so the sun won't evaporate the water. ▼

▲ Turn off the faucet instead of letting the water run while you brush your teeth.

▲ Scrub vegetables in a basin of water, not under running water.

◄ Keep a pitcher of drinking water in the refrigerator instead of running the water till it gets cold.

◄ Only run the washing machine when you have a full load.

Figure 8 There are many simple ways to conserve water around the home. *Developing Hypotheses Which of these ideas do you think would save the most water per day in your home? How could you test your hypothesis?*

of years, people have tried different methods to make salty ocean water drinkable.

Desalination The process of obtaining fresh water from salt water is called **desalination.** One method of desalination, called distillation, is to boil water so that it evaporates, leaving the salt behind. The water vapor is then condensed to produce liquid fresh water. Another method involves freezing the water, which also leaves the salt behind. Still another method is to pump water at high pressure through a very fine filter. The filter separates out pure water and returns saltier water to the ocean.

INTEGRATING CHEMISTRY

Desalination is very expensive because of the energy and equipment it requires. In spite of the cost, however, Saudi Arabia, Kuwait, Israel, and other nations in the dry Middle East depend on this technology. A few cities in the United States, such as Santa Barbara, California, have also built desalination plants.

Icebergs Some people think that icebergs are another possible source of fresh water for dry regions. Tugboats could tow a wrapped iceberg from Antarctica to a coastal area of Africa or South America. An iceberg would provide millions of liters of pure water that could be piped to shore as the iceberg melted. However, such plans raise environmental questions: How would a huge mass of ice offshore affect local weather? What would happen to living things as the ice cooled the water around it? These questions need to be answered before icebergs can be seen as a solution to Earth's future water needs.

Figure 9 The ocean is one possible source of drinking water for the future.
Applying Concepts How can ocean water be made suitable for drinking?

Section 2 Review

1. Describe a situation that could lead to a water shortage in a community.
2. Name three ways that industries can conserve water.
3. Describe the possible effects overpumping might have on an aquifer.
4. Explain how an iceberg might provide drinking water in the future.
5. **Thinking Critically Making Judgments** Do you think communities should be able to limit how often people water their lawns or wash their cars? Why or why not?

Science at Home

Place a stopper over the drain in a sink. Ask a family member to brush his or her teeth over the sink, allowing the water to run until he or she is done. Mark the level of the water in the sink with a small piece of tape. Remove the stopper and let the water drain. Replace the stopper and have the person repeat the brushing, this time turning the water on only when needed. Mark the water level with another piece of tape. Point out the difference in the amount of water used in each case.

GETTING THE SALT OUT

Desalination plants use many methods to produce fresh water from ocean water. In this lab, you will make a model of a desalination plant using the method of distillation.

Problem

How can distillation be used to obtain fresh water from salt water?

Materials

hot plate	aluminum foil	250-mL beaker
plastic spoon	water, 100 mL	shallow pan
ice	plastic tube	500-mL flask
stirring rod	rubber stopper	salt
rubber tubing, 50 cm		

Procedure

1. Pour 100 mL of water into the flask.
2. Add one spoonful of salt to the water in the flask and stir until dissolved. The solution should not be cloudy.
3. Gently insert the plastic tube through the hole of the rubber stopper. Do not force the tube into the hole; ask your teacher for help if you are having difficulty.
4. Insert one end of the plastic tube into the rubber tubing.
5. Put the rubber stopper in the flask. The bottom of the plastic tube should be above the surface of the solution.
6. Cover the beaker with aluminum foil. Press the edges of the foil against the beaker.
7. Push the free end of the rubber tubing through the center of the aluminum foil covering the top of the beaker.
8. Place the beaker in the pan, surrounded by ice.
9. Put the flask on the hot plate, keeping it away from the pan of ice. Turn the hot plate on. Bring the solution to a boil. **CAUTION:** *Do not touch the hot plate or flask. Do not allow the solution to boil completely away.*
10. Observe what happens in the flask and the beaker. Continue heating the solution until a liquid has accumulated in the beaker.
11. Turn off the hot plate and allow the flask and the beaker to cool. What is left behind in the flask? Record your observations.

Analyze and Conclude

1. What happened to the water in the flask during the boiling process? What happened inside the beaker?
2. How does the liquid collected in the beaker differ from the liquid in the flask?
3. What is the purpose of the ice in this activity?
4. **Think About It** Imagine building a desalination plant that uses the method of distillation to produce water for a city. What difficulties might you encounter in using this process on such a large scale?

More to Explore

How could you change the setup and procedure to recover fresh water from salt water without using the hot plate? Design an experiment to accomplish this goal. Obtain your teacher's permission before carrying out your experiment.

The Ogallala Aquifer

The Ogallala Aquifer lies beneath eight states of the Great Plains. It contains about 4 quadrillion liters of groundwater—about the amount of water in Lake Huron. Rainfall is scarce on the Great Plains. But by pumping water out of the aquifer, farmers can grow cotton, wheat, sorghum, and corn to feed cattle. More than one third of the nation's livestock are raised in this area.

Water in the Ogallala was trapped there during the last Ice Age, about 12,000 years ago. Now, due to the demands of irrigation, water levels are dropping much faster than the aquifer can recharge. In certain parts of the aquifer, water levels have fallen as much as 12 meters since 1980. Farmers recognize that the Ogallala cannot withstand this heavy use for long. However, not all agree on what should be done.

The Issues

Should Water Use Be Regulated? One way to reduce water use might be to charge people for water. But who owns the water and who would determine the cost? In most of the Great Plains, water has been free to anyone who dug a well on their land. To charge for water, local governments would need to construct a public water system as in most cities. This would be a very complex and costly task. Both farmers and consumers would be affected by the charge. Higher costs for growing crops would result in higher supermarket prices for grains and meat.

Should Farmers Change Their Practices? Farmers could switch to crops such as sunflowers and grains that need less water. These crops, however, are less valuable than others for producing food and for feeding livestock. As a result, they would be less profitable than traditional crops. Farmers could use water-saving methods of irrigation. Such methods are expensive to install but eventually save both water and money.

Another possibility is "dryland farming," a method that was used by pioneer farmers. This method involves keeping the soil moist using only rainwater. Because dryland farming depends on the amount of rainfall, it is unpredictable. It may not produce large harvests.

Should Current Use Continue? Many residents of the Great Plains depend on the aquifer for a living. Some people feel that farmers there must continue their present water use in order to compete with farmers elsewhere in the nation and around the world. They feel that people today should not have to suffer in order to preserve the aquifer for future generations. New sources of water may be discovered, or better methods of transporting water to the Great Plains may be developed. Better irrigation techniques that use less water may also be invented. But other people feel that since these possibilities are not certain, water use must be greatly reduced now to save the aquifer.

You Decide

1. Identify the Problem
In your own words, explain the problem facing the farmers on the Great Plains.

2. Analyze the Options
Make a chart of the solutions mentioned. List advantages and drawbacks of each. Who would benefit from each solution? Who would suffer?

3. Find a Solution
As a resident of the Great Plains, write a letter to the newspaper proposing a solution to the Ogallala problem.

DISCOVER ·······················ACTIVITY·····

Will the Pollution Reach Your Wells?

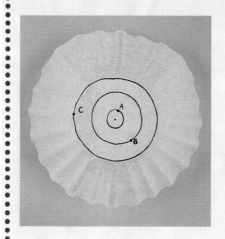

1. With a permanent marker, draw three rings on a coffee filter as shown in the picture. Draw three dots and label them A, B, and C as shown. These dots represent the locations of drinking-water supply wells.

2. Place the coffee filter on a paper plate. Moisten the coffee filter with a wet sponge. The damp coffee filter represents an aquifer.

3. Squirt five drops of food coloring onto the center of the damp coffee filter. Observe how the "pollution" travels.

Think It Over

Observing Which wells are affected by the pollution? Describe the pattern the pollution forms.

The newspaper headlines told an amazing story: "River in Flames!" "Bridges Burn As River Catches Fire!" This really happened to the Cuyahoga River in Cleveland, Ohio, in the summer of 1969. Are you wondering how a river could catch fire? What was in the Cuyahoga that allowed it to burn?

The Cuyahoga flows through a large industrial region on its way to Lake Erie. Factories along its banks used to dump their wastes into the river. Freighters spilled oil and gasoline into the water. Over time, the river became so full of chemicals and sewage that the pollution floating in it could actually burn.

Alarmed by the fire and the destruction it caused, people in Ohio began a massive campaign to clean up the Cuyahoga. Today it is safe to use for boating and fishing. The Cuyahoga River is a dramatic example of how serious water pollution can become—and of how people can work together to undo its damage.

What Is Pollution?

If you turned on your faucet and a stream of bright green water came out, you'd be fairly sure that the water contained something it shouldn't. But many things that can make water unsafe to drink don't change its color, taste, or smell. The addition of any substance that has a negative effect on water or the living things that depend on the water is called **water pollution.** Water pollution can affect surface water, groundwater, and even rain. It can result from both natural causes and human activities.

GUIDE FOR READING

◆ What are some sources of water pollution?

◆ How does agricultural runoff affect ponds and streams?

◆ How can living things help clean up polluted water?

Reading Tip As you read, make a list of sources of freshwater pollution. Write one sentence about each source.

WARNING
Fish Contaminated
DO NOT EAT

The substances that cause water pollution are called pollutants. Disease-causing organisms such as the *Cryptosporidium* you read about in Section 1 are one form of pollutant. As Figure 10 shows, other types of pollutants include toxic, or poisonous, chemicals and metals, as well as radioactive substances.

INTEGRATING LIFE SCIENCE Some types of pollutants can build up in the bodies of living things. Trace the path of one such pollutant in Figure 11. The pesticide DDT dissolves in water and is absorbed by microscopic algae. The algae, which contain only low levels of the chemical, are eaten by small water animals. When frogs or fish eat these smaller animals, they also consume the chemicals from the algae these animals had eaten. The frogs and fish are in turn eaten by birds or other animals. Each larger organism consumes a greater number of the smaller organisms, and therefore more of the DDT.

When humans eat the fish from such a pond, the toxic chemicals build up in their bodies in the same way. Over a long time, even tiny amounts of certain pollutants can build up to levels that can cause birth defects or illnesses such as cancer. Drinking impure water or eating contaminated fish are not the only ways that pollutants can affect humans. Bathing or swimming in polluted water can irritate the skin or cause more serious problems.

Point and Nonpoint Sources

To clean up a polluted body of water like the Cuyahoga River, people first need to identify the source of the pollution to prevent further damage. **The major sources of water pollution are human wastes, industrial wastes, agricultural chemicals, and runoff from roads.**

Figure 10 This table lists some examples of the different types of freshwater pollutants. *Relating Cause and Effect Why might it be helpful to know the source of a particular pollutant detected in a body of water?*

Freshwater Pollutants		
Kind of Pollutant	**Examples**	**Sources**
Disease-causing organisms	*Giardia, Cryptosporidium*, bacteria	Human wastes, runoff from livestock pens
Pesticides and fertilizers	DDT, nitrates, phosphates	Runoff from farm fields, golf courses
Industrial chemicals	PCBs, carbon tetrachloride, dioxin	Factories, industrial waste disposal sites
Metals	Lead, mercury, copper	Factories, waste disposal sites
Radioactive wastes	Uranium, carbon-14	Medical and scientific disposal sites, nuclear power plants
Petroleum products	Oil, gasoline	Road runoff, leaking underground storage tanks

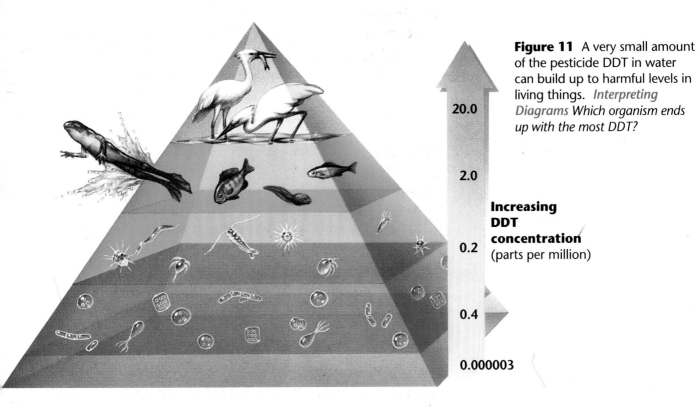

Figure 11 A very small amount of the pesticide DDT in water can build up to harmful levels in living things. *Interpreting Diagrams Which organism ends up with the most DDT?*

20.0

2.0

Increasing DDT concentration (parts per million)

0.2

0.4

0.000003

Each of these sources of pollution can be a point source or a nonpoint source, depending on how the pollution enters a body of water. For example, suppose you notice a pipe gushing white sudsy water into a river. The pipe is a **point source,** a specific source of pollution that can be identified. More often, though, the source of pollution is less obvious. Pollutants may be carried along in runoff from a farm field, a street, or a construction site. The chemicals, sewage, or radioactive materials eventually flow into a lake or river or seep into groundwater and are carried far away. It's hard to trace the exact source of this pollution. A widely spread source of pollution that can't be tied to a specific point of origin is called a **nonpoint source.**

☑ *Checkpoint* *Why are nonpoint sources difficult to identify?*

Human Wastes

Today it seems obvious that dumping human wastes into drinking water can spread disease. But scientists have only understood this connection for the last 150 years.

Dr. Snow's Discovery Cholera is a disease caused by bacteria that live in human wastes. Cholera causes people to become very dehydrated and can be fatal. In 1854, an English doctor named John Snow discovered the cause of a cholera outbreak in London. In the poorer

INTEGRATING HEALTH

Sharpen your Skills

Classifying

Classify the following as point sources or nonpoint sources of water pollution:

ACTIVITY

◆ salt used on icy roads
◆ an open drain in a sink at a paint factory
◆ a sanitary sewer pipe with a leak
◆ fertilizer sprayed onto an orchard

Give a reason why you classified each source as you did.

sections of the city, people carried water home in buckets from public wells. After 500 people in one neighborhood died in just ten days, Dr. Snow traced the cholera to a well near a pipe carrying sewage. He ended the epidemic by removing the pump handle so no one could get water from that source. Dr. Snow's work showed the danger of releasing untreated sewage into bodies of water that might be used for drinking water.

Sewage in Cities As you know, today wastewater is usually treated before being released to the environment. However, while water treatment usually kills bacteria, some viruses and parasites are able to resist chlorine and other water treatment processes. Most of these organisms come from human or animal wastes that get into the water supply.

During heavy rains and floods, sanitary sewers sometimes overflow and run into storm sewers. Since the storm sewers generally lead directly into surface water, the sewage from the sanitary sewers can pollute the water. For this reason, people are often told to boil water for drinking and cooking after a flood. The boiling kills many disease-causing organisms.

Figure 12 This engraving from the late 1800s shows people in Hamburg, Germany, getting water from a cart during a cholera epidemic. The city wells were closed, and water was brought in from the countryside.

Sewage in Rural Areas Disposing of human waste is not just a problem in big cities. In rural areas, people must be careful where they locate septic tanks. If a tank is too near a stream or on a hill, wastewater can leak into the stream or flow into the area of a well downhill.

Wastes from cattle, pigs, and chickens can also be a problem in rural areas. They contribute disease-causing bacteria and other kinds of pollution to water that runs off from pastures and barnyards.

☑ *Checkpoint Why should drinking water and sewage be kept separate?*

Industrial Wastes

Most cities and towns in the United States have wastewater treatment systems that handle sewage effectively. For this reason, water pollution by factories and mines is a more serious problem than sewage in most areas of the country. Chemicals, smoke, and heated water are three types of industrial pollutants.

Chemicals Many factory processes, especially those for making dyes and plastics or treating metals, involve toxic chemicals and strong acids. Other toxic wastes are produced as by-products, or side effects, of manufacturing and mining. Although laws now limit and control chemical pollution, some factories still release toxic chemicals directly into nearby rivers and lakes.

Another problem is leftover wastes. In the past, many industries stored toxic wastes in barrels or other containers buried underground. Over the years, however, many of these containers rusted or broke. The chemicals leaked out, polluting both the soil and the groundwater.

Figure 13 Many lakes and rivers have been polluted by wastes from nearby industries. These environmental scientists are collecting water samples from a pond for testing.

Smoke and Exhaust Many power plants and factories burn *INTEGRATING CHEMISTRY* coal or oil to fuel their processes. The engines of millions of cars, trucks, and buses burn gasoline. Every day, smoke and exhaust from these sources pour into the air, especially around large cities. When coal, oil, and gasoline are burned, molecules of the gases sulfur dioxide and nitrogen oxide are released into the atmosphere. There the sulfur and nitrogen react with water, forming sulfuric and nitric acids. The result is rain or other forms of precipitation that are more acidic than normal, called **acid rain.** When acid rain falls on lakes and ponds, the water can become so acidic that fish and other wildlife cannot survive. Acid rain also eats away the stone of buildings and statues.

Heat Pollution Think about how hot a metal slide gets on a sunny day. Imagine borrowing enough water from a swimming pool to cool the slide, and then returning the water to the pool. How would this change the swimming pool? Would you still want to jump in to cool off? The warm water would probably not be very refreshing.

Figure 14 A noisy jumble of taxis, cars, and buses crowds a city street. *Relating Cause and Effect How are these vehicles related to water pollution?*

How Do Your Algae Grow?

In this activity you will observe how fertilizers affect the growth of algae in pond water.

1. 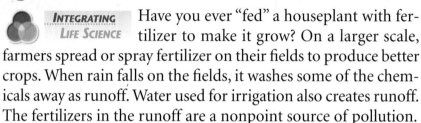 Label two jars A and B. Pour tap water into each jar until it is half full.

2. Add water from a pond or aquarium to each jar until it is three-quarters full.

3. Add 5 mL of liquid fertilizer to jar A only.

4. Cover both jars tightly and place them on a windowsill in the sunlight. Wash your hands with soap.

5. Observe the jars every day for a week.

Drawing Conclusions How did the fertilizer affect the growth of the algae in jar A? What was the purpose of jar B in this experiment?

Much of the water in factories is used to cool machinery or metal objects. Even if it contains no chemicals, the warm water alone can act as a pollutant. Many water organisms can live in only a narrow range of temperatures. Warm water released by a factory into a nearby river or pond raises the temperature of the water, sometimes enough to harm the living things there.

Agricultural Chemicals

INTEGRATING LIFE SCIENCE Have you ever "fed" a houseplant with fertilizer to make it grow? On a larger scale, farmers spread or spray fertilizer on their fields to produce better crops. When rain falls on the fields, it washes some of the chemicals away as runoff. Water used for irrigation also creates runoff. The fertilizers in the runoff are a nonpoint source of pollution.

The rich supply of nutrients from fertilizers encourages the growth of plants and algae in and around nearby bodies of water. As you learned in Chapter 2, ponds and lakes naturally change over time due to the process of eutrophication. As more plants grow in the water, dead plant material piles up on the bottom, making the water shallower and warmer. As the plant matter decays, the amount of oxygen in the water decreases. With the addition of fertilizers, this natural process speeds up. A thick, soupy scum of algae forms on top of the water. The scum blocks the sunlight and chokes the flow of water, changing the living conditions for other organisms.

Runoff and irrigation water also carry away other pollutants from farm fields. **Pesticides** are chemicals intended to kill insects and other organisms that damage crops. Pesticides may be sprayed on crops and then run off. Sometimes they are sprayed directly on ponds to kill mosquitoes. But at the same time, these chemicals can harm other insects or the animals that eat them.

✓ *Checkpoint* *How can chemicals used in agriculture reach streams, ponds, and lakes?*

Runoff from Roads

Have you ever noticed an oily sheen on a puddle in a parking lot after a rain shower? The sheen was probably caused by gasoline and motor oil that leaked from cars. When it rains, these oily substances are washed off along with the runoff. During cold winter weather, runoff also picks up the salt that is sprinkled on roads and sidewalks to melt ice. This runoff is a nonpoint source of pollution. Gasoline, oil, and salt pollute rivers and lakes that the runoff enters. These substances can also seep down into groundwater and pollute wells or even an entire aquifer.

Figure 15 A thick layer of red algae tints a pond the color of tomato soup. *Inferring What might be the cause of the algae growth in this pond?*

Cleaning Up Polluted Water

Many pollutants are eventually removed from freshwater bodies through natural cleaning processes. **Living things in lakes, streams, and wetlands filter out and break down waste materials.** For example, plant roots filter larger particles from the water. Some plants, such as water hyacinths and duckweed, can absorb metals and chemicals. And just as certain bacteria are used in purifying wastewater, some are also useful in cleaning up toxic chemicals. Bacteria that consume oil have been used to help clean up oil spills. Waste-eating bacteria may also prove to be useful in breaking down toxic chemicals in rivers and lakes.

Pollution clean-up programs can be based on such natural treatment processes. For example, both natural and artificial wetlands are being used to clean up water pollution. Wetlands have been built near coal mines to treat acidic mining runoff before it returns to the environment.

Not only living things can help clean up polluted water. Passing through the sand or rock of an aquifer naturally filters and purifies groundwater. But natural filtering cannot remove or destroy many pollutants, such as metals or manufactured chemicals. Cleaning up this kind of pollution in groundwater is very difficult. One method involves pumping polluted groundwater to the surface, sending it through a treatment plant, and returning it to a nearby lake.

Figure 16 These purple water hyacinths can be an attractive part of a cleanup program. The plants absorb certain metals and chemicals from polluted water.

Preventing Pollution

Despite the successes in cleaning up some water pollution, most pollutants are very difficult to remove. It is often easier to avoid causing the pollution in the first place. In the late 1960s, as

Figure 17 One way you can help prevent water pollution is to educate others about its causes. This student is stenciling a storm drain to remind people of its connection to a nearby river.

people became more aware of the problems of pollution, they urged the government to create laws to control pollution. The goals of those laws include the cleanup of polluted lakes and rivers, better wastewater treatment, and limits on releasing pollutants to the environment. The government also established water-quality standards and programs to clean up waste disposal sites.

Industry and Agriculture Many recycling techniques that help conserve water also help to lessen pollution. For example, factories cool water and reuse it instead of returning it to a river, reducing heat pollution. Industries also look for ways to replace toxic materials with less harmful ones. Printing inks, for instance, can be made with water instead of chemical solvents.

Farmers are trying to reduce the problem of runoff from pastures and barnyards. Some collect and reuse this water for irrigation. Other farmers plant fields of coarse grasses that filter out pollutants before the water reaches a river or pond.

What Can You Do? You can also help keep pollutants from entering the environment. Dispose of toxic substances carefully. For example, chemicals like paint and motor oil should never be poured down the drain, but instead be taken to sites that collect hazardous waste. Avoid overfertilizing lawns or gardens. Form a group of students to educate others in your community about the causes and effects of freshwater pollution. Because many kinds of water pollution are so difficult to clean up, the most important place to stop pollution is at its source.

Section 3 Review

1. List four sources of water pollution.
2. How can fertilizers cause water pollution?
3. Explain why people are often instructed to boil drinking water after a flood.
4. **Thinking Critically Making Judgments** To prevent water pollution, a factory proposes pumping its wastes into the ground instead of into a river. Would you support this change? Why or why not?

Check Your Progress

CHAPTER PROJECT 3

At this point, you should be ready to assemble your model treatment system. Does the system include at least two treatment steps? Be sure to ask an adult to help you cut materials or assemble them if necessary. (Hint: Test your treatment setup for leaks using clean tap water.)

SECTION 4 Water As an Energy Resource

DISCOVER ·········· ACTIVITY

Can Water Do Work?

1. Spread out a large plastic trash bag on the ground. On top of the bag, place several cylindrical objects such as corks, spools, marbles, balls, and empty cans.

2. Fill a plant sprayer with water. Then turn the nozzle to produce a fine mist of water. Try to move the objects with the spray of water. **CAUTION:** *Be careful of slippery wet floors if you are doing this activity indoors.*

3. Now turn the sprayer nozzle to produce a narrower stream of water. Try again to move the objects. Be sure to wipe up any spilled water when you are done.

Think It Over
Observing How does changing the nozzle opening affect the stream of water? At which setting did the objects move more easily? Why?

Picture a curving wall of concrete swooping up nearly 170 meters—taller than a 40-story building. On one side of the wall is a deep reservoir. On the other side, only a narrow river trickles between rocky canyon walls. This is Grand Coulee Dam on the Columbia River in Washington. Completed in 1942, it is still one of the largest dams in the world. Behind Grand Coulee, the water in the reservoir pushes on the concrete dam. The dam's floodgates control that awesome energy. When the gates open to release the water, the water's energy is transformed into enough electricity to light thousands of homes and businesses.

For centuries, people have used the energy of moving water to turn water wheels and run machinery. Today that energy is also a source of electrical power in many parts of the world.

Power from Moving Water

Have you ever seen a fast-moving river propel a kayaker along? If so, you know how much energy moving water can have. It can move boats, carve out canyons, and sweep away cars in a flood. The energy that sends the kayak through the rapids is kinetic

GUIDE FOR READING

◆ How does moving water produce electricity?

◆ In what ways is hydroelectric power a good source of energy?

Reading Tip Before you read the section, preview *Exploring a Hydroelectric Power Plant.* Write a list of questions you have about hydroelectric power.

Making a Water Wheel

ACTIVITY

In this activity you will see how the kinetic energy of water can do work.

1. Put on your goggles.

2. ✂ Cut an aluminum pie plate into four squares about 5 cm on a side. **CAUTION:** *Be careful not to cut yourself on the sharp edges of the pie plate.*

3. Push the sides of the aluminum squares into a foam ball as shown. Insert two toothpicks into the sides of the ball.

4. Rest the toothpicks on top of your fingers and place the blades under a stream of slowly running water.

Developing Hypotheses How would increasing the volume of water affect the speed of the water wheel? Test your hypothesis. Describe what happens to the speed of the water wheel.

---

energy. **Kinetic energy** is the form of energy that an object has when it is moving.

Energy can change from one form to another. If the water's movement is stopped, all of its energy becomes potential energy. **Potential energy** is energy that is stored and waiting to be used. To think about potential energy in another way, imagine that you're holding a baseball bat at the top of your swing. The bat at that point has potential energy. As you swing at a ball, the bat's energy becomes kinetic energy. If you hit the ball, the energy is transferred again, becoming the kinetic energy of the ball.

Hydroelectric power is electricity produced by the kinetic energy of water moving over a waterfall or a dam. To generate hydroelectric power (or "hydropower"), engineers build a dam across a river. Water backs up behind the dam, floods the valley, and creates a reservoir. Water stored behind a dam has potential energy, which is changed to kinetic energy when the water is released. **Hydroelectric power plants capture the kinetic energy of moving water and change it into electrical energy.**

How is the kinetic energy of moving water changed into the energy that lights your house and runs your computer? Follow the path of the water in *Exploring a Hydroelectric Power Plant* on the next page to see how these energy changes take place.

✓ *Checkpoint* *What type of energy does a diver have while standing at the edge of a diving board?*

The Impact of Dams

In some ways, hydroelectric power seems like an ideal way to produce electricity. **Hydroelectric power is clean, safe, and efficient. Although building a dam is expensive, the water is free and is naturally renewed by the water cycle.** Unlike power plants that burn coal or oil, hydroelectric plants do not contribute to air pollution. In the United States, hydroelectric power accounts for about 8 or 9 percent of electricity produced, while worldwide it generates about 20 percent. Some countries, such as Norway and Brazil, produce almost all their electrical energy through hydropower.

Hydroelectric plants do have limitations, however. Only certain locations are suitable for building a dam. A fast-moving river is necessary, as is an area that can be flooded to create a reservoir.

Dams and the Environment Dams affect all living things in

INTEGRATING LIFE SCIENCE the area around them. Flooding the land behind a dam can destroy wildlife habitats as well as farms and towns. What was once a fast-moving river becomes the still, deep waters of a reservoir. Some organisms

EXPLORING a Hydroelectric Power Plant

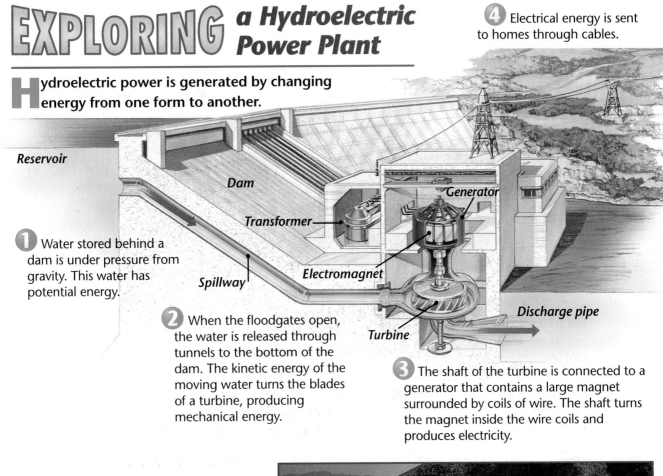

Hydroelectric power is generated by changing energy from one form to another.

4 Electrical energy is sent to homes through cables.

Reservoir

Dam

Transformer

Generator

Electromagnet

Spillway

Turbine

Discharge pipe

1 Water stored behind a dam is under pressure from gravity. This water has potential energy.

2 When the floodgates open, the water is released through tunnels to the bottom of the dam. The kinetic energy of the moving water turns the blades of a turbine, producing mechanical energy.

3 The shaft of the turbine is connected to a generator that contains a large magnet surrounded by coils of wire. The shaft turns the magnet inside the wire coils and produces electricity.

cannot survive the change. In addition, the dam is a barrier across the river. It may prevent fish from traveling to the parts of a river where they usually lay their eggs and young fish are hatched. Dams like Grand Coulee on the Columbia River, for instance, have greatly reduced the population of salmon in the river.

As a river slows down, it deposits some of the sediments it carries. These deposits can build up behind a dam instead of being carried downstream to enrich the flood plain near the river's mouth. Since the Aswan Dam was built in Egypt, for example, farmlands near the mouth of the Nile River no longer receive the rich load of nutrients the river once brought.

Displaced by a Dam How would you feel if you discovered that your riverside home would soon be dozens of meters under the water of a lake? People whose homes or farms are located

Figure 18 This photograph shows the Theodore Roosevelt Dam in Arizona. *Interpreting Photographs What natural feature of the river made this a good location to build a dam?*

Figure 19 Building the Aswan Dam meant flooding the valley that housed these statues of ancient Egyptian rulers. Piece by piece, workers carefully dismantled the great monuments and moved them to higher ground.

where a dam's reservoir is planned have had to face this issue. Large dams flood hundreds or thousands of square kilometers, covering towns and valleys with water. When the Aswan High Dam was built on the Nile, about 80,000 people had to relocate. The ancient monuments of Abu Simbel had to be moved as the water in Lake Nasser rose higher and higher.

One of the largest dams ever built is now under construction on the Yangzi River in China. The Three Gorges Dam, due to be completed in 2009, could displace more than 1.5 million people.

Benefits of Dams For countries that want to build up their industries, hydroelectric power often seems the best way to provide the electricity they need. Water power is the least expensive and least polluting large-scale energy source. Besides electricity, dams can supply water for irrigation and help in flood control.

In some places, people have suggested building small dams to supply power to a local area. Smaller dams uproot fewer people and do less harm to the environment, while still providing energy for a region to grow. However, since dams are expensive to build, small dams may not produce enough power to be worthwhile. Large dams, on the other hand, produce great amounts of power, but they also have a major effect on the land around them.

Section 4 Review

1. How does a hydroelectric plant use moving water to generate electric power?
2. Name two advantages of hydroelectric power.
3. Give one positive example and one negative example of how building a dam could affect wildlife in the area.
4. **Thinking Critically Problem Solving** Suppose you were assigned to choose a site to build a new hydroelectric plant. What features would you look for to find a good site? Be sure to consider the impact on living things as well as the physical characteristics of the site.

CHAPTER PROJECT 3

Check Your Progress
Now you are ready to test your model system, using the dirty water sample your teacher has provided. Does your treatment unit clean up the water? Measure how much of the original one liter of water is recovered. Based on your results, decide whether you need to redesign any part of your treatment system. (*Hint:* To modify your system, consider changing materials as well as adding more steps.)

SECTION 1 — Water to Drink

Key Ideas

◆ Sources of drinking water include rivers, lakes, reservoirs, and groundwater.

◆ Many communities maintain public water supplies to collect, treat, and distribute water to residents. Some homes have private wells.

◆ Most drinking water is treated to ensure that it is safe and appealing to drink.

◆ Pumps and gravity are used to increase water pressure and move water through a system of pipes.

◆ Wastewater and sewage are treated to prevent contamination of drinking water.

Key Terms

water quality	pH	hardness
concentration	filtration	flocs
coagulation	sewage	sludge
septic tank	leach field	

SECTION 2 — Balancing Water Needs

Key Ideas

◆ Water is scarce in many places, leading to competition for limited supplies.

◆ Water shortage can occur when there is too little water or too much demand in an area.

◆ Industries can conserve water by reducing water use, recycling water, and reusing water.

◆ Desalination of ocean water and icebergs are two possible future sources of fresh water.

Key Terms

drought	conservation	desalination

SECTION 3 — Freshwater Pollution

Key Ideas

◆ Sources of water pollution include human and animal wastes, industrial and agricultural chemicals, and runoff from roads.

◆ Acid rain is caused by sulfur and nitrogen from smokestacks and car exhausts.

◆ Runoff of fertilizers into bodies of water can cause plants to grow too rapidly, changing the conditions for living things there.

◆ Living organisms help to naturally remove many pollutants from water, but other pollutants are difficult to remove.

Key Terms

water pollution	point source
nonpoint source	acid rain
pesticide	

SECTION 4 — Water As an Energy Resource

INTEGRATING PHYSICS

Key Ideas

◆ Hydroelectric power plants capture the kinetic energy of moving water and change it into electrical energy.

◆ Hydroelectric power is a clean, renewable energy source, but dams are expensive to build and change the land around them.

Key Terms

kinetic energy	potential energy
hydroelectric power	

ACTIVITY

USING THE INTERNET

www.science-explorer.phschool.com

Reviewing Content

 For more review of key concepts, see the Interactive Student Tutorial CD-ROM.

Multiple Choice

Choose the letter of the best answer.

1. Chlorine is added during water treatment in order to
   a. make particles form flocs.
   b. kill disease-causing organisms.
   c. improve the taste of the water.
   d. remove objects such as fish and trash.
2. Primary treatment of wastewater typically involves
   a. adding chlorine.
   b. filtering out solids.
   c. adding sludge.
   d. adding waste-eating bacteria.
3. One process used to obtain fresh water from salt water is
   a. coagulation.   b. filtration.
   c. recharge.   d. desalination.
4. The main source of acid precipitation is
   a. smoke from coal-burning factories.
   b. pesticides sprayed in the air.
   c. runoff from farm fields.
   d. toxic chemicals buried underground.
5. Water flowing swiftly possesses
   a. mechanical energy.
   b. electrical energy.
   c. potential energy.
   d. kinetic energy.

True or False

If the statement is true, write true. If it is false, change the underlined word or words to make the statement true.

6. The <u>pH</u> of water is a measurement of the amount of calcium and magnesium.
7. Sludge is produced during the treatment of <u>drinking water</u>.
8. A drought can cause wells to dry up if the level of the water table <u>falls</u>.
9. Oily runoff from highways is an example of a <u>point</u> source of pollution.
10. Agricultural runoff containing <u>pesticides</u> often results in increased plant growth in nearby ponds and streams.

Checking Concepts

11. Describe one possible path of drinking water from its source to a home.
12. Explain how a septic system works.
13. Why are water rights an important issue in dry areas?
14. Describe one way that farmers can reduce the amount of water lost during irrigation.
15. Explain how low levels of a pollutant in a stream can have harmful effects on wildlife in and around the stream.
16. How might building a dam affect people living nearby?
17. **Writing to Learn** You have been hired as a public relations specialist for the city water department. Your first assignment is to prepare a brief fact sheet for city residents about the importance of conserving water. The fact sheet should also include some simple suggestions of ways to conserve water at home.

Thinking Visually

18. **Concept Map** Copy the concept map about freshwater pollution onto a separate sheet of paper. Complete it and add a title. (For more on concept maps, see the Skills Handbook.)

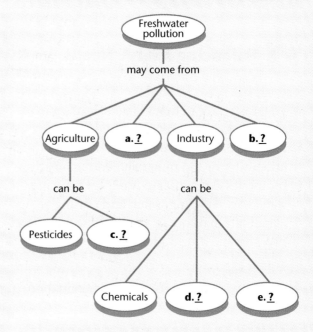

Applying Skills

A family had their drinking-water well tested to check the water quality. The test results are shown in the table below. Use the data in the table to answer Questions 19–22.

Drinking Water Sample Test Results

Lead	0.2 parts per million
Copper	0.006 parts per million
pH	5.0
Coliform count	5 out of 5 samples positive

19. Inferring The homeowners suspect that their septic tank is polluting the well. What evidence exists to support this conclusion?

20. Designing Experiments What might be the source of the lead in the water? How could you test your answer?

21. Developing Hypotheses How might the low pH of the water be related to the lead contamination?

22. Predicting The homeowners have noticed that their water does not form suds well when mixed with soap. Predict what other substances may be present in high levels in the water.

Thinking Critically

23. Relating Cause and Effect How can increased demand for water cause the ground above an aquifer to collapse?

24. Comparing and Contrasting How is the process of desalination similar to the water cycle? How is it different?

25. Making Judgments Do you think that the benefits of hydroelectric power outweigh the disadvantages? Give reasons to support your answer.

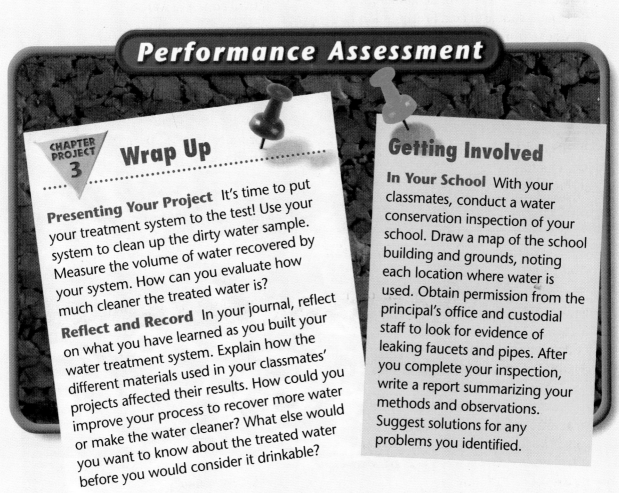

Performance Assessment

CHAPTER PROJECT 3

Wrap Up

Presenting Your Project It's time to put your treatment system to the test! Use your system to clean up the dirty water sample. Measure the volume of water recovered by your system. How can you evaluate how much cleaner the treated water is?

Reflect and Record In your journal, reflect on what you have learned as you built your water treatment system. Explain how the different materials used in your classmates' projects affected their results. How could you improve your process to recover more water or make the water cleaner? What else would you want to know about the treated water before you would consider it drinkable?

Getting Involved

In Your School With your classmates, conduct a water conservation inspection of your school. Draw a map of the school building and grounds, noting each location where water is used. Obtain permission from the principal's office and custodial staff to look for evidence of leaking faucets and pipes. After you complete your inspection, write a report summarizing your methods and observations. Suggest solutions for any problems you identified.

CHAPTER 4 Ocean Motions

WHAT'S AHEAD

SECTION 1 Wave Action

Discover How Do Waves Change a Beach?
Try This Wave Motion

Integrating Space Science
SECTION 2 Tides

Discover When Is High Tide?
Sharpen Your Skills Graphing

SECTION 3 Ocean Water Chemistry

Discover Will the Eggs Sink or Float?
Skills Lab Investigating Changes in Density

PROJECT 4

Protecting a Shoreline

The world's oceans are always in motion. Waves, tides, and currents each move Earth's waters in different ways. In this chapter you will study these movements and their power to change the land. You will build your own model of a shoreline with a lighthouse and use the model to demonstrate how some ocean motions can affect the land along the coast.

Your Goal To design and build a model ocean beach and test possible methods for preventing shoreline erosion.

To complete this project successfully, you must

- build a model beach and use it to demonstrate the effects of wave erosion
- test methods of protecting the lighthouse from damage
- follow the safety guidelines outlined in Appendix A

Get Started Begin now by previewing Figure 4 on page 118. Start thinking about how you will build a model of an ocean beach like the one in the diagram. Brainstorm a list of materials that you could use to build your model.

Check Your Progress You'll be working on this project as you study this chapter. To keep your project on track, look for Check Your Progress boxes at the following points.

Section 1 Review, page 121: Design your model beach.
Section 2 Review, page 126: Construct your model and test it.
Section 4 Review, page 140: Improve your model and test it again.

Wrap Up At the end of the chapter (page 143), you will show how well your design keeps the lighthouse from toppling into the surf.

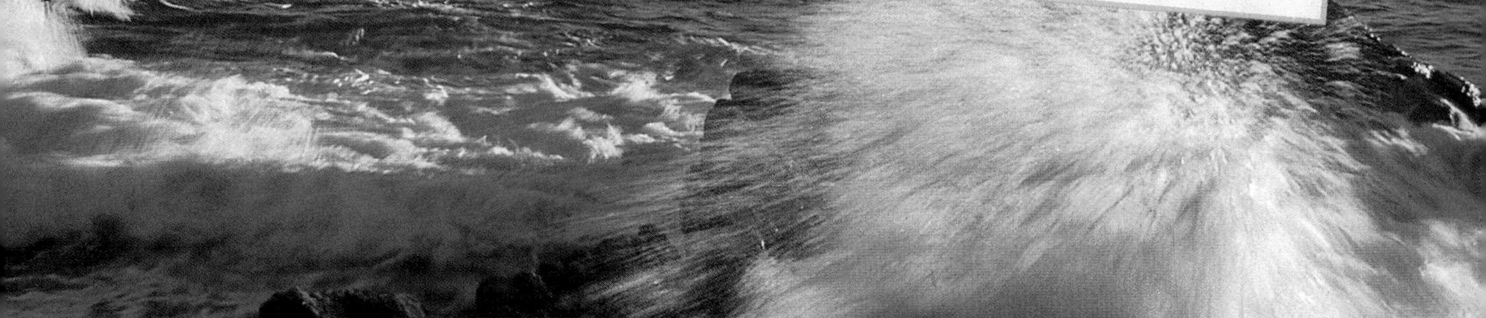

Waves crash against the rocky Maine coast. Sweeping its beacon of light across the water, the Portland Head Lighthouse warns ships of the treacherous rocks.

SECTION 4 Currents and Climate

Discover Which Is More Dense?
Sharpen Your Skills Drawing Conclusions
Real-World Lab Modeling Ocean Currents

DISCOVER · ACTIVITY · · · ·

How Do Waves Change a Beach?

1. In one end of an aluminum pan, build a "beach" of sand and pebbles. Put a book under that end of the pan to raise it about 5 centimeters.

2. Pour water slowly into the other end of the pan until it covers the edge of the sand, just as water touches the edge of a beach.

3. Place a wooden tongue depressor in the water. Move it back and forth gently in a regular rhythm to make waves in the pan. Continue for about 2 minutes.

4. Once the water has stopped moving, observe what has happened to the beach. Wash your hands when you are finished with this activity.

Think It Over

Observing How has the motion of the water changed the edge of the beach?

GUIDE FOR READING

◆ How does a wave form?

◆ How do waves change near the shore?

◆ How do waves affect beaches and coastlines?

Reading Tip Before you read, preview the diagrams and photographs in the section to see different types of wave action. Make a list of questions you have about wave motion.

Stretched flat on his surfboard, the surfer paddles out into the clear turquoise water. The surfboard bobs up and down as he awaits the perfect surfing wave. After a few minutes, he spots the telltale signs in an approaching wave. At the last possible minute before the wave crashes over him, the surfer jumps into a standing position. He balances skillfully as the energy of the wave sends the surfboard skimming down the smooth front of the curling wave.

If you've ever seen a video of surfers "catching a wave" along a Pacific beach, you know that they make this difficult sport look almost easy. But even experienced surfers can seldom predict when the next good wave will roll into shore. As you will read in this section, many different forces influence the size, shape, and timing of waves.

How Waves Form

When you watch the surfer's wave crash onto the beach, you are seeing the last step in the process of the wave's development. The process begins with wind. Without the energy of wind, the surface of the ocean would be as smooth as a mirror. **Most waves form when winds blowing across the water's surface transmit their energy to the water.** A **wave** is the movement of energy through a body of water.

Waves start in the open ocean. The size of the wave depends on the strength of the wind and on the length of time it blows. A gentle breeze creates small ripples on the surface of the water. Stronger winds create larger waves.

The size of the wave also depends on the distance over which the wind blows. Winds blowing across longer distances build up bigger waves. In the wide Pacific Ocean, a wave might travel a third of the way around the world before reaching the California coast.

Although waves may appear to carry water toward shore, the water does not actually move forward in deep water. If it did, ocean water would eventually pile up on the coasts of every continent! The energy of the wave moves toward shore, but the water itself remains where it was. You can test this for yourself by floating a piece of wood or a cork in a bowl of water. Use a spoon to make a wave in the bowl. As the wave passes, the object lurches forward a little, then bobs backward. It ends up in almost the same spot where it started.

Figure 1 A surfer cruises along the smooth front of this cresting wave. The wave's energy moves along, but the water mostly stays where it is. *Applying Concepts In which direction is the energy of this wave moving?*

Wave Motion

This activity shows how waves formed at the surface affect deeper water.

1. Fill an aquarium about three-quarters full of water.

2. Tie enough metal washers to a cork so that the cork floats about 3 cm from the bottom of the tank.

3. Repeat Step 2 with more corks so that they float 9 cm from the bottom, 15 cm from the bottom, and so on until the last cork floats on the surface.

4. Make small, steady waves in the tank by moving your hand up and down in the water. Note what happens to each cork.

5. Repeat Step 4, increasing the height of the waves by moving your hand faster.

Observing How does increasing the wave height affect the motion of each cork?

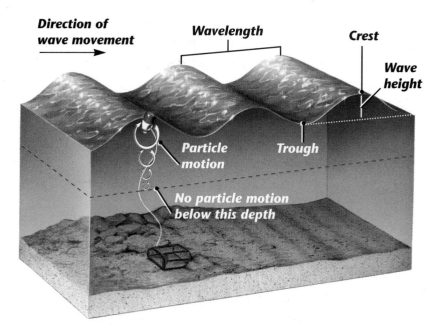

Figure 2 As a wave passes by, the water particles move in a circular motion. The buoy on the surface swings down into the trough of one wave, then back up to the crest of the next wave. Below the surface, the water particles move in smaller circles. At a depth equal to about one half the wavelength, the water particles are not affected by the surface wave.

Figure 2 shows what happens to the water as a wave travels along. As the wave passes, water particles move in a circular path. They swing forward and down with the energy of the wave, then back up to their original position.

Notice that the deeper water particles in Figure 2 move in smaller circles than those near the surface. The wind affects the water at the surface more than the deep water. Below a certain depth, the water does not move at all as the wave passes. If you were inside a submarine in deep water, you would not be able to tell whether the water above you was rough or smooth.

Describing Waves

If you ask a sailor to describe a wave, you might hear some unfamiliar terms. To a sailor, "a following sea" refers to waves traveling in the same direction as the boat. "Combers" are large, cresting waves. And "spindrift" is ocean spray torn by the wind from the surface of the waves.

Scientists have their own vocabulary of terms to describe the size and strength of waves. The name for the highest part of a wave is the **crest**. The horizontal distance between crests is the **wavelength**. Long, rolling waves with lots of space between crests have long wavelengths. Short, choppy waves have shorter wavelengths. Waves are also measured by their **frequency**, the number of waves that pass a point in a certain amount of time.

The name for the lowest part of a wave is the **trough**. The vertical distance from the crest to the trough is the **wave height**. The energy and strength of a wave depend mainly on its wave height. In the open ocean, most waves are between 2 and 5 meters high. During storms, the waves can grow much higher and more powerful.

☑ *Checkpoint* Do waves that are close together have a longer or shorter wavelength than waves that are far apart?

How Waves Change Near Shore

In deep water, waves usually travel as long, low waves called swells. As the waves approach the shore, the water becomes shallower. Follow the waves in Figure 3 as they enter the shallow water. The bottoms of the waves begin to touch the sloping ocean floor. Friction between the ocean floor and the water causes the waves to slow down. As the speed of the waves decrease, their shapes change. **Near shore, the wave height increases and the wavelength decreases.** When the wave reaches a certain height, the crest of the wave topples. The wave breaks onto the shore, forming surf.

At first, the energy of the breaking wave, or breaker, causes the water to surge up the beach. But the force of gravity pulling down on the rising water soon causes it to lose its energy. The water that moves up the beach flows back into the sea. Have you ever stood at the water's edge and felt the pull of the water rushing back out to the ocean? This pull, often called an undertow, carries shells, seaweed, and sand away from the beach. A strong undertow can be dangerous to swimmers.

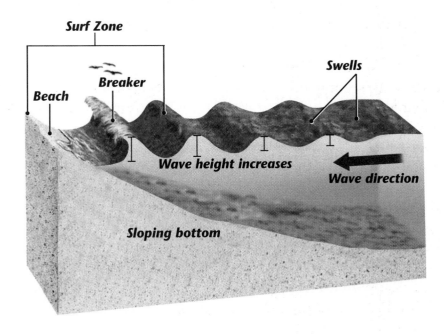

Surf Zone

Swells

Breaker

Beach

Wave height increases

Wave direction

Sloping bottom

Figure 3 Friction with the ocean floor causes waves to slow down in the shallow water near shore. The wave height increases until the waves break, forming surf. *Interpreting Diagrams What happens to the wavelength as the waves approach shore?*

How Waves Affect the Shore

What happens on shore as waves pound the beach? The diagram in Figure 4 shows some of their effects. Since wave direction at sea is determined by the wind, waves usually roll toward shore at an angle. But as they touch bottom, the shallower water slows the shoreward side of the wave first. The rows of waves gradually turn and become more nearly parallel to the shore.

Longshore Drift As the waves come into shore, water washes up the beach at an angle, carrying sand grains with it. The water and sand then run straight back down the beach. This movement of sand along the beach is called **longshore drift**. As the waves slow down, they deposit the sand they are carrying on the shallow, underwater slope in a long ridge called a **sandbar**.

Rip Currents As a sandbar grows, it can trap the water flowing along the shore. In some places, water breaks through the sandbar and begins to flow back down the sloping ocean bottom. This process creates a **rip current**, a rush of water that flows rapidly back to sea through a narrow opening. Rip currents can carry a swimmer out into deep water. Because rip currents are narrow, a strong swimmer can usually escape by swimming across the current, parallel to the beach.

☑ *Checkpoint* *In what direction does a rip current pull a swimmer?*

Figure 4 Waves approach the shore at an angle. This results in a gradual movement of sand along the beach. *Interpreting Diagrams In which direction is longshore drift moving the sand along this beach?*

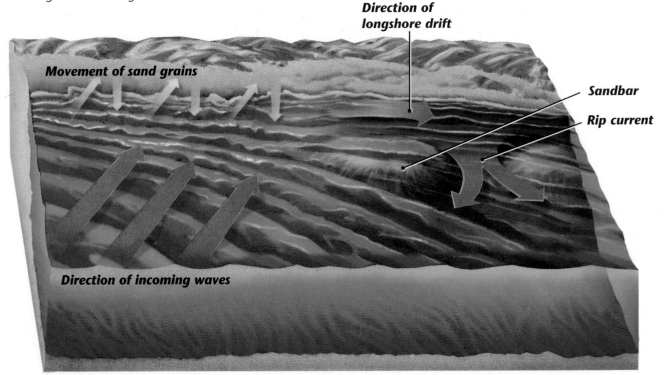

Direction of longshore drift

Movement of sand grains

Sandbar

Rip current

Direction of incoming waves

Figure 5 "The Breaking Wave off Kanagawa" is a wood-block print by the Japanese artist Hokusai.

Visual Arts
CONNECTION

The Japanese artist Hokusai (1760–1849) is well known for his land and ocean scenes. His print at the left shows a cresting wave with the snow-capped Mt. Fuji in the background.

As a teenager, Hokusai was apprenticed to a wood-block engraver. A wood-block print is made by engraving a separate block of wood for each color ink used in the picture. How many blocks do you think Hokusai needed for this print?

In Your Journal

Imagine you are writing a catalog for a museum exhibit of ocean scenes. Write a brief description of Hokusai's print for the catalog.

Waves and Beach Erosion

The boundary between land and ocean is always changing shape. If you walk on the same beach every day, you might not notice that it is changing. From day to day, waves remove sand and bring new sand at about the same rate. But if you visit a beach just once each year, you might be startled by what you see. **Waves shape a beach by eroding the shore in some places and building it up in others.**

As you learned in Chapter 2, erosion is the process of breaking up rock and carrying it away. At first, waves striking a rocky shoreline carve the rocks into tall cliffs and arches. Over many thousands of years, waves break the rocks into pebbles and grains of sand. A wide, sandy beach forms. Then the waves begin to eat away at the exposed beach. The shoreline slowly moves farther inland. Longshore drift carries the sand along the coast and deposits it elsewhere.

Reducing Erosion

Many people like to live near the ocean. But over time, erosion can wear away the beach. This threatens the homes and other buildings. To avoid losing their property, people look for ways to reduce the effect of erosion.

Groins One method of reducing erosion along a stretch of beach is to build a wall of rocks or concrete, called a **groin,** outward from the beach. The sand carried by the water piles up

Figure 6 Sand piles up against a series of groins people have built along the North Carolina coast. Building groins to stop longshore drift is one way to reduce beach erosion.

against the groins instead of moving along the shore. Figure 6 shows how groins interrupt the movement of water. However, the groins increase the amount of erosion farther down the beach.

Dunes Some natural landforms protect beaches and reduce erosion, although they can't completely stop the movement of sand. Dunes, hills of wind-blown sand covered with plants, make a beach more stable and protect the shore from erosion. The strong roots of dune plants, such as beach grass and sea oats, hold the sand in place. These plants help to slow erosion by both wind and water. But the dunes and plants can be easily destroyed by cars, bicycles, or even by many people walking over them. Without the plants to hold the sand in place, the dunes can be easily washed away by wave action.

Barrier Beaches Another natural landform that protects shorelines from wave action occurs along low-lying beaches. Long sand deposits called barrier beaches form parallel to the shore. The beaches are separated from the mainland by a shallow lagoon. Waves break against the barrier beach instead of against the land inside. For this reason, people are working to preserve natural barrier beaches like those off Cape Cod, the New Jersey shore, and the Georgia and Carolina coasts.

Figure 7 Sand dunes are a natural form of beach protection. These yellow-flowered sea oats and beach grasses anchor a dune on Cape Cod, Massachusetts.

Tsunamis

So far you have been reading about waves that are caused by the wind. Another kind of wave forms far below the ocean surface. This type of wave, called a **tsunami,** is usually caused by an earthquake on the ocean floor. The abrupt movement of the ocean floor sends pulses of energy through the water above it. When tsunamis reach the coast, they can be as devastating as an earthquake on land, smashing buildings and bridges.

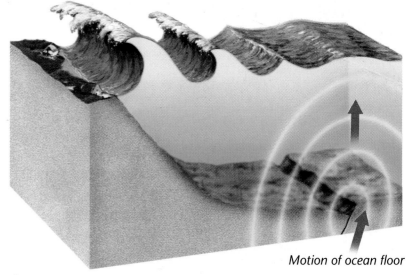

Motion of ocean floor

Despite the tremendous amount of energy a tsunami carries, people on a ship at sea may not even realize a tsunami is passing. How is this possible? A tsunami in deep water may have a wavelength of 200 kilometers or more, but have a wave height of less than a meter. But when the tsunami reaches shallow water near the coast, friction with the ocean floor causes the long wavelength to decrease suddenly. The wave height increases as the water "piles up." The tsunami becomes a towering wall of water. Some tsunamis have reached heights of 20 meters—taller than a five-story building!

Tsunamis are most common in the Pacific Ocean, often striking Alaska, Hawaii, and Japan. In 1998, tsunamis in Papua New Guinea killed more than 2,000 people. Nations are searching for ways to avoid such devastation. Some Japanese cities have built barriers designed to break up the waves. Scientists also monitor the ocean floor for warnings of earthquakes that may produce tsunamis.

Figure 8 At sea, a tsunami travels as a long, low wave. Near shore, the wave height increases suddenly. The wall of water smashes onto the land, tossing ships onto the shore and destroying buildings.
Interpreting Diagrams What is the source of a tsunami's energy?

Section 1 Review

1. Describe how ocean waves form.
2. How do wavelength and wave height change as a wave enters shallow water?
3. How does wave action cause changes in a coastline?
4. How do water particles move within a wave?
5. **Thinking Critically Relating Cause and Effect** Explain how building a groin affects the beach on each side of the groin.

Check Your Progress
You are ready to design your model ocean beach. Sketch your design. Be sure to consider what materials you will use for your shoreline and lighthouse. How will you make waves? When your design is finished, you are ready to gather your materials and construct your model. (*Hint:* Design your model, including the lighthouse, to scale.)

CHAPTER PROJECT 4

SECTION 2 Tides

DISCOVER

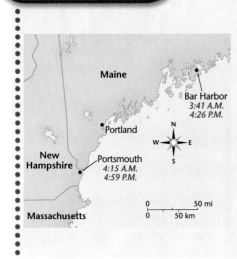

Maine

Bar Harbor
3:41 A.M.
4:26 P.M.

Portland

New Hampshire

Portsmouth
4:15 A.M.
4:59 P.M.

Massachusetts

```
0          50 mi
0      50 km
```

When Is High Tide?

Twice a day, the ocean rises and falls on the New England coast. These daily changes in water level are called tides. The map shows the times of the two high tides in each city on a particular day.

1. Calculate the length of time between the two high tides for each city. Remember to consider both hours and minutes.

2. Look at the times of the high tides in Bar Harbor and in Portsmouth. Is there a pattern in the times of the high tides?

Think It Over

Predicting Notice that the high tides for Portland are not shown. Based on the times of the other high tides on the map, predict when the high tides will occur in Portland.

GUIDE FOR READING

◆ What causes tides?

◆ How are tides a source of energy?

Reading Tip As you read, use the headings to make an outline about tides.

You're standing on a riverbank in the town of Saint John, Canada. In the distance there's a loud roaring sound, like a train approaching. Suddenly a wall of water twice your height thunders past. The surge of water rushes up the river channel so fast that it almost looks as if the river is flowing backward!

This thundering wall of water is an everyday event at Saint John. The town is located where the Saint John River enters the Bay of Fundy, an arm of the Atlantic Ocean. The Bay of Fundy is famous for its dramatic daily tides. When the tide comes in, fishing boats float on the water near the piers. But once the tide goes out, so much water flows back to sea that the boats are stranded on the muddy harbor bottom.

Figure 9 The Bay of Fundy in Canada is noted for its great differences in water level at high and low tide. **A.** Near the mouth of the bay, boats float in the Saint John River at high tide. **B.** At low tide, the boats are grounded.

What Causes Tides?

The daily rise and fall of Earth's waters on its coastlines are called **tides.** As the tide comes in, the level of the water on the beach rises gradually. When the water reaches its highest point, it is high tide. Then the tide goes out, flowing back toward the sea. When the water reaches its lowest point, it is low tide. Unlike the surface waves you read about in Section 1, tides happen regularly no matter how the wind blows. Tides occur in all bodies of water, but they are most noticeable in the ocean and large lakes.

Tides are caused by the interaction of Earth, the moon, and the sun. How can distant objects like the moon and sun influence water on Earth? The answer is gravity. Gravity is the force exerted by an object that pulls other objects toward it. Gravity keeps you and everything around you on Earth's surface. As the distance between objects increases, however, gravity's pull grows weaker.

Figure 10 shows the effect of the moon's gravity on the water on Earth's surface. The moon pulls on the water on the side closest to it (point A) more strongly than it pulls on the center of the Earth. This pull creates a bulge of water, called a tidal bulge, on the side of Earth facing the moon. The water at point C is pulled toward the moon less strongly than is Earth as a whole. This water is "left behind," forming a second bulge.

In the places in Figure 10 where there are tidal bulges (points A and C), high tide is occurring along the coastlines. In the places between the bulges (points B and D), low tide is occurring. As Earth rotates, different places on the planet's surface pass through the areas of the tidal bulges and experience the change in water levels.

☑ *Checkpoint* *What force causes the tides to occur on Earth's surface?*

Figure 10 The moon's pull on Earth's water causes tidal bulges to form on the side closest to the moon and the side farthest from the moon. *Comparing and Contrasting Where is the level of the water higher, at point C or point D?*

Graphing

ACTIVITY

This table lists the highest high tides and lowest low tides at the mouth of the Savannah River at the Atlantic Ocean in Georgia for one week. Use the data to make a graph.

Day	Highest High Tide (m)	Lowest Low Tide (m)
1	1.9	0.2
2	2.1	0.1
3	2.3	0.0
4	2.4	−0.2
5	2.5	−0.2
6	2.6	−0.3
7	1.9	0.3

1. On the horizontal axis, mark the days.

2. On the vertical axis, mark tide heights ranging from 3.0 to −1.0 meters. (*Hint:* Mark the negative numbers below the horizontal axis.)

3. Plot the tide heights for each day on the graph. Connect the high tide points with one line and the low tide points with another line.

How do the high and low tides change during the week? What type of tide might be occurring on Day 6? Explain.

The Daily Tide Cycle

As Earth turns completely around once each day, people on or near the shore observe the rise and fall of the tides as they reach the area of each tidal bulge. The high tides occur about 12 hours and 25 minutes apart in each location. As Earth rotates, eastern-most points pass through the area of the tidal bulge before points farther to the west. Therefore, high tide occurs later the farther west you go along a coastline.

In some places, the two high tides and two low tides are easy to observe each day. But in other places, the range between the water levels is less dramatic. One set of tides may even be so minimal that there appears to be only one high tide and one low tide per day. This situation is common along the coasts of Texas and western Florida, due to the gradual slope of the ocean floor in the Gulf of Mexico.

Several factors affect the height of the tide in any particular location. For example, high tide on a certain day in southern California is not necessarily the same height as high tide farther up the Pacific coast in Oregon. Landforms such as capes, peninsulas, and islands interrupt the water's movements. A basin at the mouth of a river can also increase the range of tides. As you read in Chapter 2, the speed and depth of moving water increases when it flows into a narrower channel. That is what causes the dramatic tides in the mouth of the Saint John River you read about earlier.

☑ *Checkpoint* *Describe one factor that affects the height of the tides in a particular area.*

The Monthly Tide Cycle

Even though the sun is 150 million kilometers from Earth, it is so massive that its gravity also affects the tides. The sun pulls the water on Earth's surface toward it. In Figure 11 on the facing page, you can follow the positions of the Earth, moon, and sun at different times during a month. Notice that sometimes the moon and sun pull together on Earth's waters. At other times, they pull in different directions. Changes in the positions of Earth, the moon, and the sun affect the height of the tides during a month.

Spring Tides Twice a month, at the new moon and the full moon, the sun and moon are lined up. Their combined gravitational pull produces the greatest range between high and low tide, called a **spring tide.** These tides get their name not because they occur during the season spring, but from an Old English word, *springen,* which means "to jump."

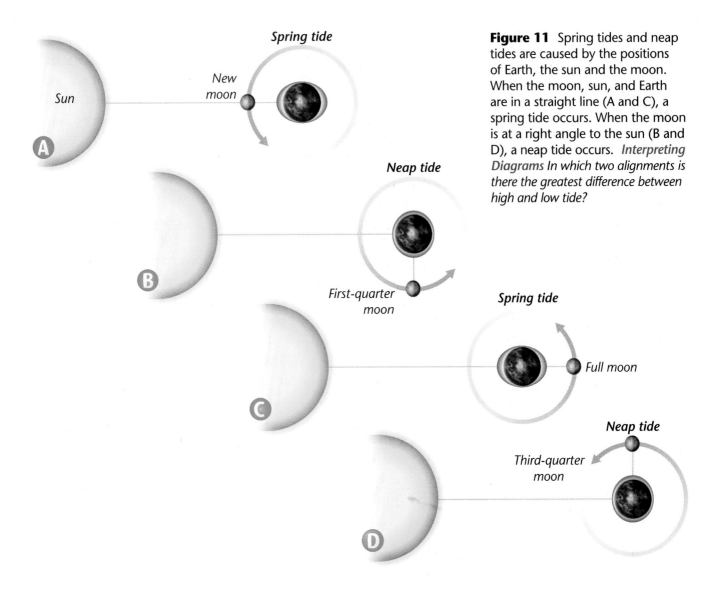

Figure 11 Spring tides and neap tides are caused by the positions of Earth, the sun and the moon. When the moon, sun, and Earth are in a straight line (A and C), a spring tide occurs. When the moon is at a right angle to the sun (B and D), a neap tide occurs. *Interpreting Diagrams In which two alignments is there the greatest difference between high and low tide?*

In the diagram:
- **A**: Sun, New moon, Spring tide
- **B**: First-quarter moon, Neap tide
- **C**: Full moon, Spring tide
- **D**: Third-quarter moon, Neap tide

Neap Tides In between spring tides, at the first and third quarters of the moon, the sun and moon pull at right angles to each other. This line-up produces a **neap tide**, a tide with the least difference between low and high tide. During a neap tide, the sun's gravity pulls some of the water away from the tidal bulge facing the moon. This acts to "even out" the water level over Earth's surface, reducing the difference between high and low tides.

Monthly Tide Tables Despite the complex factors affecting the tides, scientists can predict tides quite accurately for various locations. They combine knowledge of the movements of the moon and Earth with information about the shape of the coastline and other local conditions. If you live near the coast, your local newspaper probably publishes a tide table. Knowing the times and heights of tides is important to sailors, marine scientists, people who fish, and others who live along a coast.

Figure 12 Pulled by the tide, water rushes through this tidal power plant in France. *Making Generalizations Why are very few locations suitable for building tidal power plants?*

Energy From Tides

INTEGRATING TECHNOLOGY The movement of huge amounts of water between high and low tide are a source of potential energy—energy that is stored and waiting to be used. Engineers have designed tidal power plants that capture some of this energy as the tide moves in and out.

The first large-scale tidal power plant was built in 1967 on the Rance River in northwestern France. As high tide swirls up the river, the plant's gates open so that the water flows into a basin. As the tide retreats, the gates shut to trap the water. Gravity pulls the water back to sea through tunnels. The energy of the water moving through the tunnels powers generators that produce electricity, just as in a hydroelectric dam on a river.

Although tidal energy is a clean, renewable source of energy, it has several limitations. Harnessing tidal power is practical only where there is a large difference between high and low tides—at least 4 or 5 meters. There are very few places in the world where such a large difference occurs. Daily tides also may not occur at the time when there is a demand for electricity. However, tidal power can be a useful part of an overall plan to generate electricity that also includes other power sources between tides.

Section 2 Review

1. Explain how the moon causes a tidal bulge to form on the side of Earth closest to it.
2. How can tides be used to generate electricity?
3. Describe the positions of the sun and the moon in relation to Earth when spring tides occur.
4. **Thinking Critically Applying Concepts** Imagine that you are the captain of a fishing boat. Why would it be helpful to know the times of the tides?

Check Your Progress **CHAPTER PROJECT 4**

Now that you have built your model, plan an experiment to observe the effects of wave erosion on the shoreline. How will you measure the amount of wave action needed to topple the lighthouse? Once you have observed how waves cause shoreline erosion, repair the beach and design a way to reduce the erosion. Test your method by sending more waves against the shore. (*Hint:* For both tests, place toothpicks at regular intervals on the beach to measure erosion.)

SECTION
3 Ocean Water Chemistry

DISCOVER •• ACTIVITY

Will the Eggs Sink or Float?

1. Fill two beakers or jars with tap water.
2. Add three teaspoons of salt to one beaker. Stir until it dissolves.
3. Place a whole, uncooked egg in each jar. Handle the eggs gently to avoid breakage. Observe what happens to each egg.
4. Wash your hands when you are finished with this activity.

Think It Over

Observing Compare what happens to the two eggs. What does this tell you about the difference between salt water and fresh water?

If you've ever been swimming in the ocean and swallowed some water, you know that it is salty. Why? According to an old Swedish legend, it's all because of a magic mill. This mill could grind out anything its owner wanted, such as herring, porridge, or even gold. A greedy sea captain once stole the mill and took it away on his ship, but without finding out how to use it. He asked the mill to grind some salt but then could not stop it. The mill ground more and more salt, until the captain's ship sank from its weight. According to the tale, the mill is still at the bottom of the sea, grinding out salt!

Probably no one ever took this tale seriously, even when it was first told. The scientific explanation for the ocean's saltiness begins with the early stages of Earth's history, when the ocean covered much of the surface of the planet. Undersea volcanoes erupted, spewing chemicals into the water. Gradually, the lava from these volcanic eruptions built up areas of land. Rain fell on the bare land, washing more chemicals from the rocks into the ocean. Over time, these dissolved substances built up to the levels present in the ocean today.

GUIDE FOR READING

◆ How salty is ocean water?

◆ How do conditions in the ocean change with depth?

Reading Tip Before you read, preview the headings in the section. Then predict some characteristics of ocean water.

The Salty Ocean

Just how salty is the ocean? If you boiled a kilogram of seawater in a pot until the water was all gone, there would be about 35 grams of salts left in the bottom of the pot. **On average, one kilogram of ocean water contains about 35 grams of salts—that is, 35 parts per thousand.** The total amount of dissolved salts in water is called **salinity**.

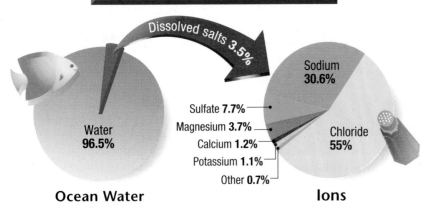

Composition of Ocean Water

Dissolved salts 3.5%

Ocean Water
Water 96.5%

Ions
Sodium 30.6%
Chloride 55%
Sulfate 7.7%
Magnesium 3.7%
Calcium 1.2%
Potassium 1.1%
Other 0.7%

Figure 13 Ocean water contains many different dissolved salts. When salts dissolve, they separate into particles called ions. *Interpreting Graphs Which ion is most common in ocean water?*

The substance you know as table salt—sodium chloride—is the salt present in the greatest amount in ocean water. When sodium chloride dissolves in water, it separates into sodium and chloride particles called ions. Other salts, such as magnesium chloride, form ions in water in the same way. Together, chloride and sodium make up almost 86 percent of the ions dissolved in ocean water, as shown in Figure 13. Ocean water also contains smaller amounts of about a dozen other ions, including magnesium and calcium, and other substances that organisms need, such as nitrogen and phosphorus.

Variations in Salinity In most parts of the ocean, the salinity is between 34 and 37 parts per thousand. But near the surface, rain, snow, and melting ice add fresh water to the ocean, lowering the salinity there. Salinity is also lower near the mouths of large rivers such as the Amazon or Mississippi. These rivers empty great amounts of fresh water into the ocean. Evaporation, on the other hand, increases salinity, since the salt is left behind as the water evaporates. For example, in the Red Sea, where the climate is hot and dry, the salinity can be as high as 41 parts per thousand. Salinity can also be higher near the poles. As the surface water freezes into ice, the salt is left behind in the remaining water.

Figure 14 These people are relaxing with the paper while floating in the water! The Dead Sea in Israel is so salty that people float easily on its surface. *Relating Cause and Effect How is Israel's hot, dry climate related to the Dead Sea's high salinity?*

Effects of Salinity Salinity affects several properties of ocean water. For instance, ocean water does not freeze until the temperature drops to about −1.9°C. The salt acts as a kind of antifreeze by interfering with the formation of ice crystals. Salt water also has a higher density than fresh water. That means that the mass of one liter of salt water is greater than the mass of one liter of fresh water. Because its density is greater, seawater has greater buoyancy. It lifts, or buoys up, less dense objects floating in it. This is why an egg floats higher in salt water than in fresh water.

INTEGRATING CHEMISTRY

Gases in Ocean Water

Just as land organisms use oxygen and other gases in the air, marine organisms use gases dissolved in ocean water. Two gases found in ocean water that are necessary for living things are oxygen and carbon dioxide.

Oxygen in seawater comes from the atmosphere and from algae in the ocean. Algae use sunlight to carry out photosynthesis, releasing oxygen into the water in the process. Oxygen is scarcer in seawater than in air and is most plentiful near the surface. Carbon dioxide, on the other hand, is about 60 times as plentiful in the oceans as in the atmosphere. Algae need carbon dioxide for photosynthesis. Animals such as corals also use carbon dioxide, which provides the carbon to build their hard skeletons.

☑ *Checkpoint* *What are two sources of the oxygen in ocean water?*

The Temperature of Ocean Water

In New England, the news reports on New Year's Day often feature the shivering members of a "Polar Bear Club" taking a dip in the icy Atlantic Ocean. Yet on the same day, people enjoy the warm waters of a Puerto Rico beach. Like temperatures on land, temperatures at the surface of the ocean vary with location and the seasons.

The broad surface of the ocean absorbs energy from the sun. Because warm water is less dense than cold water, this warm water stays as a layer on the surface. Near the equator, surface temperatures often reach 25°C, about room temperature. The temperature drops as you travel away from the equator.

The temperature of water affects the amount of dissolved oxygen it can hold. The cold waters in the polar regions contain more dissolved oxygen than warm, tropical waters. But there is still enough oxygen in tropical seas to support a variety of organisms, such as those shown in Figure 15.

Math TOOLBOX

Calculating Density

To calculate the density of a substance, divide the mass of the substance by its volume.

$$\text{density} = \frac{\text{mass}}{\text{volume}}$$

For example, one liter (L) of ocean water has a mass of 1.03 kilograms (kg). Therefore, its density is

$$\frac{1.03 \text{ kg}}{1.00 \text{ L}} = 1.03 \text{ kg/L}$$

Five liters of one type of crude oil has a mass of 4.10 kg. What is its density?

$$\frac{4.10 \text{ kg}}{5.00 \text{ L}} = 0.82 \text{ kg/L}$$

If this oil spilled on the ocean's surface, would it sink or float? Explain your answer in terms of density.

Figure 15 Both this neon-pink basslet and the lacy green sponge depend on the dissolved gases in ocean water.

EXPLORING the Water Column

Conditions change as you descend from the surface to the ocean floor.

▼ A scuba diver can descend to about 40 meters.

DEPTH

Surface Zone
Extends from surface to about 200 meters. Average temperature worldwide is 17.5°C.

0.5 km

The submersible *Alvin* can descend to about 4 kilometers. ▼

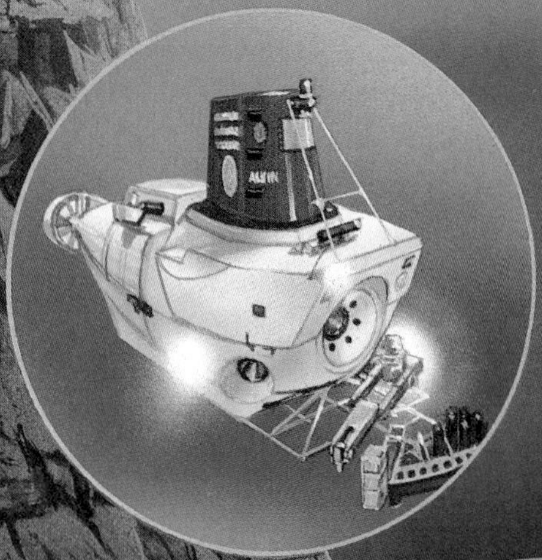

Transition Zone
Extends from bottom of surface zone to about 1 kilometer. Temperature rapidly drops to 4°C.

1.0 km

Deep Zone
Extends from about 1 kilometer to ocean floor. Average temperature is 3.5°C.

1.5 km

Color and Light
Sunlight penetrates the surface of the ocean. It appears first yellowish, then blue-green, as the water absorbs the red light. No light reaches below about 200 meters.

Temperature
Near the surface, temperature is affected by the weather above. In the transition zone, the temperature drops rapidly. In the deep zone, the water is always extremely cold.

2.0 km

P R E S S U R E   I N C R E A S E S

Salinity
Rainfall decreases salinity near the surface, while evaporation increases salinity in warm, dry areas. Below the surface zone, salinity remains fairly constant throughout the water column.

2.5 km

▼ In 1960, the submersible *Trieste* dived to a record depth of 11 kilometers.

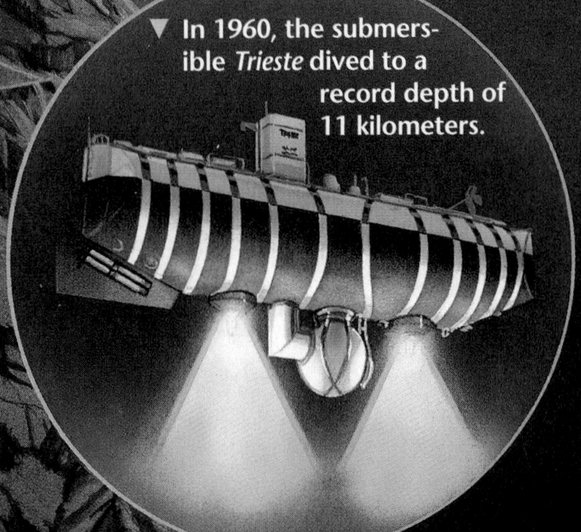

Density
The density of seawater depends on temperature and salinity. The ocean is generally least dense in the surface zone, where it is warmest. However, higher salinity also increases density. The most dense water is found in the cold deep zone.

3.0 km

3.5 km

Pressure
Pressure increases at the rate of 10 times the air pressure at sea level per 100 meters of depth.

3.8 km
Average ocean depth

4.0 km

Changes with Depth

Gazing down into the blue-green water from the deck of a ship, you might think that the vast volume of water beneath you is all the same. But in fact, conditions change dramatically from the surface to the depths. If you could descend from the surface to the ocean floor, you would pass through a vertical section of the ocean referred to as the water column. *Exploring the Water Column* shows some of the changes you would observe.

Temperature Decreases If you took temperature readings at different depths, you would observe a pattern. **Temperature decreases as you descend through the water column.** There are three temperature zones in the water column. The first zone, the surface zone, typically extends from the surface to between 100 and 500 meters. Next is the transition zone, which extends from the bottom of the surface zone to about one kilometer. The temperature drops very quickly in the transition zone, to about 4°C. Below the transition zone is the deep zone. The temperature in the deep zone is a constant 3.5°C or colder in most of the ocean.

Pressure Increases Pressure is the force exerted by the weight of water above pressing down. **Pressure increases continuously from the surface to the deepest part of the ocean.** The average depth of the ocean floor is 3.8 kilometers. There the pressure is about 400 times greater than air pressure at Earth's surface.

 INTEGRATING TECHNOLOGY Pressure is one obstacle facing scientists who want to study the ocean. A diver can descend safely only to about 40 meters. To survive in deeper water, scientists must use a submersible. A **submersible** is an underwater vehicle built of strong materials to resist pressure. In a submersible, scientists can directly observe the ocean floor, collect samples, and study deep ocean water chemistry.

Section 3 Review

1. What is the salinity of ocean water?
2. How do temperature and pressure change as you descend from the surface to the ocean floor?
3. Describe one factor that increases the salinity of seawater and one factor that decreases salinity.
4. **Thinking Critically Inferring** Would you expect the seawater just below the floating ice in the Arctic Ocean to be higher or lower in salinity than the water in the deep zone there? Explain.

Science at Home

Use a ball-point pen to poke two holes in a milk carton—one about one third of the way from the bottom and one two thirds of the way from the bottom. Cover the holes with tape and fill the carton with water. Holding the carton a meter above a sink, remove the tape and observe the streams of water. Explain that increased pressure causes the water to flow out of the bottom hole more quickly. How does this model conditions in the ocean?

Investigating Changes in Density

In this lab, you will practice the skill of controlling variables as you learn more about density.

Problem

How do various factors affect the density of ocean water?

Materials

thumbtacks	beaker, 250 mL	water
thermometer	ice	hot plate
table salt	balance	spoon
metric ruler	sharpened pencil	

unsharpened pencil with eraser
graduated cylinders, 100 mL and 250 mL

Procedure

1. Work with your group to brainstorm a list of variables that affect the density of ocean water. Some variables to consider are water temperature and salinity. As a group, choose one variable to test in this investigation.
2. One way to measure density is with a tool called a *hydrometer.* To make a hydrometer, follow the instructions on the facing page.
3. Design an experimental plan to determine how the variable you chose affects density. For example, if you have chosen temperature as your variable, you might choose to start with salt water at 0°C, then heat it to 10°C, 20°C, and 30°C. If salinity is your variable, you might start with 100 mL of tap (fresh) water and add 10 g of salt, then add another 10 g to make 20 g, then add 10 g more to make 30 g. Write out your experimental plan.

DATA TABLE

Manipulated Variable: _____

Condition Tested	Hydrometer Reading

4. List all the variables you will need to keep constant during your experiment. Revise your experimental plan and add steps to ensure that all other variables remain constant.
5. Review your plan. Make sure it includes the materials you will use and their amounts. Also make sure you have addressed all safety issues. Then check the plan with your teacher.
6. Copy the data table into your notebook.
7. Perform your experiment using the pencil hydrometer.

Analyze and Conclude

1. In your experimental plan, which variable was the manipulated variable, and which was the responding variable? Explain. (Refer to the Skills Handbook if you need more information about these types of variables.)
2. Make a graph of the data you collected in the experiment. Graph the manipulated variable on the horizontal axis. Graph the responding variable on the vertical axis.
3. How do changes in the hydrometer reading relate to density?

Making a Hydrometer

A. Begin with an unsharpened pencil. Starting 1 cm from the unsharpened end, use a second, sharpened pencil to make marks every 0.5 cm along the side of the pencil. Continue making marks until you reach the 4-cm mark.

B. Label each mark, starting at the unsharpened end of the pencil with the label 0.5.

C. Insert 3 thumbtacks as weights into the eraser end of the pencil. **CAUTION:** *Be careful not to cut yourself on the sharp points of the thumbtacks.*

D. Fill the 250-mL graduated cylinder with water at room temperature. Place the pencil in the water, eraser down.

E. Add or remove thumbtacks and adjust their placement in the eraser until the pencil floats upright, with about 2 cm sticking up above the surface of the water.

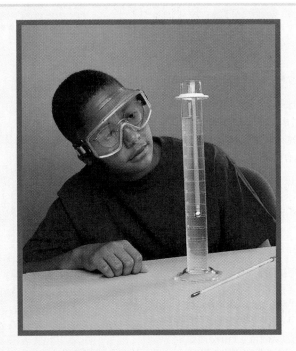

F. In your notebook, record the number next to the mark that is closest to the point where the pencil hydrometer projects from the water. As the density of the water increases, the hydrometer will float above the point you have just marked. If the water becomes less dense, the hydrometer will float below that point.

4. Use the graph to describe the relationship between the manipulated variable you tested and density.

5. Where in Earth's oceans would you find conditions like the ones that you tested?

6. **Think About It** Why is it important to make sure that all conditions other than the manipulated variable are kept constant in an experiment? How well were you able to keep the other variables constant?

More To Explore

In this experiment you observed how manipulating a particular variable affects the density of ocean water. Now conduct a second experiment, this time manipulating a different variable. As you design this experiment, make sure to control all variables except the one you are testing. Be sure to check your experimental plan with your teacher before you begin.

SECTION 4 Currents and Climate

People strolling along a Washington beach one May day in 1990 could hardly believe their eyes. Hundreds of sneakers, in all colors and sizes, were washing ashore from the Pacific Ocean. Puzzled, people gathered up the soggy shoes and took them home, wondering where the sneakers had come from. Eventually, the sneaker spill was traced to a cargo ship from South Korea. Containers had washed overboard in a storm and broken open, spilling thousands of shoes into the water.

The sneakers were a ready-made experiment for oceanographers, scientists who study the oceans. From the shoes' drifting, oceanographers could infer both the path and the speed of water movements in the Pacific. Using what they already knew about these movements, scientists made a computer model predicting when and where more sneakers would come ashore. Right on schedule, sneakers washed up in Oregon and British Columbia, Canada. The model also predicted that the shoes would turn back westward across the Pacific. Again it was correct, as some sneakers arrived in Hawaii. The shoes that did not sink could have traveled all the way back to South Korea!

Earlier in this chapter you learned how the oceans move as a result of wave action and tides. A third type of water movement is currents. A **current** is a large stream of moving water that flows through the oceans. Unlike waves, which do not actually transport water from one place to another, currents carry water great distances. Some currents move water at the surface of the ocean, while other currents move the deep water.

Surface Currents

Figure 16 shows the major surface currents in Earth's oceans. **Surface currents, which affect water to a depth of several hundred meters, are driven mainly by winds.** Following the major wind patterns of the globe, surface currents move in circular patterns in the five major ocean basins. Trace these currents on the map. Notice that most of the currents flow east or west, then double back to complete the circle.

Why do the currents move in these circular patterns? If Earth were standing still, winds and currents would flow in straight lines between the poles and the equator. But as Earth rotates, the paths of the winds and currents curve in relation to Earth's surface. This effect of Earth's rotation on the direction of winds and currents is called the **Coriolis effect** (kawr ee OH lis effect). In the Northern Hemisphere, the Coriolis effect causes the currents to curve to the right. In the Southern Hemisphere, the Coriolis effect causes the currents to curve to the left. You can see the impact of the Coriolis effect by comparing the directions of the currents in the two hemispheres on Figure 16.

Figure 16 Large surface currents generally move in circular patterns in Earth's oceans. *Interpreting Maps Name four currents that flow along the coasts of North America. State whether each current is warm or cold.*

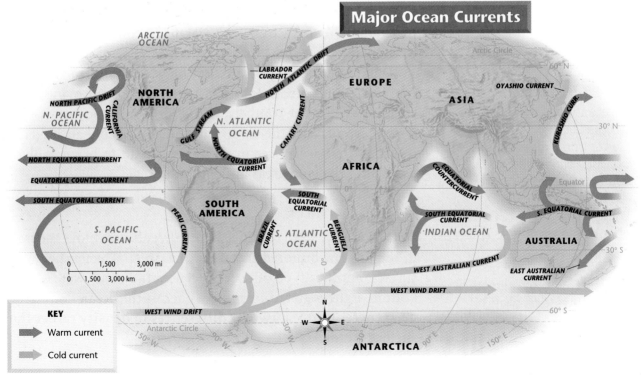

Major Ocean Currents

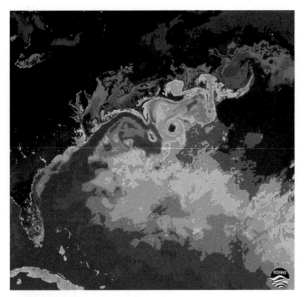

Figure 17 This satellite image of the Atlantic Ocean has been enhanced with colors that show water temperature. Red and orange indicate warmer water, while green and blue indicate colder water. The warm Gulf Stream flows around Florida as you can see in the lower left corner of the image.

The largest and most powerful surface current in the North Atlantic Ocean, the Gulf Stream, is caused by strong winds from the west. The Gulf Stream resembles a fast-moving, deep-blue river within the ocean. It is more than 30 kilometers wide and 300 meters deep, and it carries a volume of water 100 times greater than the Mississippi River. The Gulf Stream carries warm water from the Gulf of Mexico to the Caribbean Sea, then northward along the coast of the United States. Near Cape Hatteras, North Carolina, it curves eastward across the Atlantic, as a result of the Coriolis effect.

☑ *Checkpoint* **Why doesn't the Gulf Stream travel in a straight line?**

How Surface Currents Affect Climate

The Gulf Stream and North Atlantic Drift are very important to people in the city of Trondheim, Norway. Trondheim is located along Norway's western coast. Although it is very close to the Arctic Circle, winter there is fairly mild. Snow melts soon after it falls. And fortunately for the fishing boats, the local harbors are free of ice most of the winter. The two warm currents bring this area of Norway its mild climate. **Climate** is the pattern of temperature and precipitation typical of an area over a long period of time.

Currents affect climate by moving cold and warm water around the globe. In general, currents carry warm water from the tropics toward the poles and bring cold water back toward the equator. **A surface current warms or cools the air above it, influencing the climate of the land near the coast.**

Winds pick up moisture as they blow across warm-water currents. For example, the warm Kuroshio Current brings mild, rainy weather to the southern islands of Japan. In contrast, cold-water currents cool the air above them. Since cold air holds less moisture than warm air, these currents tend to bring cool, dry weather to the land areas in their path.

Deep Currents

So far you have been reading about currents that move the water in the top few hundred meters of the ocean. Deeper below the surface, another type of current causes the chilly waters at the bottom of the ocean to creep slowly across the ocean floor. **These deep currents are caused by differences in density rather than surface winds.**

Drawing Conclusions

Locate the Benguela **ACTIVITY** Current on Figure 16 on the previous page. Near the southern tip of Africa, the winds blow from west to east. Using what you have learned about surface currents and climate, what can you conclude about the impact of this current on the climate of the southwestern coast of Africa?

As you read in Section 3, the density of water depends on its temperature and its salinity. When a warm-water surface current moves from the equator toward the poles, its water gradually cools off. As ice forms near the poles, the salinity of the water increases from the salt left behind during freezing. As its temperature decreases and salinity increases, the water becomes denser and sinks. Then, the cold water flows back along the ocean floor as a deep current. Deep currents follow the hills and valleys of the ocean floor. Deep ocean currents are also affected by the Coriolis effect, which causes them to curve.

Deep ocean currents move and mix water around the world. They carry cold water from the poles back toward the equator. Deep ocean currents flow much more slowly than surface currents. They may take as long as 1,000 years to make the round trip from the pole to the equator and back again!

Upwelling

In most parts of the ocean, the surface waters do not usually mix with the deep ocean waters. However, some mixing does occur in the polar regions when the surface waters cool, sink, and form deep currents. Mixing also occurs when winds cause upwelling. **Upwelling** is the upward movement of cold water from the ocean depths. As winds blow away the warm surface water, cold water rises to replace it, as shown in Figure 18.

Upwelling brings up tiny ocean organisms, minerals, and other nutrients from the deeper layers of the water. Without this

Figure 18 As cold water rises from the deep ocean, it brings a new supply of nutrients to the surface. The nutrients feed enormous schools of fish such as these anchovies. *Relating Cause and Effect What causes cold water to rise during upwelling?*

Wind

Warm surface water

Upwelling

motion, the surface waters of the open ocean would be very scarce in nutrients. Because of the increased supply of nutrients, zones of upwelling are usually home to enormous schools of fish.

One major area of upwelling lies in the Pacific Ocean off the west coast of South America. Here, upwelling occurs when strong winds from the Andes Mountains sweep across the ocean. Huge schools of silvery anchovies thrive on the nutrients that are brought to the surface. This rich fishing area is important to millions of people who depend on it for food and jobs.

How Things Work

Modeling Ocean Currents

Why is the climate in Dublin, Ireland, so different from the climate in St. John's in Newfoundland, Canada? Since both cities are located at the same latitude, you might expect similar climate conditions in the two locations. But when it's 8°C in Dublin in January, it's usually below 0°C in St. John's. This investigation will help you understand why.

Problem

How can you model the movement of ocean water due to surface currents?

Skills Focus

making models, observing, inferring

Materials

rectangular baking tray chalk
modeling clay, 3 sticks ruler
permanent marker hole puncher
newspaper
construction paper, blue and red
jointed drinking straws, one per student
light-reflecting rheoscopic fluid, 400 mL (or water and food coloring)

Procedure

1. Cover your work area with newspaper. Place the baking tray on top of the newspaper.
2. Using the map on the facing page as a guide, draw a chalk outline of the eastern coast of North and South America on the left side of the tray. Draw the outline of the west coast of Europe and Africa on the right side of the tray.
3. Use modeling clay to create the continents, roughly following the chalk outlines you have drawn. Build the continents to a depth of about 3 cm. Press the clay tightly to the pan to form a watertight seal.
4. Fill the ocean area of your model with rheoscopic fluid (or water and food coloring) to a depth of 1 cm.
5. Place 10 blue paper punches in the ocean area marked with a blue X on the map. Place 10 red paper punches in the area marked with a red X.
6. Select a drinking straw and bend it at the joint. Write your initials on the short end of the straw with the marker.

El Niño

Changes in winds and currents can greatly impact the oceans and the neighboring land. One example is **El Niño,** an abnormal climate event that occurs every 2 to 7 years in the Pacific Ocean. El Niño begins when an unusual pattern of winds forms over the western Pacific. This causes a vast sheet of warm water to move eastward toward the South American coast. El Niño conditions can last for one to two years before the usual winds and currents return.

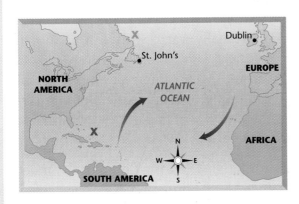

7. With a partner, simulate the pattern of winds that blow in this region of the world. One partner should position his or her straw across the westernmost bulge of Africa and blow toward the west (see arrow on map). The other partner should position his or her straw across the northern end of South America and blow toward the northeast (see arrow on map). Make sure that the straws are bent and that the short ends are parallel to the ocean surface. Both partners should begin blowing gently through the straws at the same time. Try to blow as continuously as possible for one to two minutes.

8. Observe the motion of the fluid and paper punches over the surface of the ocean. Notice what happens when the fluid and punches flow around landmasses.

Analyze and Conclude

1. Draw a map that shows the pattern of ocean currents that was produced in your model. Use red arrows to show the flow of warm water moving north from the equator. Use blue arrows to show the flow of cold water southward from the polar regions.

2. Use Figure 16 to add names to the currents you drew on your map. Which currents are warm-water currents? Which are cold-water currents?

3. Use your model to describe the relationship between winds and surface currents in the ocean.

4. Use your knowledge of ocean currents to explain why the climate in St. John's is different than the climate in Dublin.

5. **Apply** Suppose you wanted to sail to Europe from the east coast of the United States. What two natural factors could help speed up your trip? Explain your answer.

More to Explore

Use your model to simulate an upwelling off the coast of Africa. What conditions cause upwellings to occur? What are the results?

Figure 19 Heavy rains caused by El Niño washed out this road in La Honda, California, forcing homes to be evacuated. El Niño can result in severe weather all around the world.

El Niño's Impact El Niño can have disastrous consequences. For example, the arrival of El Niño's warm surface water prevents upwelling off the western coast of South America. Without the nutrients brought by upwelling, fish die or go elsewhere to find food, ruining the fishing catch that season. Seabirds, with no fish to eat, also must leave the area or starve.

El Niño has serious effects on land, too. It causes shifts in weather patterns around the world, bringing unusual and often severe conditions to different areas. For example, El Niño of 1997 and 1998 caused an unusually warm winter in the northeastern United States. However, it was also responsible for heavy rains, flooding, and mudslides in California, as well as a string of deadly tornadoes in Florida.

Forecasting El Niño Although scientists do not fully understand the conditions that create El Niño, they have been able to predict its occurrence using computer models of world climate. Knowing when El Niño will occur can reduce its impact. Scientists and public officials can plan emergency procedures and make changes to protect people and wildlife.

Section 4 Review

1. Describe how surface currents form and travel in the ocean.
2. How is heat transferred from Earth's oceans to land areas?
3. Explain how deep currents form and move in the ocean.
4. **Thinking Critically Comparing and Contrasting** Describe the similarities and differences in the movement of surface currents in the Northern Hemisphere and Southern Hemisphere.

Check Your Progress

CHAPTER PROJECT 4

This is the time to make final changes to your method of shoreline protection to further decrease erosion. Test your improved method. How much additional wave action does the lighthouse withstand? (*Hint:* Try using a combination of methods to protect the shoreline and lighthouse.)

SECTION 1 Wave Action

Key Ideas

◆ Most waves are caused by winds blowing across the surface of the water.

◆ When waves enter shallow water, the wavelength shortens and wave height increases. The wave becomes unstable and breaks on the shore.

◆ Waves erode shorelines, carving cliffs and breaking up rocks into pebbles and sand.

◆ An earthquake on the ocean floor can cause a very powerful wave called a tsunami.

Key Terms

wave	crest	wavelength
frequency	trough	wave height
longshore drift	sandbar	rip current
groin	tsunami	

SECTION 2 Tides

INTEGRATING SPACE SCIENCE

Key Ideas

◆ Tides are caused by the interaction of Earth, the moon, and the sun.

◆ There are two high tides and two low tides each day in most places.

◆ The height of tides during a month varies with changes in the positions of Earth, the moon, and the sun.

Key Terms

tide	spring tide	neap tide

SECTION 3 Ocean Water Chemistry

Key Ideas

◆ Chloride and sodium are the most abundant ions in ocean water.

◆ Salinity varies throughout the ocean, depending on the amount of evaporation or freezing, as well as the addition of fresh water from rivers or precipitation.

◆ Below the ocean surface, the water is divided into layers by temperature, with uniformly cold temperatures in deep water.

◆ Pressure increases greatly with increasing depth in the ocean.

Key Terms

salinity	submersible

SECTION 4 Currents and Climate

Key Ideas

◆ Currents are formed by Earth's rotation, winds, and differences in water temperature.

◆ The movement of warm-water and cold-water surface currents carries water around the world and influences coastal climates.

◆ Density differences between warm and cold water cause many deep-water currents in the ocean.

◆ El Niño changes the pattern of winds and currents and affects Earth's weather.

Key Terms

current	Coriolis effect	climate
upwelling	El Niño	

USING THE INTERNET *ACTIVITY*

www.science-explorer.phschool.com

Reviewing Content

 For more review of key concepts, see the Interactive Student Tutorial CD-ROM.

Multiple Choice

Choose the letter of the best answer.

1. Rolling waves with a large distance between crests have a long
   a. wave height.
   b. wavelength.
   c. frequency.
   d. trough.

2. Groins are built to reduce the effect of
   a. tsunamis.
   b. longshore drift.
   c. rip currents.
   d. deep currents.

3. At the full moon, the combined gravitational pulls of the sun and moon produce the biggest difference between low and high tide, called a
   a. surface current.
   b. neap tide.
   c. spring tide.
   d. rip current.

4. Ocean water is more dense than fresh water at the same temperature because of
   a. pressure.
   b. the Coriolis effect.
   c. upwelling.
   d. salinity.

5. Winds and currents move in curved paths because of
   a. the Coriolis effect.
   b. longshore drift.
   c. wave height.
   d. tides.

True or False

If the statement is true, write true. If it is false, change the underlined word or words to make the statement true.

6. Sand is gradually carried down the beach by <u>upwelling</u>.

7. The most common ions dissolved in ocean water are sodium and <u>potassium</u>.

8. Two gases dissolved in ocean water that are important to living things are oxygen and <u>carbon dioxide</u>.

9. As you descend deeper into the ocean, the water gets colder and pressure <u>decreases</u>.

10. <u>Currents</u> carry cold and warm ocean water around the world.

Checking Concepts

11. Explain how a rip current forms.

12. Explain how a tsunami forms and moves. Why are tsunamis so destructive?

13. Why are there two high tides a day in most places?

14. How do warm-water currents affect climate?

15. Describe the causes and result of upwelling.

16. **Writing to Learn** Imagine a beach or seashore that you have visited or would like to visit. Using what you know about wave action, write a description of the shape of the beach, sand drift, cliffs, dunes, and other features.

Thinking Visually

17. **Flowchart** Copy the flowchart about the movement of a wave onto a sheet of paper. Complete the flowchart by putting the following five steps in the correct sequence: *wave travels as low swell; wind creates ripple on ocean surface; wave breaks on shore; wavelength decreases and wave height increases; wave touches bottom in shallow water.* Add a title. (For more on flowcharts, see the Skills Handbook.)

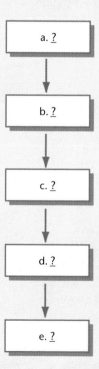

Applying Skills

The temperature readings in the table were obtained in the Atlantic Ocean near Bermuda. Use the data to answer Questions 18–20.

Depth (m)	Temp. (°C)	Depth (m)	Temp. (°C)
0	19	1,000	9
200	18	1,200	5
400	18	1,400	5
600	16	1,600	4
800	12	1,800	4

18. **Graphing** Construct a line graph using the data in the table. Plot depth readings on the horizontal axis and temperature readings on the vertical axis.

19. **Drawing Conclusions** Use your graph to identify the temperature range in the transition zone.

20. **Predicting** Predict how the ocean temperature at depths of 0 meters and at 1,400 meters would change with the seasons in this location. Explain your reasoning.

Thinking Critically

21. **Classifying** Classify these different movements of ocean water by whether each is caused by winds or not caused by winds: waves, tsunamis, tides, surface currents, deep currents, upwelling.

22. **Applying Concepts** Would you expect salinity to be high or low in a rainy ocean region near the mouth of a river? Why?

23. **Comparing and Contrasting** In what ways is the ocean at 1,000 meters deep different from the ocean at the surface in the same location?

24. **Relating Cause and Effect** How does the movement of ocean currents explain the fact that much of western Europe has a mild, wet climate?

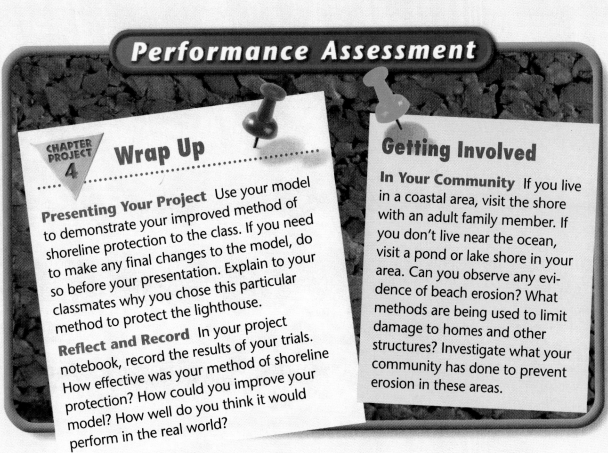

Performance Assessment

CHAPTER PROJECT 4 — Wrap Up

Presenting Your Project Use your model to demonstrate your improved method of shoreline protection to the class. If you need to make any final changes to the model, do so before your presentation. Explain to your classmates why you chose this particular method to protect the lighthouse.

Reflect and Record In your project notebook, record the results of your trials. How effective was your method of shoreline protection? How could you improve your model? How well do you think it would perform in the real world?

Getting Involved

In Your Community If you live in a coastal area, visit the shore with an adult family member. If you don't live near the ocean, visit a pond or lake shore in your area. Can you observe any evidence of beach erosion? What methods are being used to limit damage to homes and other structures? Investigate what your community has done to prevent erosion in these areas.

CHAPTER

5 Ocean Zones

WHAT'S AHEAD

 SECTION 1 **Exploring the Ocean**

Discover What Can You Learn Without Seeing?
Sharpen Your Skills Interpreting Data
Skills Lab The Shape of the Ocean Floor

Integrating Life Science
SECTION 2 **Life at the Ocean's Edge**

Discover Can Your Animal Hold On?

Integrating Life Science
SECTION 3 **The Neritic Zone and Open Ocean**

Discover How Deep Can You See?
Sharpen Your Skills Inferring

144 ◆ H

At Home in the Sea

A coral reef is a beautiful home for the organisms who dart, crawl, and hide within its lacy structure. But the reef is also a fragile place. Slight changes in water temperature and other conditions can threaten the delicate coral and the other organisms that inhabit the reef.

A coral reef is one of many different ocean habitats. From sandy tropical beaches to the cold depths of the ocean floor, organisms are able to thrive in all of them. In this chapter you will learn about the conditions in different parts of the ocean and the organisms that live there. Throughout the chapter you will work in a group to create your own model of one of the habitats.

Your Goal To build a three-dimensional model of a marine habitat and include some of the organisms that live there.

To complete the project successfully, you will need to
◆ include the significant physical features of the habitat
◆ create a life-size model of one organism that lives in the habitat
◆ write an explanation of how the organism is adapted to its habitat
◆ follow the safety guidelines in Appendix A

Get Started Begin now by previewing the visuals in the chapter to identify different ocean habitats. With your group, discuss which habitat you would like to learn more about. Begin a list of questions you have about the habitat. Also start to think about the materials you will need to build your model.

Check Your Progress You'll be working on this project as you study this chapter. To keep your project on track, look for Check Your Progress boxes at the following points.
Section 2 Review, page 161: Draw a scale diagram of your model.
Section 3 Review, page 168: Research your organism and build your model.

Wrap Up At the end of the chapter (page 179), you will display your model organism in its habitat.

The many residents of this New Guinea coral reef include golden fairy basslets, a red gorgonian sea fan, and a vibrant blue sea star.

SECTION 1 Exploring the Ocean

DISCOVER · ACTIVITY · · ·

What Can You Learn Without Seeing?

1. Your teacher will provide your group with ten plastic drinking straws and a covered box containing a mystery object. The top of the box has several holes punched in it. Using the straws as probes, try to determine the size, shape, and location of the object inside the box.

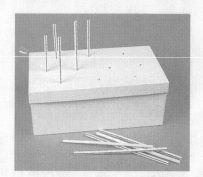

2. Based on the information you gathered, describe your object. What can you say about its length, shape, and position? Write down your hypothesis about the identity of the object.

3. Remove the box top to reveal the object.

Think It Over

Inferring Explain how you used the method of indirect observation in this activity to learn about the object.

GUIDE FOR READING

◆ What factors make ocean-floor research difficult?

◆ What processes have shaped the ocean floor?

Reading Tip As you read, make a list of features found on the ocean floor. Write one sentence about each feature.

Figure 1 This engraving shows HMS *Challenger* in the Indian Ocean in 1874, two years into its journey around the world.

Imagine going on a voyage around the world lasting three and a half years. Your assignment: to investigate "everything about the sea." Your vessel: a former warship, powered by sails and a steam engine. Its guns have been removed to make room for scientific gear. On board there are thermometers for measuring the temperature of ocean water and hundreds of kilometers of cable for lowering dredges to the bottom of the ocean. With the dredges, you scrape sand, muck, and rock from the ocean floor. You drag trawl nets behind the ship to collect ocean organisms.

The crew of a British ship, HMS *Challenger*, began such a voyage in 1872. By the end of the journey, the scientists had gathered enough data to fill 50 volumes and had collected more than 4,000 new organisms! It took 23 years to publish all the information they learned about oceanwater chemistry, currents, ocean life, and the shape of the ocean floor. The voyage of the *Challenger* was so successful that it became the model for many later ocean expeditions.

Voyages of Discovery

For thousands of years before the *Challenger* expedition, people explored the ocean. Knowledge of the ocean has always been important to the people living along its coasts. The ocean has provided food and served as a route for trade and travel to new settlements.

The Phoenicians, who lived along the Mediterranean Sea, were one of the earliest cultures to explore the oceans. By 1200 B.C., they had established sea routes for trade with the other nations around the Mediterranean. After the Phoenicians, people of many European, African, and Asian cultures sailed along the coasts to trade with distant lands.

In the Pacific Ocean around 2,000 years ago, the Polynesians left the safety of the coastline and boldly sailed into the open ocean. Their knowledge of winds and currents enabled the Polynesians to settle the scattered islands of Hawaii, Tahiti, and New Zealand.

As modern science developed and trade increased, ocean exploration changed. Nations needed accurate maps of the oceans and lands bordering them. Governments also wanted their countries to be known for new scientific discoveries. For example, in the late 1700s, the British government hired Captain James Cook to lead three voyages of exploration. Cook's crew included scientists who studied the stars and collected new species of plants and animals.

Within a century of Cook's voyages, almost all of Earth's coastlines had been mapped. Scientists then turned to the study of the ocean's waters and invented methods to explore its unknown depths. The *Challenger* expedition marked the beginning of the modern science of oceanography.

☑ *Checkpoint* *What are two reasons why people have explored the oceans?*

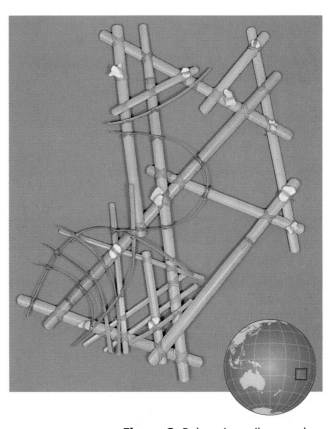

Figure 2 Polynesian sailors used stick charts to navigate the Pacific Ocean. The curved sticks represent currents and winds. The pieces of coral might represent rocks or small islands. *Interpreting Maps Use the map to explain why navigation tools were important to the Polynesians.*

Exploring the Ocean Floor

INTEGRATING TECHNOLOGY Following the *Challenger's* example, governments and universities sponsored many other major ocean research expeditions. Until recently, however, the ocean floor was unexplored, and much of the life in the oceans was unknown. Why did it take so long to reach this part of the ocean? Studying the ocean floor is difficult because the ocean is so deep—3.8 kilometers deep on average, more than twice as deep as the Grand Canyon. As you learned in Chapter 4, conditions are very harsh at such depths. First, because sunlight does not penetrate far below the surface, the deep ocean is in total darkness. Second, the water is very cold—only a few degrees above freezing. Finally, there is tremendous pressure due to the mass of water pushing down from above.

Because of the darkness, cold, and extreme pressure, scientists have had to develop technology to enable them to study the deep ocean floor. Since humans cannot survive these conditions, many of the inventions have involved indirect methods of gathering information. One of the simplest methods, used by the *Challenger's* crew, was to lower a weight on a long line into the water until the weight touched the bottom. The length of line

SCIENCE & History

Technology and Ocean Exploration

The time line includes several inventions that have helped scientists overcome the challenges of studying the ocean world.

1943 SCUBA

Jacques Cousteau and Emile Gagnan invented SCUBA, which stands for "**s**elf-**c**ontained **u**nderwater **b**reathing **a**pparatus." A tank containing compressed air is strapped to the diver's back and connected by a tube to a mouthpiece. SCUBA enables divers to explore to a depth of 40 meters.

1915   1930   1945   1960

1925 Sonar

Scientists aboard the German ship *Meteor* used sonar to map the ocean floor. They used a device called an echo sounder to produce pulses of sound. The ship's crew then timed the return of the echoes.

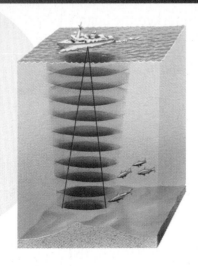

1960 Submersibles

Vehicles with very thick metal hulls protect explorers from extreme pressure and temperature, while enabling them to directly observe the ocean depths.

that got wet was approximately equal to the water's depth at that location. This method was slow and often inaccurate, as the line would descend at an angle. Nevertheless, these depth readings produced the first rough maps of the floor of the North Atlantic.

A major advance in ocean-floor mapping was sonar, a technology invented during World War I to detect submarines. **Sonar**, which stands for **so**und **na**vigation and **r**anging, is a system that uses sound waves to calculate the distance to an object. The sonar equipment on a ship sends out pulses of sound that bounce off the ocean floor. The equipment then measures how quickly the sound waves return to the ship. Sound waves return quickly if the ocean floor is close. Sound waves take longer to return if the ocean floor is farther away.

☑ *Checkpoint* How is sonar an indirect way of gathering data?

In Your Journal

Each of the inventions shown on these two pages helped solve a problem of ocean exploration. Find out more about one of these inventions. Write a short newspaper article telling the story of its development. Include details about the people who invented it and how it added to people's knowledge of the oceans.

1986

Remote Underwater Manipulator

The Remote Underwater Manipulator, or RUM III, is about the size of a small car. It is controlled by a computer aboard a ship at the surface. Without a crew, the RUM III can collect samples, take photographs, and map the ocean floor.

1975	1990	2005	2020

1978 Satellites

Seasat A was the first satellite in Earth's orbit to study the oceans. Since satellites make millions of observations a day, they provide data on rapidly changing and widespread ocean conditions. Such data include temperatures, algae growth patterns, and even the movement of large schools of fish.

1995

Gravity Mapping

The United States Navy used advanced satellite data to create a new map of the ocean floor. The satellite detected slight changes in gravity related to the shape of the ocean floor, providing accurate measurements within a few centimeters.

Features of the Ocean Floor

Once scientists were able to map the ocean floor, they discovered something surprising. The bottom of the ocean was not a flat, sandy plain stretching between the continents, as many people had thought. The deep waters hid mountain ranges bigger than any on Earth's surface, as well as deep canyons reaching into Earth's interior.

If you could take a submarine voyage along the ocean floor, what would you see? Trace your journey from the edge of one continent to another in *Exploring the Ocean Floor*.

As you leave the harbor, your submarine first passes over the **continental shelf**, a gently sloping, shallow area of the ocean floor that extends outward from the edge of a continent. At a depth of about 130 meters, the ocean floor begins to slope more steeply. This steep incline at the edge of the continental shelf is called the **continental slope**. The continental slope marks the true edge of a continent, where the rock that makes up the continent stops and the rock of the ocean floor begins.

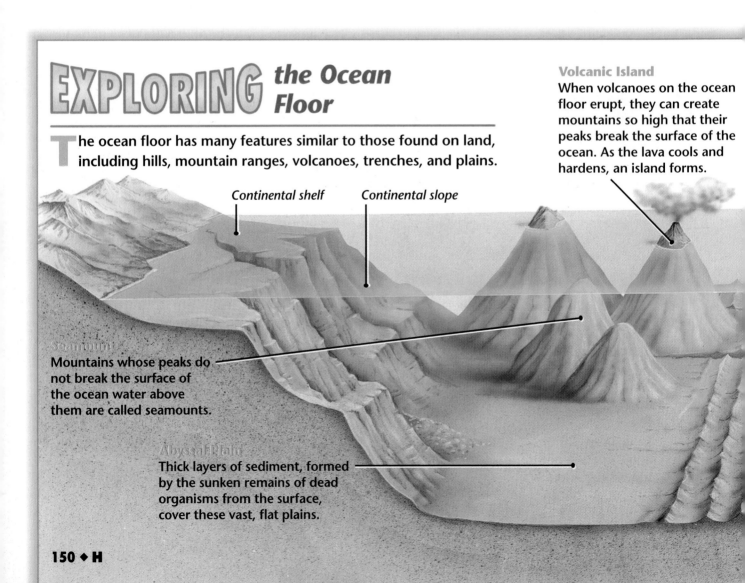

EXPLORING *the Ocean Floor*

The ocean floor has many features similar to those found on land, including hills, mountain ranges, volcanoes, trenches, and plains.

Continental shelf

Continental slope

Volcanic Island
When volcanoes on the ocean floor erupt, they can create mountains so high that their peaks break the surface of the ocean. As the lava cools and hardens, an island forms.

Seamount
Mountains whose peaks do not break the surface of the ocean water above them are called seamounts.

Abyssal Plain
Thick layers of sediment, formed by the sunken remains of dead organisms from the surface, cover these vast, flat plains.

Your submarine descends more gradually now, following the ocean floor as it slopes toward the deep ocean. After some distance, you encounter a group of mountains. Some are tall enough to break the ocean's surface, forming islands. Others, called **seamounts**, are mountains that are completely underwater. Some seamounts have flat tops because their peaks have eroded away.

Next you cross a broad area covered with thick layers of mud and silt. This smooth, nearly flat region of the ocean floor is called the **abyssal plain** (uh BIHS uhl plain). After gliding over the abyssal plain for many kilometers, you need to steer the submarine sharply upward to avoid a mountain range ahead. The **mid-ocean ridge** is a continuous range of mountains that winds around Earth, much as the line of stitches winds around a baseball. The mid-ocean ridge passes through all of Earth's oceans. Nearly 80,000 kilometers long, it is the longest mountain range on Earth.

At the top of the mid-ocean ridge, your submarine is about two kilometers above the abyssal plain, but you are still at least one kilometer below the surface. From this vantage you can see

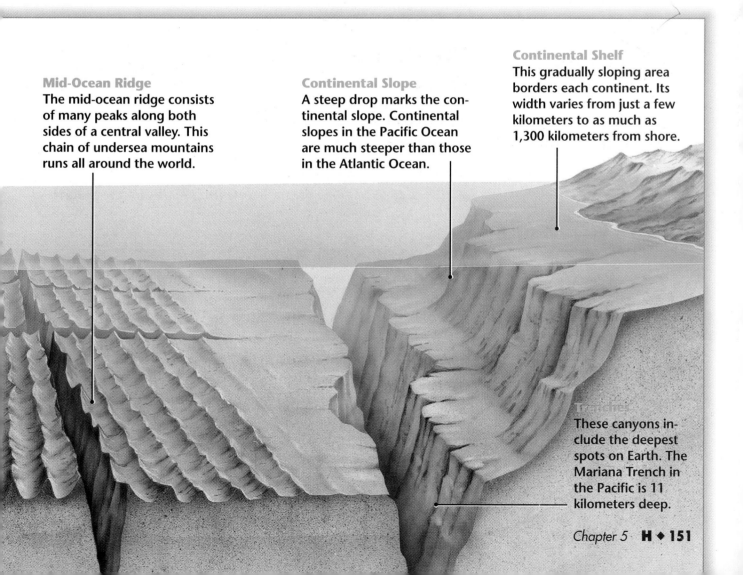

Mid-Ocean Ridge
The mid-ocean ridge consists of many peaks along both sides of a central valley. This chain of undersea mountains runs all around the world.

Continental Slope
A steep drop marks the continental slope. Continental slopes in the Pacific Ocean are much steeper than those in the Atlantic Ocean.

Continental Shelf
This gradually sloping area borders each continent. Its width varies from just a few kilometers to as much as 1,300 kilometers from shore.

Trenches
These canyons include the deepest spots on Earth. The Mariana Trench in the Pacific is 11 kilometers deep.

Interpreting Data

What is Earth's largest mountain? Use the following data to answer the question. Mauna Kea projects about 4,200 meters above sea level. Its base is on the floor of the Pacific Ocean, approximately 9,600 meters deep. Mt. Everest rises 8,850 meters from base to summit. Its base is located 100 meters above sea level. (*Hint:* Drawing a diagram may be helpful. Start with a line that represents sea level.)

Figure 3 When an undersea volcano reaches above the surface of the water, it forms an island. This peak is Mauna Kea in Hawaii.

that the mid-ocean ridge actually consists of two parallel chains of mountains separated by a central valley.

You descend from the mid-ocean ridge to another abyssal plain. Soon your submarine's lights reveal a dark gash in the ocean floor ahead of you. As you pass over it, you look down into a steep-sided canyon in the ocean floor called a **trench**. The trench is so deep you cannot see the bottom.

Your journey is nearly over as your submarine slowly climbs the continental slope. Finally you cross the continental shelf and maneuver the submarine into harbor.

✓ *Checkpoint Which ocean floor feature makes up the deepest parts of the ocean?*

Movements of the Ocean Floor

As oceanographers mapped the ocean floor, their measurements told them about the features you saw on your imaginary journey between the continents. To learn more about the floor of the deep ocean, scientists aboard a drilling ship named *Glomar Challenger*, in honor of the original *Challenger*, collected samples of the rock. They drilled the rock samples from both sides of the mid-ocean ridge in the Atlantic Ocean. Tests on the samples showed that the rock closest to the ridge had formed much more recently than the rock farther away from the ridge. This information helped explain how the ocean floor formed. To understand how, you first need to know something about Earth's structure.

Layers Inside Earth Earth consists of layers that cover the planet's center, or core. The thin, rocky, outer layer of Earth is called the crust. The thick layer between the crust and the core is the mantle. The high temperature and pressure inside Earth cause some of the material in the mantle to form a hot liquid called **magma.** Magma flows very slowly. It can escape upward through cracks in the crust and erupting volcanoes. Magma that reaches the surface is called lava. As lava cools, it forms new crust.

A Cracked Crust Earth's crust is solid rock that is broken into irregularly shaped pieces like the shell of a cracked, hard-boiled egg. The pieces of Earth's crust, along with parts of the upper mantle, are called **plates.** Such plates move slowly on the underlying portion of the mantle. About 14 major plates make up Earth's crust, as shown in Figure 4. They lie beneath the continents as well as the oceans. The plates move at an average speed of several centimeters per year—barely faster than your fingernails grow! Where two plates come together or spread apart, they create different landforms. Plate movements have shaped many of the most dramatic features of the Earth, both on land and under the ocean. **The mountain ranges of the mid-ocean ridge, trenches, and underwater volcanoes are all formed by the interactions of Earth's plates.**

Diverging Plates The mid-ocean ridge is located along the boundaries between plates that are diverging, or moving apart. Along the ridge, magma squeezes up through the cracks between

Figure 4 Earth's crust is divided into 14 major plates. *Interpreting Maps Name the plates that lie beneath parts of the continent of North America.*

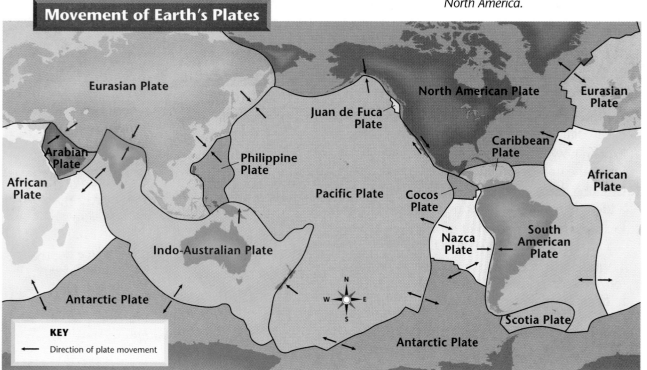

Movement of Earth's Plates

Eurasian Plate

Juan de Fuca Plate

North American Plate

Eurasian Plate

Arabian Plate

Philippine Plate

Caribbean Plate

African Plate

African Plate

Pacific Plate

Cocos Plate

Nazca Plate

South American Plate

Indo-Australian Plate

Antarctic Plate

Scotia Plate

Antarctic Plate

KEY
← Direction of plate movement

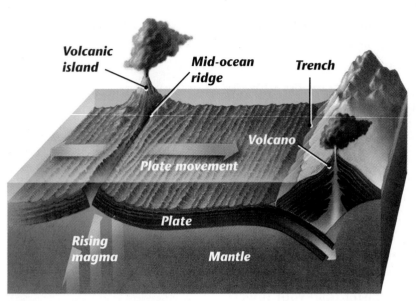

Volcanic island

Mid-ocean ridge

Trench

Volcano

Plate movement

Plate

Rising magma

Mantle

Figure 5 Where two plates diverge, magma from Earth's mantle rises up through the crack. Where two plates converge at a trench, one plate sinks under the other. *Interpreting Diagrams What happens when magma rises to Earth's surface?*

the diverging plates. As the magma hardens along the ridge, it adds a new strip of rock to the ocean floor. Each new eruption along the ridge gradually pushes the older rock away from the center of the ridge. Over many millions of years, this process, called **sea-floor spreading,** produced the ocean floor. The rock samples collected by the *Glomar Challenger* helped confirm the theory of sea-floor spreading by showing that the rocks closer to the ridge had been produced more recently than those farther away.

Converging Plates When the new ocean floor grows along the mid-ocean ridge, where does the old ocean floor farther away from the ridge go? Why doesn't Earth keep getting bigger? The answers to these questions lie in the deep ocean trenches you read about earlier. Where plates come together, or converge, one plate sinks under the other. As new rock is added at the edges of the plates along the mid-ocean ridge, old rock farther away from the mid-ocean ridge sinks into the trenches and back into Earth's interior. This process allows the ocean floor to spread while Earth itself remains the same size.

Section 1 Review

1. List three factors that make exploring the deep ocean difficult.
2. Explain how the movement of Earth's plates forms the mid-ocean ridges and trenches.
3. Describe one technique or expedition that has added to people's knowledge of the oceans.
4. Explain why Earth does not grow in size as new material is added to the ocean floor.
5. **Thinking Critically Inferring** Newly formed volcanic islands have a rich supply of minerals. Explain why this is so.

Science at Home

With a family member, choose a room in your house and make a "room-floor" map based on depth readings. Imagine that the ceiling is the ocean surface and the floor is the bottom of the ocean. Follow a straight path across the middle of the room from one wall to another. At regular intervals, use a carpenter's measuring tape to take a depth reading from the ceiling to the floor or to the top of any furniture in that spot. Plot the depths on a graph. Then challenge another family member to identify the room by looking at the graph.

THE SHAPE OF THE OCEAN FLOOR

Imagine you are an oceanographer traveling across the Atlantic along the 45° N latitude line marked on the map. You and your crew are using sonar to gather data on the depth of the ocean between Nova Scotia, Canada, and the town of Soulac on the coast of France. In this lab, you will interpret the data to create a profile of the ocean floor.

Halifax, Canada
Soulac, France
45°

Problem

How can you use data about ocean depths to determine the shape of the ocean floor?

Materials

pencil   graph paper

Procedure

1. Draw the axes of a graph. Label the horizontal axis Longitude. Mark from 65° W to 0° from left to right. Label the vertical axis Ocean Depth. Mark 0 meters at the top of the vertical axis to represent sea level. Mark –5000 meters at the bottom to represent the depth of 5000 meters below sea level. Mark depths at equal intervals along the vertical axis.

2. Examine the data in the table. The numbers in the Longitude column give the ship's location at 19 points in the Atlantic Ocean. Location 1 is Nova Scotia, and Location 19 is Soulac. The numbers in the Ocean Depth column give the depth measurements recorded at each location. Plot each measurement on your graph. Remember that the depths are represented on your graph as numbers below 0, or sea level.

3. Connect the points you have plotted with a line to create a profile of the ocean floor.

Analyze and Conclude

1. On your graph, identify and label the continental shelf and continental slope.
2. Label the abyssal plain on your graph. How would you expect the ocean floor to look there?
3. Label the mid-ocean ridge on your graph. Describe the process that is occurring there.
4. What might the feature at 10° W be? Explain.
5. **Think About It** How is it helpful to organize data into a data table or graph?

More to Explore

Use the depth measurements in the table to calculate the average depth of the Atlantic Ocean between Nova Scotia and France.

Ocean Depth Sonar Data	
Longitude	**Ocean Depth** (m)
1. 64° W	0
2. 60° W	91
3. 55° W	132
4. 50° W	73
5. 48° W	3512
6. 45° W	4024
7. 40° W	3805
8. 35° W	4171
9. 33° W	3439
10. 30° W	3073
11. 28° W	1756
12. 27° W	2195
13. 25° W	3146
14. 20° W	4244
15. 15° W	4610
16. 10° W	4976
17. 05° W	4317
18. 04° W	146
19. 01° W	0

SECTION
2 Life at the Ocean's Edge

GUIDE FOR READING

◆ What factors affect where ocean organisms live?

◆ What conditions must organisms in the rocky intertidal zone overcome?

◆ What are the major types of coastal wetlands?

Reading Tip As you read, make a list of the habitats described in this section. Write a sentence or two describing each habitat.

At first glance, a sandy ocean beach may seem lifeless. As you walk along the water's edge in the soft, wet sand, you may notice some dark, tangled seaweed that has washed up on the shore. A crab scuttles away from the pile as you walk by. Seagulls screech and swoop overhead. But for the most part, the beach appears deserted.

If you look more closely at the wet sand, you will see evidence of living things right beneath your feet. Tiny, round holes are signs of burrowing clams. These clams dig down into the sand for protection and to prevent being washed away in the waves. If you wade into the water, you may be able to spot a sand crab taking advantage of the surf to feed. The bottom half of its body buried in the sand, the crab waits for the waves to carry in a fresh supply of food for its next meal.

The organisms on this beach are well suited to the conditions there. In this section, you will learn how marine organisms have adapted to other areas where the land and ocean meet.

Living Conditions

A sandy beach is one type of marine, or ocean, habitat. Remember that an organism's habitat provides the things the organism needs to survive. An organism also must be suited to the physical conditions of the environment it lives in. **Some physical factors that determine where marine organisms can live include salinity, water temperature, light, dissolved gases, nutrients, and wave action.**

As you learned in Chapter 4, these conditions vary in different parts of the ocean. For example, salinity is lower where rivers flow into the ocean, bringing a stream of fresh

water. Salinity is higher in shallow, warm seas, where more evaporation takes place. Because cold water holds more dissolved gas than warm water, cold ocean waters contain more oxygen than tropical waters. Different organisms are suited to live in these different conditions. As a result, the same organisms do not live in every part of the ocean.

On land, most organisms live on or near the surface. The ocean, on the other hand, is a three-dimensional environment. It is inhabited by organisms at every depth. Scientists classify marine organisms according to where they live and how they move.

Plankton are tiny algae and animals that float in the water and are carried by waves and currents. Algae plankton include geometrically-shaped diatoms like those shown in Figure 6. Animal plankton include microscopic crustaceans and fish larvae. **Nekton** are free-swimming animals that can move throughout the water column. Octopus and squid, most fishes, and marine mammals such as whales and dolphins are nekton. **Benthos** are organisms that inhabit the ocean floor. Some benthos, like crabs, sea stars, and lobsters, move from place to place. Others, like sponges and sea anemones, stay in one location.

Plankton, nekton, and benthos are all found in most marine habitats. Many plankton and benthos are algae which, like plants, use sunlight to produce their own food through photosynthesis. Other plankton and benthos, as well as all nekton, are consumers. They eat either the algae or other consumers. Finally, some organisms, including many benthos, are decomposers. They break down wastes and remains of other organisms. These feeding relationships in a habitat make up a **food web**.

Figure 6 Marine organisms can be classified as plankton, nekton, or benthos. **A.** Intricate diatoms, one type of algae plankton, float on the ocean surface. **B.** These microscopic crustaceans, called copepods, are animal plankton. **C.** Free-swimming animals, such as this school of sweetlip fish, are nekton. **D.** Benthos live on the ocean floor. The sea stars and sea anemones in this colorful array are benthos.

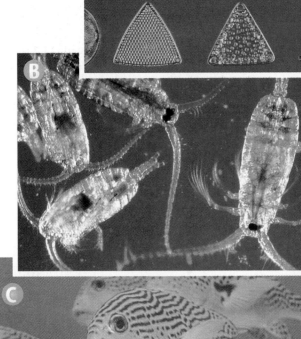

About 350 years ago, a form of poetry called *haiku* grew popular in Japan. Here is an example of a haiku about a beach.

Shining air bubbles
pushing up the hardpacked sand:
a shy clam revealed.

This poem may appear simple, but it follows a strict structure. A haiku is a 17-syllable poem written in 3 lines. There are 5 syllables in the first line, 7 syllables in the second line, and 5 syllables in the third line. A haiku should capture a moment in nature and suggest a mood or feeling.

In Your Journal

Prepare to write your own haiku about the edge of the ocean. Work with a partner to think of what you might see, hear, and feel. Review the habitats in this section for ideas. Then choose one simple, specific subject to write about. Write a draft and exchange it with your partner. After making revisions, illustrate your poem.

The first group of ocean habitats you will learn about are those found at the very edge of the ocean. The sandy beach you read about earlier is one example. Two habitats with a richer variety of life are rocky shores and salt marshes. As you read, think about how conditions in these habitats are similar, and how they are different.

☑ *Checkpoint* *Are sharks plankton, nekton, or benthos? Why?*

Rocky Shores

Imagine if your home had no walls or roof. Twice a day, a huge storm passes through, bringing a drenching downpour and winds so strong you can hardly keep your balance. At other times, the hot sun beats down, leaving you parched and dry. This is what life is like for organisms that live on rocky shores in the intertidal zone. The **intertidal zone** stretches from the highest high-tide line on land out to the point on the continental shelf exposed by the lowest low tide.

Organisms that live in the rocky intertidal zone must be able to tolerate the pounding of the waves and changes in salinity and temperature. They must also withstand periods of being underwater and periods of being exposed to the air. They must avoid drying out, hide from predators, and find food in this harsh setting. How are organisms able to survive?

Along the Rocks Rocky shores are found along much of both coasts of the United States. Figure 7 shows some of the colorful organisms that typically live along the rocky California coast.

The highest rocks, above the highest high-tide line, make up the spray zone. The spray zone is never completely covered with water, but it gets wet as the waves break against the rocks. A stripe of black algae indicates the highest high-tide line. The rocks below this level are encrusted with barnacles. Barnacles can close up their hard shells, trapping a drop of water inside to carry

Sea urchin

Sea anemones

Sea lettuce

Abalone

Brittle star

them through the dry period until the next high tide. Lower down, clumps of blue and black mussels stick out amidst the algae. The mussels produce sticky threads that harden on contact with the water, attaching the mussels to the rock. The threads are so strong that scientists are studying them as a model for new glues. The rocks are also home to flat mollusks called limpets. Limpets have a large, muscular foot to hold on tightly. They secrete drops of mucus around the edges of their shells to form a tight seal.

Algae that live in the intertidal zone are also adapted to withstand the physical conditions. Rootlike structures anchor the strands of algae firmly to the rocks. Some algae are covered with a thick layer of slime. The slime keeps the algae from drying out during low tide.

In Tide Pools When the tide goes out, some water remains in depressions among the rocks called tide pools. As the water in a tide pool is warmed by the sun, it begins to evaporate. The remaining water becomes saltier. If it rains, however, the salinity quickly decreases. Organisms in the tide pool must be able to withstand these changes in temperature and salinity, as well as the force of the waves when the tide comes in again.

Sea stars cling to the rocks with rows of tiny suction cups on their undersides. Spiny purple sea urchins crawl slowly along the bottom of the tide pool. If the bottom is sandy, sea urchins can use their spines to dig a hole in which to bury themselves during heavy surf. Under shady rock ledges, sponges and sea anemones wait for the incoming tide to bring a fresh supply of plankton and other food particles. A sea anemone may look delicate, but some can survive out of water for over two weeks. When out of the water, the anemone pulls its tentacles inside. It folds up into a round blob, resembling a rolled-up sock.

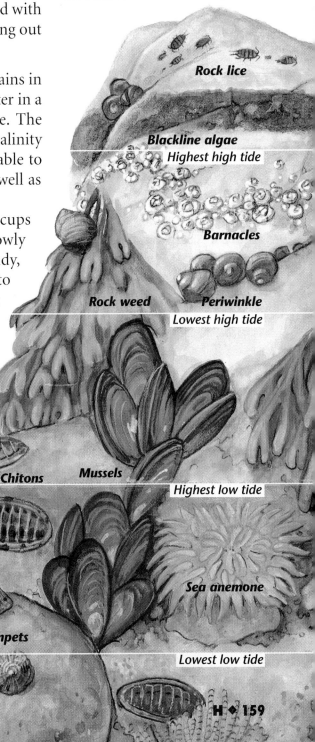

Figure 7 The constantly changing water level in the intertidal zone creates different habitats along a rocky coast. *Comparing and Contrasting* How are conditions different for organisms near the top of the rocks compared to organisms at the bottom?

Rock lice

Blackline algae
Highest high tide

Barnacles

Rock weed
Periwinkle
Lowest high tide

Chitons
Mussels
Highest low tide

Sea star

Sea anemone

Limpets

Lowest low tide

Hermit crab

Where River Meets Ocean

Other important environments along the ocean's edge are estuaries. **Estuaries** are coastal inlets or bays where fresh water from rivers mixes with the salty ocean water. Water that is partly salty and partly fresh is **brackish.**

Coastal wetlands are habitats found in and around estuaries. **Along the United States coasts, most coastal wetlands are either salt marshes or mangrove forests.** Salt marshes are especially abundant along the east coast from Massachusetts to Florida. Mangrove forests are found in the tropical waters along the southern coast of Florida and the Gulf of Mexico.

Salt Marshes A salt marsh oozes with smelly mud. Mosquitoes swarm over the water as it flows slowly through the tall, green grasses. The fresh water and tides contribute sediments, animal and plant matter, and other nutrients to the salt marsh, forming a soft, rich mud bottom.

A single plant, cordgrass, dominates the marsh. Unlike most plants, cordgrass can survive in salt water. The plant releases salt through small openings in its long, narrow leaves. The cordgrass that is not eaten by animals breaks down and is decomposed by bacteria and fungi in the water. The decomposed material supplies nutrients to organisms in the marsh.

Tidal channels run through the cordgrass. Waves break up as they enter the channels, so that organisms in the marsh are protected from the surf. Within the shelter of the marsh, fish, crabs, shrimp, and oysters hatch and feed before entering the harsher ocean environment offshore. As the tide retreats, mud flats are exposed. Hordes of crabs search for food in the rich mud. Herons, stilts, and egrets stalk across the mud to prey on the crabs and other benthos exposed by the low tide.

Mangrove Forests Mangroves—short, gnarled trees that grow well in brackish water—fringe the coastline of southern Florida. The mangroves'

Figure 8 Salt marshes and mangrove forests are two types of coastal wetlands. **A.** Salt water flows through tidal channels in a salt marsh. **B.** Arching prop roots anchor these black mangrove trees firmly in the soft, sandy soil around Florida Bay. *Making Generalizations How does the plant life in each of these habitats provide shelter for marine organisms?*

prop roots anchor the trees to the land. Mangroves can withstand all but the strongest hurricane winds. Without the mangroves to break the action of winds and waves, the coastline would change dramatically each hurricane season. The prop roots also trap sediment from the land. They create a protected nursery rich in nutrients for many young animals.

Protecting Estuaries The rivers that flow into estuaries can carry harmful substances as well as nutrients. When pollutants such as pesticides, sewage, and industrial waste get into the river water, they end up in the estuary. The pollutants change the water quality in the estuary. In turn, organisms that live in the estuary are affected. It can take many years for ocean tides to flush a heavy load of pollutants out of an estuary.

For example, Chesapeake Bay is a huge estuary located on the mid-Atlantic coast. It has been a rich source of oysters, clams, and blue crabs. However, pollutants from inland sources accumulated in the bay for many years. Their effect was to greatly reduce the number and kinds of organisms in the Chesapeake. When people realized the threat to the estuary, they took action. The water quality of rivers that empty into Chesapeake Bay is now regulated by law. Cleanup efforts have reduced much of the pollution in the bay. Today, organisms like the blue crab are making a comeback.

Figure 9 A crabber in Chesapeake Bay pulls up the last trap of the day. As the health of the estuary improves, the blue crab population is growing again.

Section 2 Review

1. Name five physical factors that affect organisms in marine habitats.

2. Describe conditions in the rocky intertidal zone.

3. List two ways that salt marshes and mangrove forests are alike and two ways they are different.

4. Thinking Critically Making Judgments A builder has proposed filling in a salt marsh to create a seaside resort. What positive and negative impacts might this proposal have on wildlife, local residents, and tourists? Would you support the proposal? Why or why not?

Check Your Progress

CHAPTER PROJECT 5
Your group should now select the marine environment you will create. Measure the space where you will build your model. Make a list of the physical features you will need to represent. Draw a scale diagram of your model and show it to your teacher. Label the different features and note the materials you will use. (*Hint:* Draw your sketch on graph paper to plan its size to fit the space.)

SECTION 3 The Neritic Zone and Open Ocean

DISCOVER ·········· ACTIVITY····

How Deep Can You See?

1. With a permanent marker, divide a white plastic lid into four quarters. Shade in two quarters as shown.

2. ✂ Use a pair of scissors to carefully poke a small hole in the center of the lid.

3. Tie a piece of string to a paper clip. Place the clip underneath the lid and thread the string up through the hole.

4. Tape the string tightly to a meterstick so that the lid presses against the bottom of the meterstick.

5. Fill a large, deep bucket with tap water.

6. While stirring the water, add one teaspoon of flour to represent the dissolved substances in seawater. The water should be slightly cloudy.

7. Lower the lid into the water so that it is 5 cm below the surface. Note whether the lid is still visible in the water.

8. Lower the lid 10 cm below the surface, then 15 cm, and so on until the lid is no longer visible.

Think It Over

Observing At what depth could you no longer see the lid? Based on your results, how do you think visibility changes with depth in the ocean?

GUIDE FOR READING

◆ What conditions in the neritic zone support organisms?

◆ Where do algae live in the open ocean?

◆ How do hydrothermal vents support organisms?

Reading Tip Before you read, preview Figure 10 on the facing page. Predict how the neritic zone and open ocean are similar and how they are different.

Floating mats of golden-brown, leaflike fronds on the ocean surface mark the location of a kelp forest. Diving below the surface, you find yourself surrounded by tall, swaying stalks of giant kelp. Sunlight filters through the water, producing a greenish light. As you pull yourself hand over hand down one of the kelp strands, you notice small bulbs at the base of each frond. You pinch one of the bulbs, and a bubble of gas escapes. These bulbs keep the heavy kelp fronds upright in the water.

The kelp forest is full of life. Bright-orange sheephead fish dart past you. Young sea lions chase each other around the kelp stalks. A sea otter, surrounded by a stream of bubbles, dives past you, down to the rocky bottom. When it rises, the otter is clutching a sea star between its paws. On the surface again, you watch the sea otter as it rolls onto its back among the kelp. The otter deftly uses its paws to scoop out the meat from the soft underside of the sea star.

◀ Sea otter eating a sea star

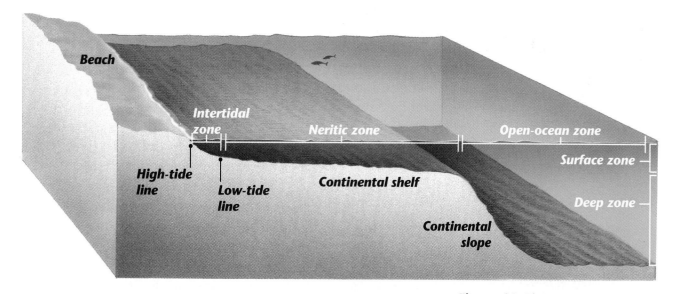

Figure 10 The ocean zone closest to land is the intertidal zone, which is bounded by the high-tide and low-tide lines. Next is the neritic zone, followed by the open-ocean zone, which makes up most of the world's oceans. The open ocean is divided by depth into the surface zone and the deep zone.
Interpreting Diagrams Which zones lie over the continental shelf?

A kelp forest is one habitat found in the neritic zone. The **neritic zone** is the part of the ocean that extends from the low-tide line out to the edge of the continental shelf. Beyond the edge of the continental shelf lies the **open-ocean zone.** Locate the neritic and open-ocean zones in Figure 10. In this section you will learn how organisms are adapted to the conditions in these zones, from the sunlit surface waters to the coldest depths.

Conditions in the Neritic Zone

A huge variety of organisms are found in the neritic zone, more than in any other area of the ocean. Most of the world's major fishing grounds are found in this zone. What makes the neritic zone home to so many living things? The answer has to do with its location over the continental shelf. **The shallow water over the continental shelf receives sunlight and a steady supply of nutrients washed from the land into the ocean.** The light and nutrients enable large plantlike algae, such as the giant kelp, to grow. These algae serve as a food source and shelter for other organisms.

In many parts of the neritic zone, upwelling currents bring additional nutrients from the bottom to the surface. These nutrients support large numbers of plankton, which form the base of ocean food webs. Schools of fish such as sardines and anchovies feed on the plankton. Major fisheries in upwelling areas include Monterey Canyon off the California coast, Newfoundland's Grand Banks, and Georges Bank off the New England coast.

Two diverse habitats typically found within the neritic zone are kelp forests and coral reefs. As you read about each, think about how they are similar and how they are different.

Checkpoint What are two ways that nutrients may be supplied to the neritic zone?

Figure 11 Light streams through a forest of giant kelp and shadowy rockfish near Monterey, California. The closeup shows the gas-filled bulbs that keep the kelp upright in the water.

Life in a Kelp Forest

Kelp forests grow in cold neritic waters, such as those along the Pacific coast from Alaska to Mexico. These large, heavy algae require a solid, rocky bottom to anchor their stalks. A bundle of rootlike strands called a **holdfast** attaches the algae to the rocks. A stalk of giant kelp can grow to 30 meters in length. The gas-filled bulbs shown in the closeup to the left keep the heavy kelp stalk upright in the water.

The kelp use the sunlight and dissolved gases in the neritic zone to produce their own food. The kelp also provide a habitat for many other organisms. The curtains of kelp hide young gray whales from predators while their mothers are feeding. Sea slugs and snails live amid the tangle of the holdfasts.

Sea otters play a particularly important role in the kelp forest. In addition to eating abalone, sea otters feed on sea urchins, which eat the kelp. In areas where sea otters have disappeared, armies of sea urchins have devoured the kelp. The once-thriving forest has become a barren rocky zone.

Coral Reefs

Although a coral reef may look as if it is made of rock, it is actually made of living things. Coral reefs are created by colonies of tiny coral animals, each of which is not much larger than a pencil eraser. The coral animals produce a hard structure that surrounds their soft bodies. After the coral dies, the empty structure remains. New coral animals attach and grow on top of it. Over many years, a reef is built. Most of the coral reefs that exist today were begun about 5,000 to 10,000 years ago.

Microscopic algae live within the bodies of the coral animals and provide food for them. Because the algae require warm temperatures and sunlight, coral reefs can only form in shallow, tropical ocean waters. The reefs grow above continental shelves or around volcanic islands, where the water is shallow.

In areas where the seafloor is sinking, a reef may develop over time into an atoll. An **atoll** is a ring-shaped reef surrounding a shallow lagoon. Figure 12 shows the development of an atoll. It begins as a fringing reef that closely surrounds the edges of the island. As the reef grows upward, the island sinks, and a barrier reef forms. Water separates the top of the barrier reef from the land. The island continues to sink until it is eventually underwater, forming the atoll.

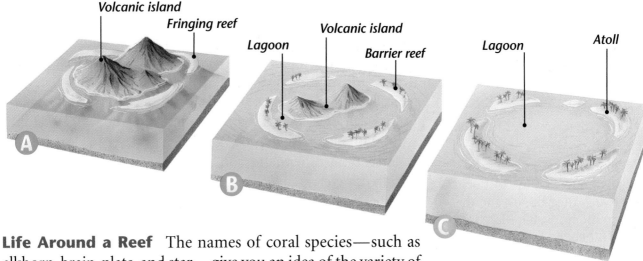

Volcanic island
Fringing reef

Lagoon
Volcanic island
Barrier reef

Lagoon
Atoll

A

B

C

Life Around a Reef

The names of coral species—such as elkhorn, brain, plate, and star—give you an idea of the variety of shapes coral can form. Many animals live in and around the crevices of the reef, including octopuses, spiny lobsters, shrimp, toothy moray eels, and fish in all colors and sizes. Parrotfish like the one in Figure 13 scrape coral off the reef to eat. The parrot-fish grind up the broken coral inside their bodies, producing the fine, soft sand commonly found around the reef.

Coral Reefs and Humans

Coral reefs are natural aquarium exhibits, displaying a colorful diversity of life to be enjoyed and studied. Reefs also protect coastlines during violent storms. The reefs break up the surf, preventing waves from severely eroding the land. However, human activities can harm the fragile reefs. Boat anchors dragging across a reef can damage it. Divers can accidentally break off pieces of the reef. Even brushing against the reef can harm some of the coral animals. Because coral only grows a few millimeters a year, a reef cannot quickly recover.

Changes in water temperature and clarity also affect coral reefs. For example, if the water becomes too warm, the corals release the algae that live inside them. Cloudy water endangers the algae by reducing the amount of light that reaches them. If sediments produced by storms or human activities bury a reef, the algae in the living coral cannot survive. Without the algae, the coral animals do not grow well and eventually die.

Today many people understand the importance of coral reefs and try to protect them. Many reef areas have been designated as marine sanctuaries, which limits the amount of diving and other activity allowed near the reef. Scientists worldwide are also studying the effects of temperature change and pollution on the reefs to better protect them.

☑ *Checkpoint* *How can human activities impact a coral reef?*

Figure 12 An atoll develops in stages. **A.** A fringing reef closely surrounds an island. **B.** As the island sinks, a lagoon forms inside the barrier reef. **C.** Finally, the island sinks below the surface, leaving a ring-shaped atoll. *Interpreting Diagrams In which stage is the reef the youngest?*

Figure 13 A parrotfish delicately nibbles away at a coral reef in the Red Sea. Reefs provide a habitat for many fish and other marine organisms.

ACTIVITY

To keep from sinking, many plankton rely on the friction between their bodies and the surrounding water. More friction is needed to stay afloat in warm water than in denser cold water. One of the copepods below is found in tropical ocean waters, while the other is found near the poles. Which do you think is which? Explain your reasoning. (*Hint:* More streamlined shapes create less friction with their surroundings.)

Conditions in the Open Ocean

The open ocean begins where the neritic zone ends, at the edge of the continental shelf. Diving into the open ocean is like descending a long staircase with a light only at the very top. Light from the sun only penetrates a short distance into the water, typically to a depth of less than 200 meters. If the water is cloudy with sediment, sunlight does not reach as deep. In clear tropical waters, on the other hand, some light may reach as deep as a few hundred meters.

The fact that only a small portion of the open ocean receives sunlight is one way it differs from the neritic zone. Another difference is the amount of dissolved nutrients in the water. While the neritic zone receives a constant supply of nutrients from shore, dissolved nutrients are less abundant in the open ocean. As a result, the open ocean zone supports fewer organisms.

The Surface Zone The surface zone extends as far as sunlight reaches below the surface. **The surface zone is the only part of the open ocean that receives enough sunlight to support the growth of algae.** These microscopic algae are the base of open-ocean food webs. Animal plankton that feed on algae include tiny crustaceans called copepods, shrimp-like krill, and the young of many ocean animals such as crabs, mollusks, and fishes.

Figure 15 on the facing page shows an Arctic food web. Each organism in this food web depends either directly or indirectly on the plankton. Throughout the ocean, plankton are a source of food for other organisms of all sizes. If you think of sharks as sharp-toothed, meat-eating hunters, you might be surprised to learn that the biggest sharks of all feed entirely on tiny plankton! Whale sharks, which can grow to more than 10 meters long, strain plankton from the water. Many whales feed only on plankton as well, including Earth's largest animal, the blue whale.

The Deep Zone When you explored the water column in Chapter 4, you observed that the ocean became darker and colder as you descended. Because of its harsh conditions, the deep ocean is often compared to a desert. Compared to other land and ocean environments, few organisms live in the deep zone. But unlike a desert baking under the bright sun, the deep ocean is cold, dark, and wet.

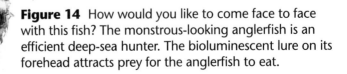

Figure 14 How would you like to come face to face with this fish? The monstrous-looking anglerfish is an efficient deep-sea hunter. The bioluminescent lure on its forehead attracts prey for the anglerfish to eat.

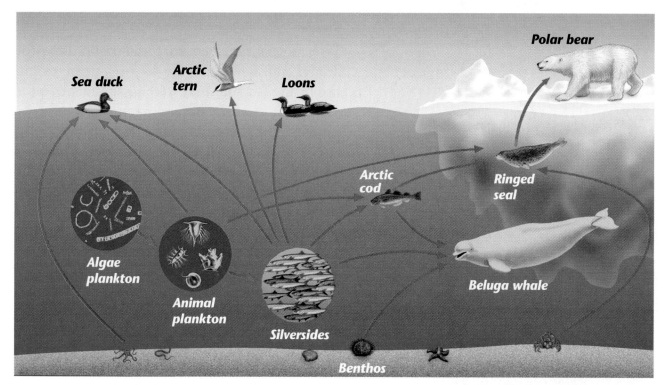

Figure 15 This marine food web includes typical organisms found in the Arctic Ocean. The arrows indicate what each organism eats. *Interpreting Diagrams* *Which organisms feed directly on the Arctic cod? Which organisms depend indirectly on the cod?*

Finding food in the darkness is a challenge. Many deep-sea fishes produce their own light. The production of light by living things is called **bioluminescence.** Some fishes use chemical reactions to produce their own light, like fireflies on land. Other fishes have colonies of bioluminescent bacteria living in pockets on their bodies. Still others have light-producing organs. The anglerfish, for example, has a light organ on its head. The fish lurks in the shadows below the pool of light. Shrimp and fishes that are attracted to the light become the anglerfish's prey.

Because the food supply in most of the deep ocean is much more limited than in shallower water, animals in this zone must be good hunters to survive. The gaping mouths of many deep-sea fishes are filled with fang-like teeth. Rows of sharp teeth stick out at angles, ensuring that any animal it bites cannot escape.

☑ *Checkpoint* *Why do very few organisms live in the deep zone?*

Hydrothermal Vents

As the submersible *Alvin* descended to a depth of 2,500 meters into the Galápagos Rift in the Pacific Ocean one day in 1977, the scientists aboard could hardly believe their eyes. Outside the submersible, the headlights revealed a bizarre scene. Clouds of black water billowed up from chimney-shaped structures on the ocean floor. Meter-long tubes with gaping, lipstick-red ends swayed in the water. White crabs scuttled over the rocks, crawling around clams as big as dinner plates.

Figure 16 Giant tube worms cluster around a hydrothermal vent on the deep ocean floor.

The scientists were surprised not only by the strange appearance of these deep-sea creatures, but also by the fact that they were so abundant. In the deepest parts of the ocean, organisms tend to be very small and slow-moving because food is so rare. The number, size, and variety of organisms were unusually large for such a deep part of the ocean. What could these organisms find to eat so far from sunlight?

The strange community the scientists in *Alvin* observed was located around a hydrothermal vent. A **hydrothermal vent** is an area where ocean water sinks through cracks in the ocean floor, is heated by the underlying magma, and rises again through the cracks. These vents are located along ocean ridges, where the plates are moving apart and new ocean floor is forming.

The heated water coming from a vent carries gases and minerals from Earth's interior. **The chemical nutrients in the heated water support the unique group of organisms that are found around hydrothermal vents.** Bacteria feed directly on the chemical nutrients that are spewed out of the vents. Like the algae in the surface zone that use sunlight to produce food, these bacteria use the chemicals to produce food. They form the base of the food web at a hydrothermal vent.

Other organisms, like the giant clams, feed on the bacteria. The red-tipped tube worms are supplied with food by bacteria living within their tissues. Meanwhile, the scuttling crabs feed on the remains of the other inhabitants in their unusual habitat.

Section 3 Review

1. Describe the physical conditions in the neritic zone.
2. What factor limits where algae are found in the open ocean?
3. What is the source of nutrients for organisms around a hydrothermal vent?
4. Explain how bioluminescence is important to some fish that live in the deep ocean.
5. **Thinking Critically Relating Cause and Effect** When forests on a tropical island are cut down, the soil is more easily eroded. Explain how this could affect a coral reef near the island.

Check Your Progress CHAPTER PROJECT 5

By now you should have selected an organism to model. Research your organism to determine its size and other physical characteristics. How does the organism survive in its marine habitat? Check your plan for constructing the organism with your teacher. Your group should also begin building your model habitat. Make sure you have collected all the necessary materials before you begin building.

4 Resources From the Ocean

DISCOVER ···································· ACTIVITY····

Is It From the Ocean?

1. Your teacher will give you some labels from common household products. Read the ingredient information on each label.

2. Divide the products into two piles—those you think include substances that come from the ocean and those that do not.

Think About It

Classifying For each product that you classified as coming from the ocean, name the item from the ocean that is used to produce it. In what ocean zone is it found?

When European explorers began sailing to North America, they were astounded by the huge number of codfish that lived off its eastern coast. One traveler reported that this area was so "swarming with fish that they could be taken not only with a net but in baskets let down and weighted with a stone." Others reported sailing through schools of cod so thick they slowed the boats down!

This cod fishery stretched from Newfoundland to a hook of land appropriately named Cape Cod. For more than 400 years, the seemingly endless supply of "King Cod" supported a thriving fishing industry. But beginning in the early 1900s, fishing crews had to work harder to catch the same amount of cod. As the fishing grew more difficult each year, it became clear that the cod were disappearing. With the price of cod rising, there was more competition to catch the fewer fish available. In 1992, the Canadian government had to declare the fishery closed.

No one knows for sure how long it will take the cod population to fully recover. Scientists are studying cod and other fisheries to learn how to preserve them for future generations.

Living Resources

Cod are just one example of a living resource from the ocean. How many other kinds of seafood

GUIDE FOR READING

◆ How does the supply of fish in a fishery change from year to year?

◆ Who controls and protects ocean resources?

Reading Tip Before you read, rewrite the headings in the section as how, why, or what questions. As you read, look for answers to those questions.

Figure 17 Big catches of cod like this one from Georges Bank, off the New England coast, have become less common since the early 1900s.

have you tasted: tuna, shrimp, flounder, lobster, clams, squid, oysters, seaweed, or mussels? These foods and the many others that come from the ocean make up about five percent of the world's total food supply.

Harvesting Fish Just six species make up the majority of fishes harvested for eating: herring, sardine, anchovy, cod, pollock, and mackerel. Locate the world's major fisheries in Figure 18. You can see that they are all located close to coasts. Nearly all fishes caught are harvested from coastal waters or areas of upwelling. These waters contain nutrients and plankton on which they feed.

If used wisely, fisheries naturally renew themselves each year. **New fish are born, replacing those that are caught, but only as long as the fishery is not overfished. Overfishing causes the supply of fish to decrease.** Overfishing has become a problem as better technology has enabled people to catch large numbers of fish very quickly. For example, some fishing fleets have electronic equipment that allows them to locate schools of fish precisely. They can be caught faster than they can reproduce. Once this occurs, it begins a cycle that leads to fewer and fewer fish each season. Eventually, the fishery may be depleted, like the cod fishery you read about earlier.

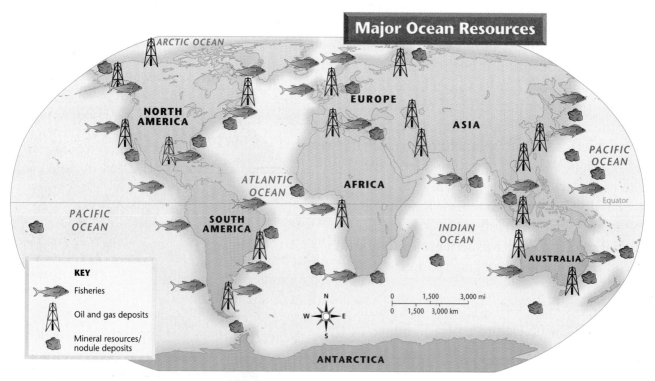

Figure 18 All over the world, the oceans are an important source of food, oil and gas, and minerals. *Interpreting Maps Where are Africa's major fisheries located?*

Aquaculture As fish stocks become depleted, **aquaculture,** the farming of saltwater and freshwater organisms, is likely to become more common. Aquaculture has been practiced in some Asian countries for centuries. This process involves creating an environment for the organisms and controlling nutrient levels, water temperature, light, and other factors to help them thrive. Oysters, abalone, and shrimp have successfully been farmed in artificial saltwater ponds and protected bays. Even landlocked regions can produce seafood using aquaculture. For example, salmon are now being raised in Nebraska fields that once were cattle ranches.

INTEGRATING TECHNOLOGY

Other Ocean Products People harvest ocean organisms for many purposes besides food. For example, algae is an ingredient in many household products. Its gelatin-like texture makes it an ideal base for detergents, shampoos, cosmetics, paints, and even ice cream! Sediments containing the hard fragments of diatoms are used for abrasives and polishes. Many researchers believe that other marine organisms may be important sources of chemicals for medicines in the future.

☑ *Checkpoint* How are fisheries naturally renewed each year?

Mineral Resources

In addition to living organisms, the ocean contains valuable nonliving resources. Some of these are found within ocean water itself. Chapter 3 described how fresh water can be extracted from ocean water in the process of desalination. Desalination provides fresh water for many dry areas and islands. When the fresh water is removed from ocean water, the salts that are left behind are also a valuable resource. Over half of the world's supply of magnesium, a strong, light metal, is obtained from seawater in this way.

A second source of nonliving resources is the ocean floor. From the layer of sediments covering the continental shelves, gravel and sand are mined for use in building construction. In some areas of the world diamonds and gold are mined from sand deposits. Metals such as manganese also accumulate on the ocean floor. The metals concentrate around pieces of shell, forming black lumps called **nodules** (NAHJ oolz). Because they sometimes occur in waters as deep as 5,000 meters, recovering the nodules is a difficult process. The technology to gather them is still being developed.

Not all nations have agreed on who owns the rights to nodules and other resources on the deep ocean floor. Some feel the

TRY THIS

Seaweed Candy

Make this Asian dessert **ACTIVITY** to discover one way to eat algae. Remember to prepare food only in a non-science classroom. Be sure to get permission before using a stove.

2 blocks of agar (one 0.5-ounce package)
1 cup sugar
4 cups guava juice or other fruit juice
food coloring

1. Rinse the agar, a substance obtained from algae.

2. Break agar into cubes and place them in a saucepan.

3. Put on your goggles. Add the sugar and juice to the pan. Bring the mixture to a boil. Turn down the heat and cook, stirring, until the agar dissolves.

4. Remove pan from heat and stir in a few drops of food coloring. Pour the mixture into a shallow pan. Let cool.

5. Refrigerate candy until firm.

6. Cut into blocks and serve.

Inferring What purpose does the agar serve in this recipe? What purposes do the sugar and juice serve?

Figure 19 Lit up like a city at night, this Norwegian oil-drilling platform rises above the icy waters of the North Sea. Hundreds of people may live and work aboard such an oil rig.

nations who find and recover the minerals should own them. Others feel that this is unfair to nations who cannot yet afford the technology to obtain a share of these resources.

Fuels From the Ocean Floor

Another type of nonliving resource forms from the remains of dead marine organisms. These remains sink to the bottom of the ocean, where they are buried by sediments. As more sediments accumulate, the buried remains decompose. Over hundreds of thousands of years, the heat and pressure from the overlying layers gradually transform the remains into oil and natural gas.

As you know, many organisms live in the part of the ocean above the continental shelf. The thick sediments on the continental shelves bury the remains of living things. As a result, the richest deposits of oil and gas are often located on the continental shelves.

Oil rigs like the one in Figure 19 drill the rocky ocean floor as much as 300 meters below the surface. Imagine trying to dig a hole in the concrete bottom of a swimming pool, while standing on a raft floating on the surface of the water. You can see why drilling the ocean floor is very difficult! Ocean drilling is made even harder by strong currents, winds, and violent storms.

☑ *Checkpoint* *What is the source of the oil and gas deposits on the ocean floor?*

Ocean Pollution

It was once thought that the ocean was so vast that people could not damage it by throwing wastes into it. This is partially true—the ocean is a self-cleaning system that can absorb some wastes without permanent damage. But dumping large amounts of wastes into the ocean threatens many marine organisms.

Recall that water pollution is the addition of any substance that has a negative effect on the living things that depend on the water. Most ocean pollution comes from the land. Although some is the result of natural occurrences, most pollution is related to human activities.

Natural Sources Some pollution is the result of weather. For example, heavy rains wash fresh water into estuaries and out into the water offshore. This surge of fresh water pollutes the ocean by lowering its salinity. A sudden change in salinity may kill ocean animals that are unable to adjust to it.

Human Sources Pollutants related to human activities include sewage, chemicals, and trash dumped into coastal waters. Chemicals that run off fields and roads often end up in the ocean. These substances can harm ocean organisms directly. The pollutants can also build up in their bodies and poison other animals, including people, that feed on them. Trash can cause serious problems, too. Seals, otters, and other marine mammals that need to breathe air can get tangled in old fishing lines or nets and drown. Other animals are harmed when they swallow plastic bags that block their stomachs.

Oil Spills One major threat to ocean life is oil pollution. When an oil tanker or drilling platform is damaged, oil leaks into the surrounding ocean. Oil is harmful to many organisms. It coats the bodies of marine mammals and birds. This destroys their natural insulation and affects their ability to float. The oil is also harmful to animals that swallow it.

Figure 20 Removing oil from a beach is a difficult, messy chore. This cleanup worker is using absorbent mops to remove oil from the sand. In the closeup, two more workers try to clean oil from a bird's beak and feathers. *Inferring What might have caused this oil pollution?*

Figure 21 Flags fly outside the United Nations headquarters in New York City. The United Nations develops policies on the use of the oceans by countries. *Applying Concepts Why can't each nation make its own laws regarding ocean resources?*

Interestingly, there is a natural cleaning process that slowly takes place after oil spills. Certain bacteria that live in the ocean feed on the oil and multiply. It takes many years, but eventually an oil-covered beach can become clean again. This has happened even in the portions of the Prince William Sound in Alaska that were blanketed with oil from the 1989 wreck of the oil tanker *Exxon Valdez.*

Protecting Earth's Oceans

Who owns the ocean and its resources? Who has the responsibility of protecting them? These are questions that nations have been struggling to answer for hundreds of years. **Because the world ocean is a continuous body of water that has no boundaries, it is difficult to determine who, if anyone, should control portions of it. Nations must cooperate to manage and protect the oceans.**

The United Nations has established different boundaries in the oceans. According to one treaty, a nation now controls the first 22 kilometers out from its coasts. The nation also controls resources in the waters or on the continental shelf within 370 kilometers of shore. This treaty leaves approximately half of the ocean's surface waters as "high seas," owned by no nation. Ownership of the ocean floor beneath the high seas is still under debate.

Other international efforts have resulted in cooperation aimed at reducing ocean pollution. Examples include the establishment of marine refuges and regulations for building safer oil tankers.

Section 4 Review

1. How can overfishing affect a fishery?
2. Explain why international cooperation is necessary to solve many problems related to ocean resources.
3. Name a nonliving resource found in the ocean. Where is it located? How is it obtained and used?
4. **Thinking Critically Making Judgments** Should mineral resources on the ocean floor belong to whomever finds them, or to the closest nation? Consider each position and write a short paragraph stating your opinion.

Science at Home

Have a family member hook one end of a rubber band around his or her wrist. Stretch the rubber band across the back of the hand and hook the free end over three fingers as shown. Now ask the person to try to remove the rubber band without using the other hand. Explain that this shows how difficult it is for seals or dolphins to free themselves from a plastic beverage ring or piece of net. Can you propose any ways to reduce this threat to marine mammals?

SCIENCE AND SOCIETY

Shrimp Farms—At What Cost to the Environment?

About one quarter of the world's shrimp are raised on shrimp farms. Many shrimp farms are created by clearing trees from mangrove forests and digging shallow, fenced-in ponds. Farmers then fill the ponds with ocean water and shrimp larvae. After about six months, when the shrimp are big enough to sell, the farmers drain the pond water back into the ocean.

To grow healthy shrimp, farmers often add fertilizers, medicines, and pesticides to the ponds. When the pond water is released to the ocean, these chemicals can harm other animals. The United Nations has estimated that 25 percent of the world's mangrove forests have been destroyed as a result of shrimp farming. As awareness of the environmental impact of shrimp farms has grown, the industry has come under attack.

▲ Shrimp farmer in Malaysia

The Issues

How Important Is Shrimp Farming? For many people in the world, shrimp is more than luxury food: It is a staple of their diet and their main source of animal protein. The demand for shrimp currently is greater than the natural supply in Earth's oceans. To meet the demand, many countries, including the United States, have turned to shrimp farming. Shrimp farms provide needed food and jobs that some people believe are worth a certain amount of damage to the environment. They feel it is not possible to have shrimp farms that are both highly productive and environmentally safe.

Can the Pollution Be Reduced? Shrimp farmers are exploring ways to reduce the impact of their farms on the coastal environment. Better pond construction can help stop chemicals from leaking into the surrounding waters. Some governments recognize the importance of mangrove forests in providing a habitat for many species and in protecting the shoreline. These governments have passed laws regulating where shrimp farms may be built. Farmers must investigate the impact their ponds will have on nearby mangrove forests and get approval before choosing a location. These methods of reducing environmental damage, however, are expensive and time-consuming for the shrimp farmers.

Should Farmers Use Alternative Methods? In some parts of Asia, a less destructive method of shrimp farming has been practiced for centuries. Raising shrimp in ditches dug around clusters of mangroves provides the young shrimp with a natural nutrient supply that includes debris from the trees. A gate keeps the shrimp from escaping into the ocean and also allows the motion of the tides to replenish the water in the ditches. The disadvantage of this method is that it is much less profitable than the constructed shrimp ponds. Many shrimp farmers could not afford to switch to this method. If they did, the price of shrimp worldwide would rise.

You Decide

1. Identify the Problem

In your own words, summarize the problem facing shrimp farmers.

2. Analyze the Options

Make a list of the solutions mentioned. List the advantages and drawbacks of each. Who would benefit from each plan? Who might suffer?

3. Find a Solution

Write a brochure or pamphlet for shrimp farmers that states your proposed solution to their problem. After you have written the text, illustrate your brochure.

CLEANING UP AN OIL SPILL

Oil Spill in Bay

An oil tanker hit a reef yesterday, spilling thousands of barrels of crude oil into the water. Cleanup efforts will begin today. Workers must race against time to save birds and sea otters. With stormy weather forecasted, however, scientists expect considerable damage. Volunteers are needed to help clean up.

Imagine that you are a volunteer helping to clean up an oil spill. In this activity, you will use a variety of materials to remove as much oil as possible from the water and to keep oil from reaching the beach. You will also see how oil affects animals that are exposed to a spill.

Problem

How can an oil spill be cleaned up?

Skills Focus

making models, forming operational definitions

Materials

water	shallow pan	vegetable oil
feather	paper cup	plastic dropper
paper towels	cotton balls	wooden sticks
marking pen	graduated cylinder, 100 mL	

Procedure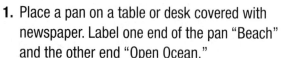

1. Place a pan on a table or desk covered with newspaper. Label one end of the pan "Beach" and the other end "Open Ocean."
2. Pour water into the pan to a depth of 2 cm.
3. Gently pour 20 mL of vegetable oil into the center of the pan. Record your observations.
4. Dip a feather and your finger into the oil. Observe how each is affected by the oil.
5. Try to wipe oil off the feather and your finger using paper towels. Record whether any oil is left on the feather or your skin.
6. Now try to clean up the spill. Record your observations with each step. First, using the wooden sticks, try to keep the oil from reaching the "beach." Next, gently blow across the surface of the water from the "open ocean" side to simulate wind and waves. Then use the cotton balls, paper towels, and dropper to recover as much of the oil as possible.
7. When you are finished, dispose of the oil and used items in the paper cup. Wash your hands.

Analyze and Conclude

1. How successful were you in cleaning up the oil? Is the water as clean as it was at the start?
2. How well were you able to keep the oil from reaching the beach? Describe how useful the different materials were in cleaning up the oil.
3. Describe what happened when you cleaned the feather and your finger. What might happen to fish, birds, and other animals if they were coated with oil as a result of an oil spill?
4. Predict how storms with strong winds and waves would affect the cleanup of an oil spill.
5. **Apply** Look at the used cleanup materials in the paper cup. What additional problems for cleanup crews does this suggest?

Getting Involved

One way to reduce the threat of oil spills is to transport less oil across the oceans. To make that possible, people would need to use less oil in their daily lives. Oil is used to heat homes, to produce gasoline, and to make products such as plastics and textiles. List at least three ways to reduce the amount of oil you and your family use.

SECTION 1 — Exploring the Ocean

Key Ideas

◆ Technology such as sonar enables scientists to study the deep ocean floor despite the darkness, cold, and extreme pressure there.

◆ The ocean floor has features similar to those found on the continents, including plains, mountain ranges, volcanoes, and trenches. These landforms are all formed by the interactions of Earth's moving plates.

◆ In the process of sea-floor spreading, new rock forms at the edges of diverging plates, and old rock sinks between converging plates.

Key Terms

sonar	continental shelf	continental slope
seamount	abyssal plain	mid-ocean ridge
trench	magma	plates
sea-floor spreading		

SECTION 2 — Life at the Ocean's Edge

INTEGRATING LIFE SCIENCE

Key Ideas

◆ Physical factors that affect marine organisms include salinity, water temperature, light, dissolved gases, nutrients, and wave action.

◆ Organisms in the rocky intertidal zone must be able to tolerate the pounding of the waves, as well as being both underwater and exposed to the air for long periods of time.

◆ Coastal wetlands include salt marshes and mangrove forests.

Key Terms

plankton	nekton	benthos
food web	intertidal zone	estuary
brackish		

SECTION 3 — The Neritic Zone and Open Ocean

INTEGRATING LIFE SCIENCE

Key Ideas

◆ The neritic zone receives sunlight and nutrients washed from the land. Habitats in this zone include kelp forests and coral reefs.

◆ The thin layer of sunlit water at the surface is the only part of the open ocean that can support algae, which need the sunlight to produce food. Other marine organisms depend on the food made by algae.

◆ The chemical nutrients in the hot water around a hydrothermal vent support the organisms that live around the vent.

Key Terms

neritic zone	open-ocean zone
holdfast	atoll
bioluminescence	hydrothermal vent

SECTION 4 — Resources From the Ocean

Key Ideas

◆ If used wisely, fisheries are a renewable resource. New fish will replace those that are caught, but only if overfishing does not reduce the population too severely.

◆ Nonliving resources from the ocean include dissolved substances in seawater and minerals and fuels from the ocean floor.

◆ Nations must cooperate to manage and protect the oceans.

Key Terms

aquaculture   nodules

ACTIVITY

USING THE INTERNET

www.science-explorer.phschool.com

Reviewing Content

For more review of key concepts, see the Interactive Student Tutorial CD-ROM.

Multiple Choice
Choose the letter of the best answer.

1. Earth's crust and upper mantle are made up of moving
   a. magma.
   b. plates.
   c. trenches.
   d. abyssal plains.

2. An area where rivers flow into the ocean and fresh water and salt water mix is a(n)
   a. tide pool.
   b. hydrothermal vent.
   c. estuary.
   d. kelp forest.

3. A tropical ocean community made by tiny animals that have algae growing in their tissues is a(n)
   a. mangrove forest.
   b. salt marsh.
   c. intertidal zone.
   d. coral reef.

4. In the open-ocean zone, organisms depend directly or indirectly on food that is made by
   a. marine mammals.
   b. nekton in the water column.
   c. plants growing on the deep ocean floor.
   d. algae near the surface.

5. Most ocean pollutants come from
   a. marine organisms.
   b. the land.
   c. the atmosphere.
   d. Earth's core.

True or False
If the statement is true, write true. If it is false, change the underlined word or words to make the statement true.

6. The mid-ocean ridge is formed where two plates <u>converge</u>.

7. The area between the high and low tide lines is the <u>neritic</u> zone.

8. Water that is partly salty and partly fresh is <u>brackish</u>.

9. A ring-shaped coral reef surrounding a lagoon is called a(n) <u>seamount</u>.

10. Many deep-sea fishes use their <u>bioluminescence</u> to attract prey.

Checking Concepts

11. Describe one method that has been used to study the ocean floor.

12. Describe three physical factors that organisms in the rocky intertidal zone must overcome.

13. Explain why estuaries are especially vulnerable to pollution.

14. Explain why scientists were surprised to discover the variety of organisms living around hydrothermal vents.

15. **Writing to Learn** Imagine that you are an "aquanaut" on a voyage of discovery across the ocean floor. Write a logbook entry that summarizes your observations as you travel from one continent to another. Include details about the shape of the ocean floor, as well as some organisms you encounter along your journey.

Thinking Visually

16. **Compare/Contrast Table** Copy the table about ocean habitats onto a separate sheet of paper. Then fill in the empty spaces and add a title. (See the Skills Handbook for more on compare/contrast tables.)

Habitat	Zone	Conditions	Organisms
Tide pool	Intertidal	a. ?	b. ?
Coral reef	c. ?	d. ?	Coral, fishes, shrimp, eels
Surface zone	Open ocean	e. ?	f. ?
Hydrothermal vent	g. ?	High pressure, dark, warm	h. ?

Applying Skills

Use the diagram of a portion of the ocean floor to answer Questions 17–19.

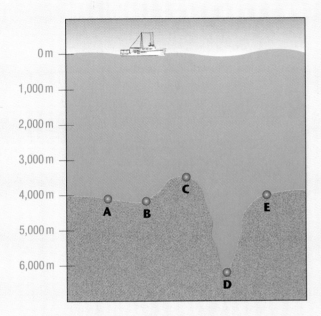

17. Interpreting Diagrams What is the approximate depth of the ocean floor at point A? At point C?

18. Inferring What might the feature between locations A and B be? The feature at point D?

19. Posing Questions What other information would help you determine whether point A or point E is closer to the mid-ocean ridge? Explain.

Thinking Critically

20. Classifying Classify each of the following organisms as plankton, nekton, or benthos: squid, sea stars, microscopic algae, whales, sea otters, anglerfish, and giant clams.

21. Making Generalizations Explain why many of the world's fisheries are located in the neritic zone.

22. Predicting Suppose the number of plankton in the ocean suddenly decreased to half their current number. Predict how this would affect other marine organisms.

23. Relating Cause and Effect How might fertilizers used on farmland result in ocean pollution near shore?

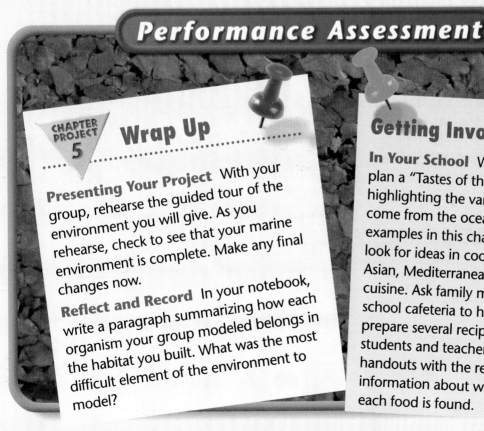

Performance Assessment

CHAPTER PROJECT 5 — Wrap Up

Presenting Your Project With your group, rehearse the guided tour of the environment you will give. As you rehearse, check to see that your marine environment is complete. Make any final changes now.

Reflect and Record In your notebook, write a paragraph summarizing how each organism your group modeled belongs in the habitat you built. What was the most difficult element of the environment to model?

Getting Involved

In Your School With your classmates, plan a "Tastes of the Sea" exhibition highlighting the variety of foods that come from the ocean. Besides the examples in this chapter, you might look for ideas in cookbooks featuring Asian, Mediterranean, and Caribbean cuisine. Ask family members and your school cafeteria to help your class prepare several recipes for other students and teachers to sample. Make handouts with the recipes and information about where in the ocean each food is found.

THE MISSISSIPPI

What would you name a river that—

- *carries about 420 million metric tons of cargo a year,*
- *drains 31 states and 2 Canadian provinces,*
- *looks like a tree that has a thin top trunk and 2 strong branches,*
- *flows at about 18,100 cubic meters of water per second?*

Native Americans called the river *misi sipi*, an Algonquin name meaning "big water," or "father of waters."

Have you ever traveled on a river or lake that feeds into the mighty Mississippi River? Perhaps you have but never realized it. The map below shows the watershed of this great river. From the west, the Missouri River — the "Big Muddy"— carries soft silt eroded from the Great Plains. The Missouri joins the Mississippi near St. Louis, turning the river's clear water to muddy brown. From the east, the Ohio River flows in from the rocky Appalachian plateau, nearly doubling the volume of water in the river. In all, the huge Mississippi watershed drains about 40 percent of the United States.

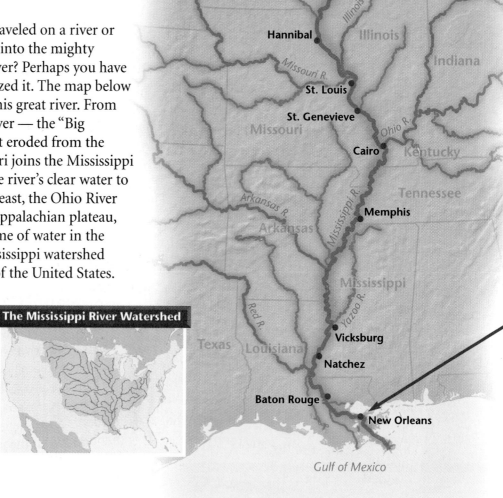

The Mississippi River starts at Lake Itasca and flows through 10 states to the Gulf of Mexico. The river is a drainage point for hundreds of tributaries in the vast Mississippi watershed. ▶

The Mississippi River Watershed

A National Trade Route

Since Native Americans settled in villages along the Mississippi around 1,200 years ago, the river has served as a water highway for trade and travel.

In the late 1600s, French explorers, fur traders, and soldiers arrived in the Mississippi Valley. They chose strategic sites for forts and fur-trading posts — Prairie du Chien, St. Louis, and St. Genevieve. At first, traders used canoes, rafts, and flatboats to carry goods downstream. But traveling up the river was difficult. Crews had to use long poles to push narrow keelboats upstream against the current.

In 1811, the arrival of *The New Orleans*, the first steamboat on the Mississippi River, changed the river forever. Within 40 years, there were hundreds more steamboats and many new river towns. On the upper Mississippi, the city of Minneapolis grew up around flour mills near the falls. Farther downstream, Memphis became a center for transporting cotton. Later, it was a stopping point for showboats and musicians. New Orleans quickly became a world port. It received cotton, tobacco, and sugar cane from southern plantations and exported corn, wheat and indigo to Europe. Imported luxury items, such as soap, coffee, shoes, and textiles, traveled upstream from the port of New Orleans. Up and down the river townspeople eagerly waited for the cry, "Steamboat comin'!"

▲ St. Anthony Falls is the northernmost point of navigation on the Mississippi.

▲ Crews in flatboats rode the river currents, steering with long oars.

▲ New Orleans has been a major trading port since its founding in 1718.

Social Studies Activity

Use the map to choose a city on the Mississippi River to learn about. Imagine that you are an early settler in the city. Write a letter to convince relatives to move to your city. Before writing, learn about the history, founding, and trade of the city. Look for answers to the following questions:

◆ Who founded the city? When was the city founded? Why did settlers decide to move there? Where did they come from?

◆ What part did the Mississippi River play in the city's founding?

◆ What other physical features were important to the city?

◆ Where did the city's name come from?

◆ What products were grown, bought, or sold there?

Taming the River

Navigating the sandbars, shallow water, and rocky rapids on the upper Mississippi River was treacherous for captains of ships and barges in the 1800s. To make traveling easier, engineers in the early 1900s built a "water staircase," a series of 29 locks and dams between Minneapolis, Minnesota, and Alton, Illinois, above St. Louis. A lock is an enclosed basin, with gates at each end. Locks allow engineers to raise or lower the water level in a certain area of the river. Between the locks on the upper Mississippi, the river forms wide pools of quiet water, maintaining a channel deep enough for large boats.

Use the diagrams to trace how a boat "locks through" as it travels upstream. This technology allowed boats to travel to cities on the upper Mississippi. ▶

① The lock gate opens. Your boat moves in and you tie up to the wall.

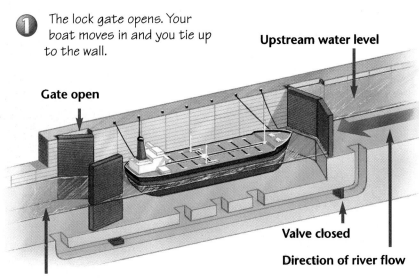

Gate open

Upstream water level

Valve closed

Direction of river flow

Downstream water level

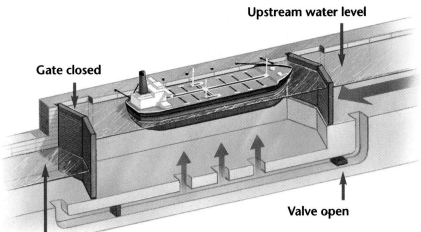

Upstream water level

Gate closed

Valve open

Downstream water level

② The gate closes, and water pours in. As water fills the lock—like a bathtub filling—it lifts the boat a meter or more. When the water in the lock is even with the water level upstream, the gates at the upstream end open. You untie your boat and move out into the river.

If you were going downstream, you would "lock through" in reverse. The water would empty out of the lock, lowering the water level to match the level downstream.

Science Activity

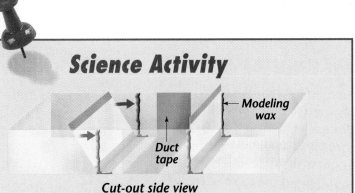

Modeling wax

Duct tape

Cut-out side view

Use a cardboard milk container to build a working model of a lock. Set up your lock following the illustration. Then demonstrate how your lock works, using a cork or pen cap as your ship and sailing it through the lock.

All Aboard

The whistle blows. The gleaming white steamboat pulls away from the dock just below Fort Snelling, Minnesota. You head downstream toward New Orleans. As you watch the paddlewheel splashing in the water, you think of the old-time steamboats that carried passengers up and down the Mississippi River in the 1800s.

Today you are cruising at a speed of 11.3 kilometers per hour. You want to stay awake until you enter Lock 3 at Red Wing, Minnesota. It's 4:30 P.M. on Monday now. You know that it's about 78.8 kilometers to Red Wing. It should take about 7 hours to reach the lock. So you'll be there at 11:30 P.M. and through the lock by midnight.

As your boat travels along the river, it will follow the schedule you see on this page. The highlight of your trip will be Mark Twain's hometown of Hannibal, Missouri. You will arrive there on Friday.

Look at the Upper Mississippi River schedule to answer the questions below. Distances are given from Fort Snelling.

◆ What is your average speed between Dubuque and Hannibal? Use the following equation:

$$speed = \frac{distance}{time}$$

Round to the nearest tenth.

◆ How long will you spend in Prairie du Chien?

◆ About how long does it take to travel from Prairie du Chien to Dubuque?

MISSISSIPPI RIVERBOAT SCHEDULE
MAY to SEPTEMBER

UPPER MISSISSIPPI RIVERBOAT SCHEDULE

Port	Arrival Time	Departure Time	Distance From Fort Snelling
Fort Snelling, MN		4:30 P.M. Mon.	0 km
Lock 3, Red Wing, MN	11:30 P.M. Mon.	12:00 midnight	78.8 km
Prairie du Chien, WI	11:00 P.M. Tues.	10:30 A.M. Wed.	337.8 km
Dubuque, IA	6:30 P.M. Wed.	7:00 P.M. Wed.	426.3 km
Hannibal, MO	1:00 A.M. Fri.	———	863.9 km

LOWER MISSISSIPPI RIVERBOAT SCHEDULE

Port	Arrival Time	Departure Time	Distance From Fort Snelling
Hannibal, MO		6 P.M. Fri.	863.9 km
Lock 26 at Alton, IL	a. ?	b. ?	1033 km
St. Louis, MO	c. ?	d. ?	1070.7 km
Cape Girardeau, MO	6:30 A.M. Sun.	———	e. ?

Math Activity

Now complete the riverboat schedule for the Lower Mississippi. Your boat will leave Hannibal at 6 P.M. Friday and will travel at a speed of 14.7 kilometers per hour for the rest of the journey.

◆ When will you arrive at Lock 26?

◆ You spend 34 minutes in the lock. When will you depart from Lock 26? Your boat travels on. When will it arrive in St. Louis?

◆ The boat will spend 4 hours in St. Louis and head to Cape Girardeau, arriving at 6:30 A.M. Sunday. How far is it from St. Louis to Cape Girardeau?

Mark Three! Mark Twain!

To steer a boat on the Mississippi, early riverboat pilots had to memorize landmarks at every bend and curve of the river, going both upstream and down. They had to know where the channel was deep enough for the boat, where the current was strong, where there were sandbars or sunken logs.

When Samuel Clemens was growing up in the small river town of Hannibal, Missouri, his ambition was to become a Mississippi River steamboat pilot. He was a pilot for a while. Later he became one of America's most famous writers, using the pen name Mark Twain. In the passage below from his book *Life on the Mississippi*, Twain describes a lesson he learned from an experienced pilot, Mr. Bixby.

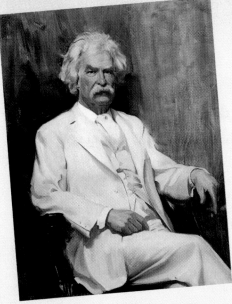

What's in a Name?

Mark Twain's name comes from a term that steamboat crews used to measure the depth of river water. *Twain* means "two." Dropping a weighted line, they would call out the depth: "Mark twain!"—2 fathoms deep; "Mark three!"—3 fathoms deep. (Note: One fathom equals 1.8 meters.)

"My boy," [Bixby said] "you've got to know the shape of the river perfectly. It is all there is left to steer by on a very dark night. Everything else is blotted out and gone. But mind you, it hasn't the same shape in the night that it has in the daytime."

"How on earth am I ever going to learn it, then?"

"How do you follow a hall at home in the dark? Because you know the shape of it. You can't see it."

"Do you mean to say that I've got to know all the million trifling variations of shape in the banks of this interminable [endless] river as well as I know the shape of the front hall at home?"

"On my honor, you've got to know them better than any man ever did know the shapes of the halls in his own house."

"I wish I was dead!"

"Now I don't want to discourage you, but —. . . . You see, this has got to be learned; there isn't any getting around it. . .

The river is a very different shape on a pitch-dark night from what it is on a starlight night. All shores seem to be straight lines, then, and mighty dim ones, too; and you'd run them for straight lines, only you know better. . . . Then there's your gray mist. You take a night when there's one of these grisly, drizzly gray mists, and then there isn't any particular shape to a shore. A gray mist would tangle the head of the oldest man that ever lived. Well, then, different kinds of moonlight change the shape of the river in different ways. You see —"

"Oh, don't say any more, please! Have I got to learn the shape of the river according to all these five hundred thousand different ways? If I tried to carry all that cargo in my head, it would make me stoop-shouldered."

"No! You only learn the shape of the river; and you learn it with such absolute certainty that you can always steer by the shape that's in your head, and never mind the one that's before your eyes."

Language Arts Activity

Read the excerpt, focusing on what the dialogue tells you about the characters of Mark Twain and Mr. Bixby.

◆ What lesson does Mark Twain learn?

◆ How does Mr. Bixby feel about the Mississippi River? How can you tell?

Now, use dialogue to write an ending to this riverboat excerpt. Before you begin writing, think carefully about the characters, setting, and your conclusion.

Riverboat captains were licensed to navigate the river. ▶

Tie It Together

Celebrate the River

Plan a class fair featuring cities on the Mississippi River today, such as St. Louis (above). Set up a booth for each city and create a travel brochure to persuade people to visit.

As a team, choose a city to represent. Then divide up tasks so different members find information on the following topics:

◆ Interesting attractions and events that your city offers— zoos, museums, parks, sports events, music festivals, and so on.

◆ Influences of different groups on the city's food, customs, music, and architecture.

◆ Physical features of the area around the city.

◆ Famous people—writers, political figures, entertainers—who lived there.

◆ Historic places to visit, such as monuments, houses, battlefields, and statues.

◆ Illustrations and pictures of special attractions.

◆ Maps of walking tours and historic areas.

◆ Native plants and animals in the area.

Before starting your brochure, decide which attractions to highlight. Think of a slogan for your travel campaign. If you wish, make a poster. Celebrate life on the river today.

Think Like a Scientist

Although you may not know it, you think like a scientist every day. Whenever you ask a question and explore possible answers, you use many of the same skills that scientists do. Some of these skills are described on this page.

Observing

When you use one or more of your five senses to gather information about the world, you are **observing**. Hearing a dog bark, counting twelve green seeds, and smelling smoke are all observations. To increase the power of their senses, scientists sometimes use microscopes, telescopes, or other instruments that help them make more detailed observations.

An observation must be factual and accurate—an exact report of what your senses detect. It is important to keep careful records of your observations in science class by writing or drawing in a notebook. The information collected through observations is called evidence or data.

Inferring

When you explain or interpret an observation, you are **inferring**, or making an inference. For example, if you hear your dog barking, you may infer that someone is at your front door. To make this inference, you combine the evidence—the barking dog— and your experience or knowledge—you know that your dog barks when strangers approach—to reach a logical conclusion.

Notice that an inference is not a fact; it is only one of many possible explanations for an observation. For example, your dog may be barking because it wants to go for a walk. An inference may turn out to be incorrect even if it is based on accurate observations and logical reasoning. The only way to find out if an inference is correct is to investigate further.

Predicting

When you listen to the weather forecast, you hear many predictions about the next day's weather—what the temperature will be, whether it will rain, and how windy it will be. Weather forecasters use observations and knowledge of weather patterns to predict the weather. The skill of **predicting** involves making an inference about a future event based on current evidence or past experience.

Because a prediction is an inference, it may prove to be false. In science class, you can test some of your predictions by doing experiments. For example, suppose you predict that larger paper airplanes can fly farther than smaller airplanes. How could you test your prediction?

ACTIVITY Use the photograph to answer the questions below.

Observing Look closely at the photograph. List at least three observations.

Inferring Use your observations to make an inference about what has happened. What experience or knowledge did you use to make the inference?

Predicting Predict what will happen next. On what evidence or experience do you base your prediction?

Classifying

Could you imagine searching for a book in the library if the books were shelved in no particular order? Your trip to the library would be an all-day event! Luckily, librarians group together books on similar topics or by the same author. Grouping together items that are alike in some way is called **classifying**. You can classify items in many ways: by size, by shape, by use, and by other important characteristics.

Like librarians, scientists use the skill of classifying to organize information and objects. When things are sorted into groups, the relationships among them become easier to understand.

Classify the objects in the photograph into two groups based on any characteristic you choose. Then use another characteristic to classify the objects into three groups. **ACTIVITY**

Making Models

This student is using a model to demonstrate what causes day and night on Earth. What do the flashlight and the tennis ball in the model represent? **ACTIVITY**

Have you ever drawn a picture to help someone understand what you were saying? Such a drawing is one type of model. A model is a picture, diagram, computer image, or other representation of a complex object or process. **Making models** helps people understand things that they cannot observe directly.

Scientists often use models to represent things that are either very large or very small, such as the planets in the solar system, or the parts of a cell. Such models are physical models—drawings or three-dimensional structures that look like the real thing. Other models are mental models—mathematical equations or words that describe how something works.

Communicating

Whenever you talk on the phone, write a letter, or listen to your teacher at school, you are communicating. **Communicating** is the process of sharing ideas and information with other people. Communicating effectively requires many skills, including writing, reading, speaking, listening, and making models.

Scientists communicate to share results, information, and opinions. Scientists often communicate about their work in journals, over the telephone, in

letters, and on the Internet. They also attend scientific meetings where they share their ideas with one another in person.

On a sheet of paper, write out clear, detailed directions for tying your shoe. Then exchange directions with a partner. Follow your partner's directions exactly. How successful were you at tying your shoe? How could your partner have communicated more clearly? **ACTIVITY**

Making Measurements

When scientists make observations, it is not sufficient to say that something is "big" or "heavy." Instead, scientists use instruments to measure just how big or heavy an object is. By measuring, scientists can express their observations more precisely and communicate more information about what they observe.

Measuring in SI

The standard system of measurement used by scientists around the world is known as the International System of Units, which is abbreviated as SI (in French, *Système International d'Unités*). SI units are easy to use because they are based on multiples of 10. Each unit is ten times larger than the next smallest unit and one tenth the size of the next largest unit. The table lists the prefixes used to name the most common SI units.

Common SI Prefixes

Prefix	Symbol	Meaning
kilo-	k	1,000
hecto-	h	100
deka-	da	10
deci-	d	0.1 (one tenth)
centi-	c	0.01 (one hundredth)
milli-	m	0.001 (one thousandth)

Length To measure length, or the distance between two points, the unit of measure is the **meter (m)**. One meter is the approximate distance from the floor to a doorknob. Long distances, such as the distance between two cities, are measured in kilometers (km). Small lengths are measured in centimeters (cm) or millimeters (mm). Scientists use metric rulers and meter sticks to measure length.

Common Conversions

1 km = 1,000 m
1 m = 100 cm
1 m = 1,000 mm
1 cm = 10 mm

The larger lines on the metric ruler in the picture show centimeter divisions, while the smaller, unnumbered lines show millimeter divisions. How many centimeters long is the shell? How many millimeters long is it? **ACTIVITY**

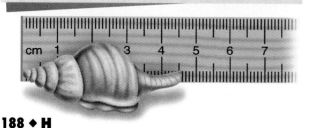

Liquid Volume To measure the volume of a liquid, or the amount of space a liquid takes up, you will use a unit of measure known as the **liter (L)**. One liter is the approximate volume of a medium-sized carton of milk. Smaller volumes are measured in milliliters (mL). Scientists use graduated cylinders to measure liquid volume.

Common Conversion

1 L = 1,000 mL

The graduated cylinder in the picture is marked in milliliter divisions. Notice that the water in the cylinder has a curved surface. This curved surface is called the *meniscus*. To measure the volume, you must read the level at the lowest point of the meniscus. What is the volume of water in this graduated cylinder? **ACTIVITY**

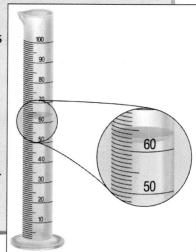

Mass To measure mass, or the amount of matter in an object, you will use a unit of measure known as the **gram (g)**. One gram is approximately the mass of a paper clip. Larger masses are measured in kilograms (kg). Scientists use a balance to find the mass of an object.

Common Conversion

1 kg = 1,000 g

The electronic balance displays the mass of an apple in kilograms. What is the mass of the apple? Suppose a recipe for applesauce called for one kilogram of apples. About how many apples would you need?

Temperature
To measure the temperature of a substance, you will use the **Celsius scale**. Temperature is measured in degrees Celsius (°C) using a Celsius thermometer. Water freezes at 0°C and boils at 100°C.

ACTIVITY
What is the temperature of the liquid in degrees Celsius?

Converting SI Units

To use the SI system, you must know how to convert between units. Converting from one unit to another involves the skill of **calculating**, or using mathematical operations. Converting between SI units is similar to converting between dollars and dimes because both systems are based on multiples of ten.

Suppose you want to convert a length of 80 centimeters to meters. Follow these steps to convert between units.

1. Begin by writing down the measurement you want to convert—in this example, 80 centimeters.
2. Write a conversion factor that represents the relationship between the two units you are converting. In this example, the relationship is *1 meter = 100 centimeters*. Write this conversion factor as a fraction, making sure to place the units you are converting from (centimeters, in this example) in the denominator.

3. Multiply the measurement you want to convert by the fraction. When you do this, the units in the first measurement will cancel out with the units in the denominator. Your answer will be in the units you are converting to (meters, in this example).

Example

80 centimeters = ____?____ meters

$$80 \text{ centimeters} \times \frac{1 \text{ meter}}{100 \text{ centimeters}} = \frac{80 \text{ meters}}{100}$$

$$= 0.8 \text{ meters}$$

Convert between the following units.
1. 600 millimeters = __?__ meters
2. 0.35 liters = __?__ milliliters
3. 1,050 grams = __?__ kilograms

Conducting a Scientific Investigation

In some ways, scientists are like detectives, piecing together clues to learn about a process or event. One way that scientists gather clues is by carrying out experiments. An experiment tests an idea in a careful, orderly manner. Although all experiments do not follow the same steps in the same order, many follow a pattern similar to the one described here.

Posing Questions

Experiments begin by asking a scientific question. A scientific question is one that can be answered by gathering evidence. For example, the question "Which freezes faster— fresh water or salt water?" is a scientific question because you can carry out an investigation and gather information to answer the question.

Developing a Hypothesis

The next step is to form a hypothesis. A **hypothesis** is a prediction about the outcome of the experiment. Like all predictions, hypotheses are based on your observations and previous knowledge or experience. But, unlike many predictions, a hypothesis must be something that can be tested. A properly worded hypothesis should take the form of an *If . . . then* statement. For example, a hypothesis might be *"If I add salt to fresh water, then the water will take longer to freeze."* A hypothesis worded this way serves as a rough outline of the experiment you should perform.

Designing an Experiment

Next you need to plan a way to test your hypothesis. Your plan should be written out as a step-by-step procedure and should describe the observations or measurements you will make.

Two important steps involved in designing an experiment are controlling variables and forming operational definitions.

Controlling Variables In a well-designed experiment, you need to keep all variables the same except for one. A **variable** is any factor that can change in an experiment. The factor that you change is called the **manipulated variable.** In this experiment, the manipulated variable is the amount of salt added to the water. Other factors, such as the amount of water or the starting temperature, are kept constant.

The factor that changes as a result of the manipulated variable is called the responding variable. The **responding variable** is what you measure or observe to obtain your results. In this experiment, the responding variable is how long the water takes to freeze.

An experiment in which all factors except one are kept constant is a **controlled experiment**. Most controlled experiments include a test called the control. In this experiment, Container 3 is the control. Because no salt is added to Container 3, you can compare the results from the other containers to it. Any difference in results must be due to the addition of salt alone.

Forming Operational Definitions
Another important aspect of a well-designed experiment is having clear operational definitions. An **operational definition** is a statement that describes how a particular variable is to be measured or how a term is to be defined. For example, in this experiment, how will you determine if the water has frozen? You might decide to insert a stick in each container at the start of the experiment. Your operational definition of "frozen" would be the time at which the stick can no longer move.

EXPERIMENTAL PROCEDURE

1. Fill 3 containers with 300 milliliters of cold tap water.

2. Add 10 grams of salt to Container 1; stir. Add 20 grams of salt to Container 2; stir. Add no salt to Container 3.

3. Place the 3 containers in a freezer.

4. Check the containers every 15 minutes. Record your observations.

Interpreting Data

The observations and measurements you make in an experiment are called data. At the end of an experiment, you need to analyze the data to look for any patterns or trends. Patterns often become clear if you organize your data in a data table or graph. Then think through what the data reveal. Do they support your hypothesis? Do they point out a flaw in your experiment? Do you need to collect more data?

Drawing Conclusions

A conclusion is a statement that sums up what you have learned from an experiment. When you draw a conclusion, you need to decide whether the data you collected support your hypothesis or not. You may need to repeat an experiment several times before you can draw any conclusions from it. Conclusions often lead you to pose new questions and plan new experiments to answer them.

Is a ball's bounce affected by the height from which it is dropped? Using the steps just described, plan a controlled experiment to investigate this problem. **ACTIVITY**

Thinking Critically

Has a friend ever asked for your advice about a problem? If so, you may have helped your friend think through the problem in a logical way. Without knowing it, you used critical-thinking skills to help your friend. Critical thinking involves the use of reasoning and logic to solve problems or make decisions. Some critical-thinking skills are described below.

Comparing and Contrasting

When you examine two objects for similarities and differences, you are using the skill of **comparing and contrasting**. Comparing involves identifying similarities, or common characteristics. Contrasting involves identifying differences. Analyzing objects in this way can help you discover details that you might otherwise overlook.

ACTIVITY Compare and contrast the two animals in the photo. First list all the similarities that you see. Then list all the differences.

Applying Concepts

When you use your knowledge about one situation to make sense of a similar situation, you are using the skill of **applying concepts**. Being able to transfer your knowledge from one situation to another shows that you truly understand a concept. You may use this skill in answering test questions that present different problems from the ones you've reviewed in class.

ACTIVITY You have just learned that water takes longer to freeze when other substances are mixed into it. Use this knowledge to explain why people need a substance called antifreeze in their car's radiator in the winter.

Interpreting Illustrations

Diagrams, photographs, and maps are included in textbooks to help clarify what you read. These illustrations show processes, places, and ideas in a visual manner. The skill called **interpreting illustrations** can help you learn from these visual elements. To understand an illustration, take the time to study the illustration along with all the written information that accompanies it. Captions identify the key concepts shown in the illustration. Labels point out the important parts of a diagram or map, while keys identify the symbols used in a map.

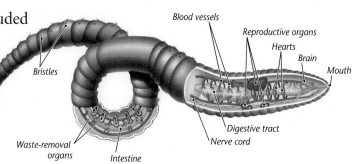

Blood vessels
Reproductive organs
Hearts
Brain
Mouth
Bristles
Digestive tract
Nerve cord
Waste-removal organs
Intestine

▲ **Internal anatomy of an earthworm**

ACTIVITY Study the diagram above. Then write a short paragraph explaining what you have learned.

Relating Cause and Effect

If one event causes another event to occur, the two events are said to have a cause-and-effect relationship. When you determine that such a relationship exists between two events, you use a skill called **relating cause and effect**. For example, if you notice an itchy, red bump on your skin, you might infer that a mosquito bit you. The mosquito bite is the cause, and the bump is the effect.

It is important to note that two events do not necessarily have a cause-and-effect relationship just because they occur together. Scientists carry out experiments or use past experience to determine whether a cause-and-effect relationship exists.

ACTIVITY You are on a camping trip and your flashlight has stopped working. List some possible causes for the flashlight malfunction. How could you determine which cause-and-effect relationship has left you in the dark?

Making Generalizations

When you draw a conclusion about an entire group based on information about only some of the group's members, you are using a skill called **making generalizations**. For a generalization to be valid, the sample you choose must be large enough and representative of the entire group. You might, for example, put this skill to work at a farm stand if you see a sign that says, "Sample some grapes before you buy." If you sample a few sweet grapes, you may conclude that all the grapes are sweet—and purchase a large bunch.

ACTIVITY A team of scientists needs to determine whether the water in a large reservoir is safe to drink. How could they use the skill of making generalizations to help them? What should they do?

Making Judgments

When you evaluate something to decide whether it is good or bad, or right or wrong, you are using a skill called **making judgments**. For example, you make judgments when you decide to eat healthful foods or to pick up litter in a park. Before you make a judgment, you need to think through the pros and cons of a situation, and identify the values or standards that you hold.

ACTIVITY Should children and teens be required to wear helmets when bicycling? Explain why you feel the way you do.

Problem Solving

When you use critical-thinking skills to resolve an issue or decide on a course of action, you are using a skill called **problem solving**. Some problems, such as how to convert a fraction into a decimal, are straightforward. Other problems, such as figuring out why your computer has stopped working, are complex. Some complex problems can be solved using the trial and error method—try out one solution first, and if that doesn't work, try another. Other useful problem-solving strategies include making models and brainstorming possible solutions with a partner.

Organizing Information

As you read this textbook, how can you make sense of all the information it contains? Some useful tools to help you organize information are shown on this page. These tools are called *graphic organizers* because they give you a visual picture of a topic, showing at a glance how key concepts are related.

Concept Maps

Concept maps are useful tools for organizing information on broad topics. A concept map begins with a general concept and shows how it can be broken down into more specific concepts. In that way, relationships between concepts become easier to understand.

A concept map is constructed by placing concept words (usually nouns) in ovals and connecting them with linking words. The most general concept word is placed at the top, and the words become more specific as you move downward. The linking words, which are written on a line extending between two ovals, describe the relationship between the two concepts they connect. If you follow any string of concepts and linking words down the map, it should read like a sentence.

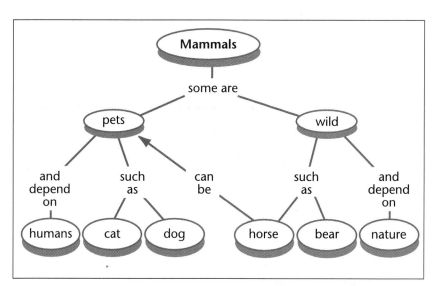

Some concept maps include linking words that connect a concept on one branch of the map to a concept on another branch. These linking words, called cross-linkages, show more complex interrelationships among concepts.

Compare/Contrast Tables

Compare/contrast tables are useful tools for sorting out the similarities and differences between two or more items. A table provides an organized framework in which to compare items based on specific characteristics that you identify.

To create a compare/contrast table, list the items to be compared across the top of a table. Then list the characteristics that will form the basis of your comparison in the left-hand

Characteristic	Baseball	Basketball
Number of Players	9	5
Playing Field	Baseball diamond	Basketball court
Equipment	bat, baseball, mitts	basket, basketball

column. Complete the table by filling in information about each characteristic, first for one item and then for the other.

Venn Diagrams

Another way to show similarities and differences between items is with a Venn diagram. A Venn diagram consists of two or more circles that partially overlap. Each circle represents a particular concept or idea. Common characteristics, or similarities, are written within the area of overlap between the two circles. Unique characteristics, or differences, are written in the parts of the circles outside the area of overlap.

To create a Venn diagram, draw two overlapping circles. Label the circles with the names of the items being compared. Write the

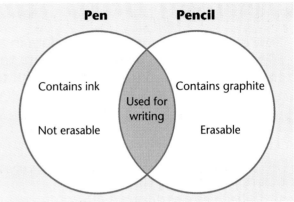

unique characteristics in each circle outside the area of overlap. Then write the shared characteristics within the area of overlap.

Flowcharts

A flowchart can help you understand the order in which certain events have occurred or should occur. Flowcharts are useful for outlining the stages in a process or the steps in a procedure.

To make a flowchart, write a brief description of each event in a box. Place the first event at the top of the page, followed by the second event, the third event, and so on. Then draw an arrow to connect each event to the one that occurs next.

Preparing Pasta

Boil water
↓
Cook pasta
↓
Drain water
↓
Add sauce

Cycle Diagrams

A cycle diagram can be used to show a sequence of events that is continuous, or cyclical. A continuous sequence does not have an end because, when the final event is over, the first event begins again. Like a flowchart, a cycle diagram can help you understand the order of events.

To create a cycle diagram, write a brief description of each event in a box. Place one event at the top of the page in the center. Then, moving in a clockwise direction around an imaginary circle, write each event in its proper sequence. Draw arrows to connect each event to the one that occurs next to form a continuous circle.

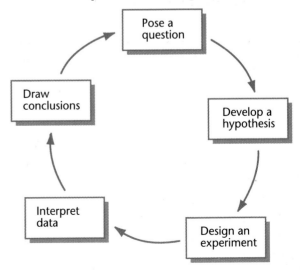

Steps in a Science Experiment

Creating Data Tables and Graphs

How can you make sense of the data in a science experiment? The first step is to organize the data to help you understand them. Data tables and graphs are helpful tools for organizing data.

Data Tables

You have gathered your materials and set up your experiment. But before you start, you need to plan a way to record what happens during the experiment. By creating a data table, you can record your observations and measurements in an orderly way.

Suppose, for example, that a scientist conducted an experiment to find out how many Calories people of different body masses burn while doing various activities. The data table shows the results.

Notice in the data table that the manipulated variable (body mass) is the heading of one column. The responding variable (for Experiment 1, the number of Calories burned while bicycling) is the heading of the next column. Additional columns were added for related experiments.

CALORIES BURNED IN 30 MINUTES OF ACTIVITY			
Body Mass	Experiment 1 Bicycling	Experiment 2 Playing Basketball	Experiment 3 Watching Television
30 kg	60 Calories	120 Calories	21 Calories
40 kg	77 Calories	164 Calories	27 Calories
50 kg	95 Calories	206 Calories	33 Calories
60 kg	114 Calories	248 Calories	38 Calories

Bar Graphs

To compare how many Calories a person burns doing various activities, you could create a bar graph. A bar graph is used to display data in a number of separate, or distinct, categories. In this example, bicycling, playing basketball, and watching television are three separate categories.

To create a bar graph, follow these steps.

1. On graph paper, draw a horizontal, or *x*-, axis and a vertical, or *y*-, axis.
2. Write the names of the categories to be graphed along the horizontal axis. Include an overall label for the axis as well.
3. Label the vertical axis with the name of the responding variable. Include units of measurement. Then create a scale along the axis by marking off equally spaced numbers that cover the range of the data collected.
4. For each category, draw a solid bar using the scale on the vertical axis to determine the appropriate height. For example, for bicycling, draw the bar as high as the 60 mark on the vertical axis. Make all the bars the same width and leave equal spaces between them.
5. Add a title that describes the graph.

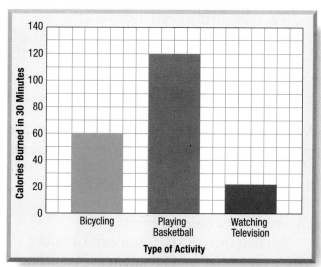

Calories Burned by a 30-kilogram Person in Various Activities

Line Graphs

To see whether a relationship exists between body mass and the number of Calories burned while bicycling, you could create a line graph. A line graph is used to display data that show how one variable (the responding variable) changes in response to another variable (the manipulated variable). You can use a line graph when your manipulated variable is *continuous*, that is, when there are other points between the ones that you tested. In this example, body mass is a continuous variable because there are other body masses between 30 and 40 kilograms (for example, 31 kilograms). Time is another example of a continuous variable.

Line graphs are powerful tools because they allow you to estimate values for conditions that you did not test in the experiment. For example, you can use the line graph to estimate that a 35-kilogram person would burn 68 Calories while bicycling.

To create a line graph, follow these steps.

1. On graph paper, draw a horizontal, or *x*-, axis and a vertical, or *y*-, axis.
2. Label the horizontal axis with the name of the manipulated variable. Label the vertical axis with the name of the responding variable. Include units of measurement.
3. Create a scale on each axis by marking off equally spaced numbers that cover the range of the data collected.
4. Plot a point on the graph for each piece of data. In the line graph above, the dotted lines show how to plot the first data point (30 kilograms and 60 Calories). Draw an imaginary vertical line extending up from the horizontal axis at the 30-kilogram mark. Then draw an imaginary horizontal line extending across from the vertical axis at the 60-Calorie mark. Plot the point where the two lines intersect.

Effect of Body Mass on Calories Burned While Bicycling

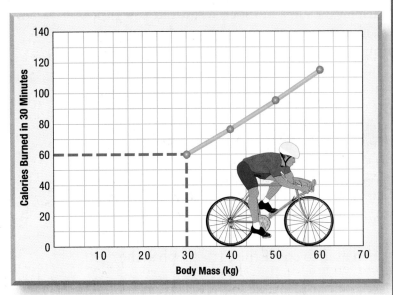

5. Connect the plotted points with a solid line. (In some cases, it may be more appropriate to draw a line that shows the general trend of the plotted points. In those cases, some of the points may fall above or below the line.)
6. Add a title that identifies the variables or relationship in the graph.

ACTIVITY

Create line graphs to display the data from Experiment 2 and Experiment 3 in the data table.

ACTIVITY

You read in the newspaper that a total of 4 centimeters of rain fell in your area in June, 2.5 centimeters fell in July, and 1.5 centimeters fell in August. What type of graph would you use to display these data? Use graph paper to create the graph.

Circle Graphs

Like bar graphs, circle graphs can be used to display data in a number of separate categories. Unlike bar graphs, however, circle graphs can only be used when you have data for *all* the categories that make up a given topic. A circle graph is sometimes called a pie chart because it resembles a pie cut into slices. The pie represents the entire topic, while the slices represent the individual categories. The size of a slice indicates what percentage of the whole a particular category makes up.

The data table below shows the results of a survey in which 24 teenagers were asked to identify their favorite sport. The data were then used to create the circle graph at the right.

Sports That Teens Prefer

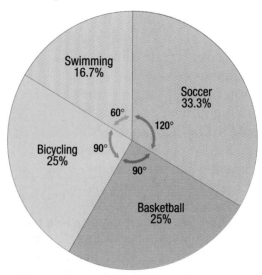

FAVORITE SPORTS	
Sport	Number of Students
Soccer	8
Basketball	6
Bicycling	6
Swimming	4

To create a circle graph, follow these steps.

1. Use a compass to draw a circle. Mark the center of the circle with a point. Then draw a line from the center point to the top of the circle.

2. Determine the size of each "slice" by setting up a proportion where x equals the number of degrees in a slice. (NOTE: A circle contains 360 degrees.) For example, to find the number of degrees in the "soccer" slice, set up the following proportion:

$$\frac{\text{students who prefer soccer}}{\text{total number of students}} = \frac{x}{\text{total number of degrees in a circle}}$$

$$\frac{8}{24} = \frac{x}{360}$$

Cross-multiply and solve for x.

$$24x = 8 \times 360$$
$$x = 120$$

The "soccer" slice should contain 120 degrees.

3. Use a protractor to measure the angle of the first slice, using the line you drew to the top of the circle as the 0° line. Draw a line from the center of the circle to the edge for the angle you measured.

4. Continue around the circle by measuring out the size of each slice with the protractor. Start measuring from the edge of the previous slice so the wedges do not overlap. When you are done, the entire circle should be filled in.

5. Determine the percentage of the whole circle that each slice represents. To do this, divide the number of degrees in a slice by the total number of degrees in a circle (360), and multiply by 100%. For the "soccer" slice, you can find the percentage as follows:

$$\frac{120}{360} \times 100\% = 33.3\%$$

6. Use a different color to shade in each slice. Label each slice with the name of the category and with the percentage of the whole it represents.

7. Add a title to the circle graph.

In a class of 28 students, 12 students **ACTIVITY** take the bus to school, 10 students walk, and 6 students ride their bicycles. Create a circle graph to display these data.

Laboratory Safety

Safety Symbols

These symbols alert you to possible dangers in the laboratory and remind you to work carefully.

Safety Goggles Always wear safety goggles to protect your eyes in any activity involving chemicals, flames or heating, or the possibility of broken glassware.

Lab Apron Wear a laboratory apron to protect your skin and clothing from damage.

Breakage You are working with materials that may be breakable, such as glass containers, glass tubing, thermometers, or funnels. Handle breakable materials with care. Do not touch broken glassware.

Heat-resistant Gloves Use an oven mitt or other hand protection when handling hot materials. Hot plates, hot glassware, or hot water can cause burns. Do not touch hot objects with your bare hands.

Heating Use a clamp or tongs to pick up hot glassware. Do not touch hot objects with your bare hands.

Sharp Object Pointed-tip scissors, scalpels, knives, needles, pins, or tacks are sharp. They can cut or puncture your skin. Always direct a sharp edge or point away from yourself and others. Use sharp instruments only as instructed.

Electric Shock Avoid the possibility of electric shock. Never use electrical equipment around water, or when the equipment is wet or your hands are wet. Be sure cords are untangled and cannot trip anyone. Disconnect the equipment when it is not in use.

Corrosive Chemical You are working with an acid or another corrosive chemical. Avoid getting it on your skin or clothing, or in your eyes. Do not inhale the vapors. Wash your hands when you are finished with the activity.

Poison Do not let any poisonous chemical come in contact with your skin and do not inhale its vapors. Wash your hands when you are finished with the activity.

Physical Safety When an experiment involves physical activity, take precautions to avoid injuring yourself or others. Follow instructions from your teacher. Alert your teacher if there is any reason you should not participate in the activity.

Animal Safety Treat live animals with care to avoid harming the animals or yourself. Working with animal parts or preserved animals also may require caution. Wash your hands when you are finished with the activity.

Plant Safety Handle plants in the laboratory or during field work only as directed by your teacher. If you are allergic to certain plants, tell your teacher before doing an activity in which those plants are used. Avoid touching harmful plants such as poison ivy, poison oak, or poison sumac, or plants with thorns. Wash your hands when you are finished with the activity.

Flames You may be working with flames from a lab burner, candle, or matches. Tie back loose hair and clothing. Follow instructions from your teacher about lighting and extinguishing flames.

No Flames Flammable materials may be present. Make sure there are no flames, sparks, or other exposed heat sources present.

Fumes When poisonous or unpleasant vapors may be involved, work in a ventilated area. Avoid inhaling vapors directly. Only test an odor when directed to do so by your teacher, and use a wafting motion to direct the vapor toward your nose.

Disposal Chemicals and other laboratory materials used in the activity must be disposed of safely. Follow the instructions from your teacher.

Hand Washing Wash your hands thoroughly when finished with the activity. Use antibacterial soap and warm water. Lather both sides of your hands and between your fingers. Rinse well.

General Safety Awareness You may see this symbol when none of the symbols described earlier appears. In this case, follow the specific instructions provided. You may also see this symbol when you are asked to develop your own procedure in a lab. Have your teacher approve your plan before you go further.

Science Safety Rules

To prepare yourself to work safely in the laboratory, read over the following safety rules. Then read them a second time. Make sure you understand and follow each rule. Ask your teacher to explain any rules you do not understand.

Dress Code

1. To protect yourself from injuring your eyes, wear safety goggles whenever you work with chemicals, burners, glassware, or any substance that might get into your eyes. If you wear contact lenses, wear your safety goggles and notify your teacher.
2. Wear a lab apron or coat whenever you work with corrosive chemicals or substances that can stain.
3. Tie back long hair to keep it away from any chemicals, flames, or equipment.
4. Remove or tie back any article of clothing or jewelry that can hang down and touch chemicals, flames, or equipment. Roll up or secure long sleeves.
5. Never wear open shoes or sandals.

General Precautions

6. Read all directions for an experiment several times before beginning the activity. Carefully follow all written and oral instructions. If you are in doubt about any part of the experiment, ask your teacher for assistance.
7. Never perform activities that are not assigned or authorized by your teacher. Obtain permission before "experimenting" on your own. Never handle any equipment unless you have specific permission.
8. Never perform lab activities without direct supervision.
9. Never eat or drink in the laboratory.
10. Keep work areas clean and tidy at all times. Bring only notebooks and lab manuals or written lab procedures to the work area. All other items, such as purses and backpacks, should be left in a designated area.
11. Do not engage in horseplay.

First Aid

12. Always report all accidents or injuries to your teacher, no matter how minor. Notify your teacher immediately about any fires.
13. Learn what to do in case of specific accidents, such as getting acid in your eyes or on your skin. (Rinse acids from your body with lots of water.)
14. Be aware of the location of the first-aid kit, but do not use it unless instructed by your teacher. In case of injury, your teacher should administer first aid. Your teacher may also send you to the school nurse or call a physician.
15. Know the location of emergency equipment, such as the fire extinguisher and fire blanket, and know how to use it.
16. Know the location of the nearest telephone and whom to contact in an emergency.

Heating and Fire Safety

17. Never use a heat source, such as a candle, burner, or hot plate, without wearing safety goggles.
18. Never heat anything unless instructed to do so. A chemical that is harmless when cool may be dangerous when heated.
19. Keep all combustible materials away from flames. Never use a flame or spark near a combustible chemical.
20. Never reach across a flame.
21. Before using a laboratory burner, make sure you know proper procedures for lighting and adjusting the burner, as demonstrated by your teacher. Do not touch the burner. It may be hot. And never leave a lighted burner unattended!
22. Chemicals can splash or boil out of a heated test tube. When heating a substance in a test tube, make sure that the mouth of the tube is not pointed at you or anyone else.
23. Never heat a liquid in a closed container. The expanding gases produced may blow the container apart.
24. Before picking up a container that has been heated, hold the back of your hand near it. If you can feel the heat on the back of your hand, the container is too hot to handle. Use an oven mitt to pick up a container that has been heated.

Using Chemicals Safely

25. Never mix chemicals "for the fun of it." You might produce a dangerous, possibly explosive substance.

26. Never put your face near the mouth of a container that holds chemicals. Never touch, taste, or smell a chemical unless you are instructed by your teacher to do so. Many chemicals are poisonous.

27. Use only those chemicals needed in the activity. Read and double-check labels on supply bottles before removing any chemicals. Take only as much as you need. Keep all containers closed when chemicals are not being used.

28. Dispose of all chemicals as instructed by your teacher. To avoid contamination, never return chemicals to their original containers. Never simply pour chemicals or other substances into the sink or trash containers.

29. Be extra careful when working with acids or bases. Pour all chemicals over the sink or a container, not over your work surface.

30. If you are instructed to test for odors, use a wafting motion to direct the odors to your nose. Do not inhale the fumes directly from the container.

31. When mixing an acid and water, always pour the water into the container first and then add the acid to the water. Never pour water into an acid.

32. Take extreme care not to spill any material in the laboratory. Wash chemical spills and splashes immediately with plenty of water. Immediately begin rinsing with water any acids that get on your skin or clothing, and notify your teacher of any acid spill at the same time.

Using Glassware Safely

33. Never force glass tubing or thermometers into a rubber stopper or rubber tubing. Have your teacher insert the glass tubing or thermometer if required for an activity.

34. If you are using a laboratory burner, use a wire screen to protect glassware from any flame. Never heat glassware that is not thoroughly dry on the outside.

35. Keep in mind that hot glassware looks cool. Never pick up glassware without first checking to see if it is hot. Use an oven mitt. See rule 24.

36. Never use broken or chipped glassware. If glassware breaks, notify your teacher and dispose of the glassware in the proper broken-glassware container. Never handle broken glass with your bare hands.

37. Never eat or drink from lab glassware.

38. Thoroughly clean glassware before putting it away.

Using Sharp Instruments

39. Handle scalpels or other sharp instruments with extreme care. Never cut material toward you; cut away from you.

40. Immediately notify your teacher if you cut your skin when working in the laboratory.

Animal and Plant Safety

41. Never perform experiments that cause pain, discomfort, or harm to mammals, birds, reptiles, fishes, or amphibians. This rule applies at home as well as in the classroom.

42. Animals should be handled only if absolutely necessary. Your teacher will instruct you as to how to handle each animal species brought into the classroom.

43. If you know that you are allergic to certain plants, molds, or animals, tell your teacher before doing an activity in which these are used.

44. During field work, protect your skin by wearing long pants, long sleeves, socks, and closed shoes. Know how to recognize the poisonous plants and fungi in your area, as well as plants with thorns, and avoid contact with them.

45. Never eat any part of an unidentified plant or fungus.

46. Wash your hands thoroughly after handling animals or the cage containing animals. Wash your hands when you are finished with any activity involving animal parts, plants, or soil.

End-of-Experiment Rules

47. After an experiment has been completed, clean up your work area and return all equipment to its proper place.

48. Dispose of waste materials as instructed by your teacher.

49. Wash your hands after every experiment.

50. Always turn off all burners or hot plates when they are not in use. Unplug hot plates and other electrical equipment. If you used a burner, check that the gas-line valve to the burner is off as well.

Glossary

A

abyssal plain A smooth, nearly flat region of the deep ocean floor. (p. 151)

acid rain Rain that is more acidic than normal, caused by the release of molecules of sulfur dioxide and nitrogen oxide into the air. (p. 101)

aquaculture The farming of saltwater and freshwater organisms. (p. 171)

aquifer An underground layer of rock or soil that holds water. (p. 72)

artesian well A well in which water rises because of pressure within the aquifer. (p. 73)

atoll A ring-shaped coral island. (p. 164)

B

benthos Organisms that live on the bottom of the ocean or other body of water. (p. 157)

bioluminescence The production of light by living things. (p. 167)

brackish Water that is partly salty and partly fresh, characteristic of estuaries. (p. 160)

C

capillary action The combined force of attraction among water molecules and with the molecules of surrounding materials. (p. 25)

climate The pattern of temperature and precipitation typical of an area over a long period of time. (p. 136)

coagulation The process by which particles in a liquid clump together; a step in the water treatment process. (p. 85)

concentration The amount of one substance in a certain volume of another substance. (p. 84)

condensation The process by which a gas changes to a liquid. (p. 27)

conservation The process of using a resource wisely so it will not be used up. (p. 92)

continental shelf A gently sloping, shallow area of the ocean floor that extends outward from the edge of a continent. (p. 150)

continental slope A steep incline leading down from the edge of the continental shelf. (p. 150)

controlled experiment An experiment in which all factors except one are kept constant. (p. 191)

Coriolis effect The effect of Earth's rotation on the direction of winds and currents. (p. 135)

crest The highest point of a wave. (p. 116)

current A large stream of moving water that flows through the ocean. (p. 135)

D

delta The area of sediment deposits that build up near a river's mouth. (p. 50)

deposition The process by which soil and fragments of rock are deposited in a new location. (p. 45)

desalination The process of obtaining fresh water from salt water by removing the salt. (p. 94)

divide A ridge of land that separates one watershed from another. (p. 45)

drought A water shortage caused by scarce rainfall in a particular area. (p. 91)

E

El Niño An abnormal climate event that occurs every 2 to 7 years in the Pacific Ocean, causing changes in winds, currents, and weather patterns. (p. 139)

erosion The process by which fragments of soil and rock are broken off from the ground surface and carried away. (p. 45)

estuary A coastal inlet or bay where fresh water from rivers mixes with salty ocean water. (p. 160)

eutrophication The process by which nutrients in a lake build up over time, causing an increase in the growth of algae. (p. 57)

evaporation The process by which molecules at the surface of a liquid absorb enough energy to change to the gaseous state. (p. 27)

F

filtration The process of passing water through a series of screens that allow the water through, but not larger solid particles. (p. 85)

flocs Sticky globs created by adding a chemical such as alum during water treatment. (p. 85)

flood plain A broad, flat valley through which a river flows. (p. 50)

food web The feeding relationships in a habitat. (p. 157)

frequency The number of waves that pass a specific point in a given amount of time. (p. 116)

G

geyser A type of hot spring in which the water is under pressure and bursts periodically into the air. (p. 74)

glacier A huge mass of ice and snow that moves slowly over the land. (p. 65)

groin A stone or concrete wall built out from a beach to reduce erosion. (p. 119)

groundwater Water that fills the cracks and pores in underground soil and rock layers. (p. 22)

H

habitat The place where an organism lives and that provides the things it needs to survive. (p. 20)

hardness The level of the minerals calcium and magnesium in water. (p. 84)

headwaters The many small streams that come together at the source of the river. (p. 48)

holdfast A bundle of rootlike strands that attaches algae to the rocks. (p. 164)

hydroelectric power Electricity produced by the kinetic energy of water moving over a waterfall or dam. (p. 106)

hydrothermal vent An area where ocean water sinks through cracks in the ocean floor, is heated by the underlying magma, and rises again through the cracks. (p. 168)

hypothesis A prediction about the outcome of an experiment. (p. 190)

impermeable Characteristic of materials through which water does not easily pass, such as clay and granite. (p. 69)

intertidal zone The area that stretches from the highest high-tide line on land out to the point on the continental shelf exposed by the lowest low tide. (p. 158)

irrigation The process of supplying water to areas of land to make them suitable for growing crops. (p. 17)

kinetic energy The form of energy that an object has when it is moving. (p. 106)

leach field The ground area around a septic tank through which wastewater filters after leaving the tank. (p. 89)

levee A long ridge formed by deposits of sediments alongside a river channel. (p. 52)

longshore drift The movement of sand along a beach; caused by waves coming into shore at an angle. (p. 118)

magma Hot, liquid substance that makes up part of Earth's mantle. (p. 153)

manipulated variable The one factor that a scientist changes during an experiment. (p. 191)

meander A looping curve formed in a river as it winds through its flood plain. (p. 50)

mid-ocean ridge The continuous range of mountains on the ocean floor that winds around Earth. (p. 151)

mouth The point where a river flows into another body of water. (p. 50)

neap tide A tide with the least difference between low and high tide that occurs when the sun and moon pull at right angles to each other. (p. 125)

nekton Free-swimming animals that can move throughout the water column. (p. 157)

neritic zone The part of the ocean that extends from the low-tide line out to the edge of the continental shelf. (p. 163)

nodule A lump formed when metals such as manganese build up around pieces of shell on the ocean floor. (p. 171)

nonpoint source A widely spread source of pollution that is difficult to link to a specific point of origin, such as road runoff. (p. 99)

open-ocean zone The area of the ocean beyond the edge of the continental shelf. (p. 163)

operational definition A statement that describes how a particular variable is to be measured or a term is to be defined. (p. 191)

oxbow lake The crescent-shaped, cutoff body of water that remains after a river carves a new channel. (p. 50)

permeable Characteristic of materials that allow water to easily pass through them, such as sand and gravel. (p. 69)

pesticide A chemical intended to kill insects and other organisms that damage crops. (p. 102)

pH How acidic or basic a substance is, measured on a scale of 1 (very acidic) to 14 (very basic). (p. 83)

photosynthesis The process by which plants use water, plus carbon dioxide and energy from the sun, to make food. (p. 19)

plankton Tiny algae and animals that float in water and are carried by waves and currents. (p. 157)

plate One of the major pieces that make up Earth's upper layer. (p. 153)

point source A specific source of pollution that can be identified, such as a pipe. (p. 99)

polar molecule A molecule that has electrically charged areas. (p. 24)

pores Tiny openings in and between particles of rock and soil which may contain air or water. (p. 69)

potential energy Energy that is stored and waiting to be used. (p. 106)

precipitation Water that falls to Earth as rain, snow, sleet, or hail. (p. 34)

recharge New water that enters an aquifer from the surface. (p. 73)

reservoir A natural or artificial lake that stores water for human use. (p. 56)

responding variable The factor that changes as a result of changes to the manipulated variable in an experiment. (p. 191)

rip current A rush of water that flows rapidly back to sea through a narrow opening. (p. 118)

runoff Water that flows over the ground surface rather than soaking into the ground. (p. 43)

·········· S ··········

salinity The total amount of dissolved salts in a water sample. (p. 127)

sandbar A ridge of sand deposited by waves as they slow down near shore. (p. 118)

saturated zone A layer of permeable rock or soil in which the cracks and pores are totally filled with water. (p. 69)

sea-floor spreading The process by which new material is added to the ocean floor along the boundary between diverging plates. (p. 154)

seamount A mountain on the ocean floor that is completely underwater. (p. 151)

sediments The particles of rock and soil that are moved by water or wind, resulting in erosion and deposition. (p. 45)

septic tank An underground tank containing bacteria that treat wastewater as it passes through. (p. 89)

sewage Water containing human wastes. (p. 87)

sludge Deposits of fine solids that settle out from wastewater during the treatment process. (p. 88)

solution A mixture that forms when one substance dissolves another. (p. 25)

solvent A substance that dissolves another substance, forming a solution. (p. 25)

sonar A system that uses sound waves to calculate the distance to an object, which gets its name from sound navigation and ranging. (p. 149)

specific heat The amount of heat needed to increase the temperature of a certain mass of substance by 1°C. (p. 29)

spring A place where groundwater bubbles or flows out of cracks in the rocks. (p. 74)

spring tide A tide with the greatest difference between high and low tide that occurs when the sun and the moon are aligned in a line with Earth. (p. 124)

state A form of matter; solid, liquid, or gas. (p. 26)

submersible An underwater vehicle built of strong materials to resist pressure at depth. (p. 131)

surface tension The tightness across the surface of water that is caused by the polar molecules pulling on each other. (p. 24)

·········· T ··········

tides The daily rise and fall of Earth's waters on shores. (p. 123)

transpiration The process by which plants release water vapor through their leaves. (p. 33)

trench A deep canyon in the ocean floor. (p. 152)

tributary A smaller stream or river that feeds into a main river. (p. 44)

trough The lowest point of a wave. (p. 117)

tsunami A giant wave caused by an earthquake on the ocean floor. (p. 121)

·········· U ··········

unsaturated zone A layer of rocks and soil above the water table in which the pores contain air as well as water. (p. 69)

upwelling An upward flow of cold water from the ocean depths. (p. 137)

·········· V ··········

variable Any factor that can change as part of an experiment. (p. 191)

·········· W ··········

water cycle The continuous process by which water moves through the living and nonliving parts of the environment. (p. 32)

water pollution The addition of any substance that has a negative effect on water or the living things that depend on the water. (p. 97)

water quality The degree of purity of water, determined by measuring the substances in water, besides water molecules. (p. 82)

watershed The land area that supplies water to a river system. (p. 44)

water table The top of the saturated zone, or depth to the groundwater in an aquifer. (p. 69)

water vapor The invisible, gaseous form of water. (p. 20)

wave The movement of energy through a body of water. (p. 115)

wave height The vertical distance from the crest of a wave to the trough. (p. 117)

wavelength The horizontal distance between two wave crests. (p. 116)

wetland An area of land that is covered with a shallow layer of water during some or all of the year. (p. 59)

Index

Acknowledgments

Illustration

Patrice Rossi Calkin: 50, 58
Warren Cutler: 6, 7, 54–55, 62–63, 158–159
John Edwards & Associates: 99, 116, 117, 118, 121, 123, 125, 137, 154, 163
GeoSystems Global Corporation: 21, 44, 63 t, 135, 153, 170
Andrea Golden: 8, 24, 25, 27, 34, 36, 37, 61, 72
Martucci Design: 20, 179, 196, 197, 198
Paul Mirocha: 167
Morgan Cain & Associates: 86, 93, 102, 106, 188 bl, 188 br, 189 tl, 189 bl
Morgan Cain & Associates (Chris Forsey): 148, 150–151, 165
Matt Myerchak: 76, 110, 142, 195
Ortelius Design Inc.: 16, 18, 19, 57, 96, 122, 139, 147, 155
Matthew Pippin: 22, 33, 48–49, 69, 73, 77, 85, 88, 89, 107, 130
J/B Woolsey Associates (Mark Desman): 166, 192
Rose Zgodzinski: 128

Photography

Photo Research Paula Wehde

Cover Design Bruce Bond
Cover Image ©Tony Rostron/Panoramic Images

Nature of Science
Page 10, 11, 12 b, Courtesy of Cindy Lee Van Dover; **12 t,** Emory Kristof/National Geographic Image Collection; **13,** Woods Hole Oceanographic Institution.

Chapter 1
Pages 14-15, Randy Linchs/Sharpshooters; **16 b,** Uniphoto; **17 tl,** Peter Menzel/Stock Boston; **17 tr,** Foodpix; **18 t,** O. Louis Mazzatenta/National Geographic Image Collection; **18 b,** Liba Taylor/Corbis; **19 t,** Tom Bean/TSI; **19 b,** Gianni Dagli Orti/Corbis; **23,** Russ Lappa; **24 b,** Stephen Dalton/Photo Researchers; **25 inset** Tom Bean/The Stock Market; **25 b,** Mark & Audry Gibson/The Stock Market; **27 l,** Steven C. Kaufman/Peter Arnold; **27 m,** Chris Soresen/the Stock Market; **27 r,** Japack/Leo de Wys; **28 b,** Neal Mishler/Natural Selection; **29 t,** D. Adams/Picture Perfect Images; **29 b,** Russ Lappa; **31 b,** **32 t,** Richard Haynes; **32 b,** Michael Giannechini/Photo Researchers; **34 t,** John Shaw/Tom Stack & Associates; **35 t,** **37 t,** Japack/Leo de Wys.

Chapter 2
Pages 40-41, Dave Johnston/Picture Cube; **42 t,** Russ Lappa; **42 inset,** Wernher Krutein/Gamma-Liaison; **42 m,** Superstock; **43,** Paul Barton/The Stock Market; **45,** Jacques Jangoux/TSI; **47,** Mark Thayer; **48 l,** Michael Durham/ENP; **48 b,** Darrell Gulin/TSI; **49 l,** Harry Engels/Animals Animals; **49 r,** Hal Horwitz/Corbis; **51 inset,** Gregory Foster/Gamma-Liaison; **51** Bill Gillette/Gamma-Liaison; **52,** Les Stone/Sygma; **53 t,** Russ Lappa; **53 b,** Annie Griffiths Belt/Aurora; **56 l,** David L. Brown/The Stock Market; **56 r,** John Shaw/Tom Stack & Associates; **57,** George Holton/Photo Researchers; **59 t,** Russ Lappa; **59 b,** Helen Cruickshank/Photo Researchers; **60 l,** Breck P. Kent/Animals Animals; **60 r, 204,** Greg Vaughn/Tom Stack & Associates; **61,** John Eastcott/Yva Momatiuk/Earth Scenes; **64,** Patrick M. Rose/Save the Manatee; **65 t,** Richard Haynes; **65 b,** Ralph A. Clevenger/Westlight; **66 t,** Don Pitcher/Stock Boston; **66 bl,** Hulton Getty/TSI; **66 br,** Superstock; **67,** Ralph A. Clevenger/Westlight; **68 t,** Richard Haynes; **68 b,** Tim Olive/Sharpshooters; **71,** Mark Thayer; **74,** Barbara Filet/TSI; **75,** R. Clevenger/Westlight.

Chapter 3
Pages 78-79, Jeremy Horner/Corbis; **80,** Russ Lappa; **81,** Guy Marche/TSI; **82,** Michael Newman/Photo Edit; **87 b,** Deborah Davis/Photo Edit; **87 t,** Ted Horowitz/The Stock Market; **90 t,** Russ Lappa; **90 b,** Laura Sikes/Sygma; **91,** Calvin Larsen/Photo Researchers; **92,** Russ Lappa; **94 t,** Peter Skinner/Photo Researchers; **94 b, 95, 97t,** Russ Lappa; **97,** Seth Resnick/Stock Boston; **100,** Corbis/Bettmann; **101 t,** Mugshots/The Stock Market; **101 b,** Wayne Eastep/TSI; **103 t,** Carson Baldwin/Earth Scenes; **103 b,** John Eastcott/Yva Momatiuk/Stock Boston; **104,** Peter Essick/Aurora; **105 t,** Russ Lappa; **105 b,** I. Burgum/P. Boorman/TSI; **107 b,** Robert K. Grubbs/Photo Network; **108,** George Gerster/Photo Researchers; **109 b,** Deborah David/Photo Edit; **109 t,** Mugshots/Stock Market.

Chapter 4
Pages 112-113, Seigried Layda/TSI; **114 t,** Richard Haynes; **114-115 b,** Aaron Chang/The Stock Market; **119 t,** ©1996 The Art Institute of Chicago, Clarence Buckingham Collection; **119 b,** Russ Lappa; **120 t,** Eric Horan/Gamma Liaison; **120 b,** Grace Davies/New England Stock; **122, 123,** Gene Ahrens/Bruce Coleman; **126,** Maher Attar/Sygma; **127 t,** Richard Haynes; **127 b,** Russ Lappa; **128,** Alon Reininger/The Stock Market; **129,** Corel; **131,** Russ Lappa; **133,** Mark Thayer; **134 b,** Russ Lappa; **134 t,** Richard Haynes; **136,** Raven/Explorer/Photo Researchers; **137 br,** Carol Roessler/Animals Animals; **140,** Ryan Ott/AP Photo.

Chapter 5
Pages 144-145, Fred Bavendam; **146 t,** Russ Lappa; **146 b,** The Granger Collection; **147,** Courtesy, Peabody Essex Museum, Salem, MA; **148,** Norbert Wu/The Stock Market; **149 t,** Scripps Oceanographic Institution; **149 b,** Scott Camanzine/Photo Researchers; **152,** Ted Streshinsky/Corbis; **154,** Russ Lappa; **156,** Richard Dunoff/The Stock Market; **157 tr,** E.R. Degginger/Photo Researchers; **157 mr,** Tim Heller/Mo Yung Productions; **157 br,** Doug Perrine/Innerspace Visions; **157 bl,** F. Stuart Westmorland/Photo Researchers; **160 bl,** Maresa Pryor, **br,** Peter Weiman **both** Earth Scenes; **161 t,** Lynda Richardson/Corbis; **161 b,** Andy Mertinez/Photo Researchers; **162 t,** Richard Haynes; **162 b,** Jeff Foott/Tom Stack & Associates; **164 l,** Chuck Davis/TSI; **164 r,** Randy Morse/Tom Stack & Associates; **165,** Mike Bacon/Tom Stack & Associates; **166,** Norbert Wu; **168,** D. Foster/WHOI/Visuals Unlimited; **169 t,** Richard Haynes; **169 b,** Nathan Benn/Stock Boston; **171,** Russ Lappa; **172,** Arnulf Husmo/TSI; **173 l,** Bob Torrez/TSI; **173 r,** Bill Nation/Sygma; **174 t,** Jake Evans/TSI; **174 b,** Richard Haynes; **175,** Tim Hauf/Visuals Unlimited; **177 l,** Doug Perrine/Innerspace Visions; **177 r,** Randy Morse/Tom Stack & Associates.

Interdisciplinary Exploration
Page 181 t, The Granger Collection; **181 m,** North Wind Picture Archives; **181 b,** University Art Collection, Tulane; **183,** Richard Pasley/Liaison International; **184,** Art Resource; **185 t,** North Wind Picture Archives; **185 b,** Chromo Sohm/Photo Researchers.

Skills Handbook
Page 186, Mike Moreland/Photo Network; **187 t,** Foodpix; **187 m,** Richard Haynes; **187 b,** Russ Lappa; **190,** Richard Haynes; **192,** Ron Kimball; **193,** Renee Lynn/Photo Researchers.